Praise for Engage, The Trainer's Guide to Learning

"The success achieved by Jeanine O'Neill-Blackwell and
has been nothing short of amazing and this book details how the 4M... ...
venue. Readers will find it easy to understand, practical, down-to-earth, and eminently transferable into
all learning situations."
~ Dr. Bernice McCarthy, creator of the 4MAT® model and
author of many books, including *About Learning* and *About Teaching*

"I have witnessed the 4MAT model shared in this book create amazing results in all learning situations: from
intimate technical workshops to highly engaging multi-day conferences with tens of thousands of participants.
Engage, The Trainer's Guide to Learning Styles is an easy-to-apply guide for learning how to create learning
experiences that captivate and transform."
~ Scott Buchanan, Vice Chairman of the Professional Beauty Association

"As training and development professionals, we are continually looking for the latest and greatest tools to
increase learning impact. Seldom does the thought process involve taking a step back and truly assessing the
role the trainer plays in the transfer of knowledge. *Engage, The Trainer's Guide to Learning Styles* provides
an insightful approach to explore the trainer's preferred style, strengths and potential gaps. This is an
essential element in successful learning and development solutions. This book is a great resource
for development of others and self."
~ Jana Svoboda, Learning and Development Manager, Cabela's Sporting Goods

"It is not over-reaching to say that adopting the 4MAT model can transform
an organization's training department."
~ Brian Johnson, Director of Corporate Training and Development, Holland America Lines

"4MAT gave us a common language and frame for being equally adept at designing both the "know-how" and
"how to" of leadership development. In fact, an epiphany that many of us have had with all of our experience,
education and training is that activity doesn't necessarily equal application. Unless your objective is to teach
learners how to discuss or create dialogue, a 'talking, discussing activity' is not necessarily one that provides
learners with adequate practice to develop the capability you're trying to develop."
~ Davida Sharpe, Director of Programs and Services,
Global Product Development, The Center for Creative Leadership

"In our company, we don't make an impact unless we make a connection. 4MAT is our 'go to' model for
crafting every learning interaction with our customers from workshop design to keynote preparation. This has
made a huge difference in the quality of the connections with our customers. The simplicity and organization of
Engage, The Trainer's Guide to Learning Styles makes creating brain-based learning intuitive and easy.
This is my new by-my-side training reference guide."
~ Virginia Meyer, Co-Founder and COO of redCHOCOLATE®

"As we trained our design and delivery faculty in 4MAT, one of the more senior faculty members shared with
the whole class that this was the best internal training he had experienced in CCL [The Center for Creative
Leadership] and that what made it the best was that it provided us with a common language for talking about
the designs we create. With 4MAT, we could have substantive conversations about the work we shared."
~ David Horth, Senior Fellow and Senior Designer, The Center for Creative Leadership

About Pfeiffer

Pfeiffer serves the professional development and hands-on resource needs of training and human resource practitioners and gives them products to do their jobs better. We deliver proven ideas and solutions from experts in HR development and HR management, and we offer effective and customizable tools to improve workplace performance. From novice to seasoned professional, Pfeiffer is the source you can trust to make yourself and your organization more successful.

Essential Knowledge Pfeiffer produces insightful, practical, and comprehensive materials on topics that matter the most to training and HR professionals. Our Essential Knowledge resources translate the expertise of seasoned professionals into practical, how-to guidance on critical workplace issues and problems. These resources are supported by case studies, worksheets, and job aids and are frequently supplemented with CD-ROMs, websites, and other means of making the content easier to read, understand, and use.

Essential Tools Pfeiffer's Essential Tools resources save time and expense by offering proven, ready-to-use materials—including exercises, activities, games, instruments, and assessments—for use during a training or team-learning event. These resources are frequently offered in looseleaf or CD-ROM format to facilitate copying and customization of the material.

Pfeiffer also recognizes the remarkable power of new technologies in expanding the reach and effectiveness of training. While e-hype has often created whizbang solutions in search of a problem, we are dedicated to bringing convenience and enhancements to proven training solutions. All our e-tools comply with rigorous functionality standards. The most appropriate technology wrapped around essential content yields the perfect solution for today's on-the-go trainers and human resource professionals.

Essential resources for training and HR professionals

ENGAGE

ENGAGE

The Trainer's Guide to Learning Styles

Jeanine O'Neill-Blackwell

Pfeiffer™

Published by Pfeiffer

An Imprint of Wiley

One Montgomery Street, Suite 1200, San Francisco, CA 94104-4594

www.pfeiffer.com

For additional copies/bulk purchases of this book in the U.S. please contact 800-274-4434.

Pfeiffer books and products are available through most bookstores. To contact Pfeiffer directly call our Customer Care Department within the U.S. at 800-274-4434, outside the U.S. at 317-572-3985, fax 317-572-4002, or visit www.pfeiffer.com.

Pfeiffer also publishes its books in a variety of electronic formats and by print-on-demand. Some material included with standard print versions of this book may not be included in e-books or in print-on-demand. If the version of this book that you purchased references media such as a CD or DVD that was not included in your purchase, you may download this material at http://booksupport.wiley.com. For more information about Wiley products, visit www.wiley.com.

Library of Congress Cataloging-in-Publication Data

O'Neill-Blackwell, Jeanine.
  Engage : the trainer's guide to learning styles / Jeanine O'Neill-Blackwell.
     pages cm
  Includes bibliographical references and index.
    ISBN 978-1-118-02943-5 (pbk.); 978-1-118-22231-7 (ebk); 978-1-118-23604-8 (ebk.); 978-1-118-26085-2 (ebk.)
  1. Training. 2. Learning. I. Title.
  LB1027.47.O64 2012
  370.15'23—dc23   2012005811

Acquiring Editor: Matt Davis   Production Editor: Kelsey McGee
Marketing Manager: Brian Grimm   Editor: Rebecca Taff
Director of Development: Kathleen Dolan Davies   Editorial Assistant: Michael Zelenko
Developmental Editor: Susan Rachmiller   Manufacturing Supervisor: Becky Morgan
V10009158_041619

To Maw Maw, for teaching that brilliance shows up in many forms.

Contents

Chapter 1: What Are Your Natural Training Strengths? ⋯⋯⋯⋯⋯⋯⋯⋯⋯ 1

The Trainer's Strengths • Job of the Trainer • Value of This Book • Let's Get Started: Taking the Training Style Inventory® (TRSI®) • The Four Training Approaches • Four Trainer Type Assessments • Your Learning Style: What You Look for, You Find • Common Descriptions of Ideal Learning Environments • Your Style: The Four Parts of the Learning Cycle • Summary • Identifying Areas of Opportunity • FAQs • Reflect • Act

Chapter 2: The Four Learning Styles in the Room ⋯⋯⋯⋯⋯⋯⋯⋯⋯⋯⋯ 33

What Is Learning? • Your Learning Style • The 4MAT® Learning Styles • Understanding Your Thinking Map • Thinking Strengths of Each Style • Functional Strengths of Each Style • How Your Training Style Relates to the Needs of Each Learning Style • Summary • FAQs • Reflect • Act

Chapter 3: 4MAT: The Four Steps of the Learning Cycle ⋯⋯⋯⋯⋯⋯⋯⋯ 65

A Brief Tour of the Brain • Brain Research on Learning • The Four Steps • Using the 4MAT Model to Design Learning • The First Step: Engage • The Second Step: Share • The Third Step: Practice • The Fourth Step: Perform • Summary • Reflect • Act

Chapter 4: Engage: The Art of Creating Powerful Openings ⋯⋯⋯⋯⋯⋯ 83

What Happens in Engage • Focus 1: Gaining Attention by Linking to What Learners Already Know • Focus 2: Using Questions to Provoke Reflection, Generate Dialogue, and Guide the Movement of the Group • Focus 3: Creating a Safe Learning Environment • Five Ways to Enhance Learner Safety While Building a Sense of Community • Summary • Reflect • Act • Examples of Engage Activities

Chapter 5: Share: Animating the Learning Content ⋯⋯⋯⋯⋯⋯⋯⋯⋯⋯ 125

Two Channels of Delivery: Visual and Verbal • The Verbal Channel: How to Organize Your Lecture • The Visual Channel: Animating Lecture Using Visual Strategies • Animating Lecture with Visual Organizers • Animating Lecture with PowerPoint • Summary • Reflect • Act • Examples of Share Activities

Chapter 6: Practice: Building Mastery Through Application ⋯⋯⋯⋯⋯⋯ 183

Designing Outcome-Based Practice Activities • Facilitating (Setting Up) Activities Effectively • Observing Application • Coaching and Debriefing • Using Questions to Focus the Learner's Attention • Coaching Assessment Tool • Strategies That Work in Practice • Summary • Reflect • Act • Examples of Practice Activities

Foreword

This book will enhance the ability of readers to understand their preferred approach to learning, their most comfortable way to take in new knowledge and information, as well as their preferred way to acquire new skills. The 4MAT® System is used for professional development in the fields of education, in corporate and government training and delivery at both teaching and training levels as well as administrative and leadership levels.

Instructional design, team processing, leadership skills, communication, conflict resolution, decision making, problem solving, and creativity are the major emphases of the 4MAT model. 4MAT encourages organizations to use multiple methods of problem solving and communication to help tap into the full potential of individuals.

The success achieved by Jeanine O'Neill-Blackwell and the 4MAT 4Business® team in the business world has been nothing short of amazing, and this book details how the 4MAT Learning Cycle resonates in that venue. Readers will find it easy to understand, practical, down-to-earth, and eminently transferable into all learning situations.

The 4MAT Learning Cycle and resultant learning styles encompass the natural learning act. The model is based on deep and solid theoretical findings that follow exactly how the brain learns, yet it is elegantly simple. It is a system of cognitive organization, a framework for the intuiting and thinking brain, and a transformation for people who go through it; transformative because it begins where people are and their connections to their past experiences and takes them into their futures armed to generate new learning results. It moves through the twin dimensions of receiving knowledge and information and producing effective adaptations.

The significance of this book rests on the following premises on which it is based:

- That people approach learning in different ways.
- That these differences are profound.
- That learning is a natural cycle that encompasses these differences.
- That our feeling and thinking brains go through the exact same cycle.
- That the key to continuous learning is to understand how this cycle works, and that high learning skill is traveling this cycle with ease.

It is with great pride that I endorse this adaptation of 4MAT for the corporate world.

Bernice McCarthy
Barrington, Illinois
November 2011

Acknowledgments

This book is a product of the contribution of many people. Some contributed directly to the words and images in this book and others in indirect, yet equally important, ways.

I am especially grateful to:

Terry, Madison, Mackensie, and Riley for listening, supporting, and being interested in what I love.

Our clients who have tested and refined the strategies shared in this book, especially Aveda, the Center for Creative Leadership, Grundfos Pumps, and Holland Cruises for sharing their 4MAT® successes and lessons learned so that others might benefit from their experience.

The thousands of educators and trainers who have embraced the 4MAT model.

The Wiley team, especially Matt Davis and Michael Zelenko, for seeing the vision.

Mark Morrow, for making the connections that made this book a reality.

The entire 4MAT global team.

Jennifer Boudreaux, for being all things that I am not.

Danielle Marks, for being a Zen-like creative partner who told the visual part of this story.

Edwin Neill II, my mentor and missed friend, for creating an environment that enabled me to discover my love of learning.

Bernice McCarthy, creator of the 4MAT model, for her commitment to honoring the potential of every human being.

"What you are the world is". And without your transformation there can be no transformation of the world."

~ J. Krishnamurti (1895 – 1986)

Introduction

When you reflect back over your career can you recall a particularly transformative learning experience—one that made a significant impact on your life? I bet you can. Most people can spend a few moments on this exercise and generate a powerful example. What was it about this experience that impacted you?

I can recall a transformational moment that occurred during a visionary presentation on leading organizational learning. The insight I gained in that experience completely changed the way I viewed the role learning played in an organization. I was inspired to change my approach to leading training and development in the organization I worked in at the time.

While most of us can identify a transformative learning experience in our lives, many of us would be hard pressed to identify more than a few that occurred in a formal learning environment. Not only are some formal learning experiences less than "transformational," but many are downright boring and include a wide range of attention-sapping barriers to effective learning which you have likely experienced. The reading of the PowerPoint® slides, the endless lecture on product features, the page-by-page review of a policy manual, and even the well-intentioned use of irrelevant games that promote "learner-centered training" often have a mind-numbing effect. No wonder many learners groan at the prospect of attending training.

So what distinguishes a transformational learning experience from a mind-numbing one? Clearly, the person designing and delivering the learning experience holds the key to making every training event an effective and even transformational learning experience. As a learning professional or someone recruited to design and/or deliver some form of training, the idea that you (the designer or trainer) hold the power to transform may be a bit overwhelming. After all, isn't the ability to move others in this way (to lead, engage, inspire) a gift of natural talent? While it's true that some people are naturally gifted at engaging others, the focus of this book is to demonstrate how you can build on a natural cycle of learning that empowers anyone to lead inspiring and engaging learning experiences. Once you learn what happens in this learning cycle and how to lead learners through the cycle consistently, you will find yourself among the (rock star) ranks of those you once thought truly gifted.

IT'S ABOUT YOUR STRENGTHS

The first step in becoming a creator of transformational learning experiences is identifying and applying your natural learning strengths to help you:

- gain the learner's attention,
- share information in a compelling way,
- inspire action, and
- make a difference in the lives of your learners.

The next step is building a thorough understanding of the four primary ways your audience prefers to take in and make meaning of new information. We call these preferences "learning styles." In this step, you will discover how your strengths relate to each learning style. The final step focuses on implementing a plan for maximizing your strengths and adapting your natural learning style to generate the greatest learning impact while reaching all learning styles.

Let's explore how we will do this:

STEP 1–DISCOVER YOUR TRAINING STRENGTHS

Current brain research informs us that there are four distinct parts of a universal learning cycle that must happen for true learning to occur. When one part of the cycle is missing, learning impact suffers. The 4MAT model explored in this book was created by Dr. Bernice McCarthy in 1979. McCarthy combined her learning theory studies with the hemisphericity (right brain and left brain) work of Nobel Prize winner Roger Sperry. She drew on the research of Carl Jung, Jean Piaget, Lev Vygotsky, John Dewey, Kurt Lewin, and David Kolb to create an instructional system that would move learners through the complete learning cycle using strategies that would appeal to all learning styles.

Since 1979, over one million people have discovered their natural learning, leading, and training strengths through 4MAT strengths assessment tools. Hundreds of thousands of trainers and educators all over the world have experienced the 4MAT instructional model in professional development programs in the fields of education, corporate and government training at both teaching and training levels, as well as administrative and leadership levels.

The 4MAT model that we will explore in this book addresses each step in the learning cycle with specific details on what the learner is doing in each part of the cycle and what the trainer must do to successfully move the learner through the cycle. You'll discover how to lead learners through this cycle when designing and delivering training using the 4MAT skills and tools.

In this book, you'll find a unique passcode to gain access to the 4MAT Training Style Inventory® (TRSI). The Training Style Inventory measures your preference and natural strength in four distinct training approaches. When you complete the Training Style Inventory, you will receive an in-depth analysis of your training strengths and an action guide to maximize your unique strengths.

What you will likely discover is that there are parts of the process of designing and leading learning in which you are naturally strong, maybe even gifted. There are some areas where you have to work harder and focus conscious attention around to do well. And there are some parts of this process that you may avoid altogether. To reach every learner and ensure that you generate real learning results, you must have a threshold level of competency in all four parts of the learning cycle. The trick is figuring out how to apply your natural strengths and use them to reach that threshold in the parts of the learning cycle you might normally struggle with or avoid altogether. With a bit of conscious intention, you can expand your natural strengths to engage, captivate, and empower all learning styles.

STEP 2–UNDERSTAND ALL LEARNING STYLES AND HOW YOUR OWN STYLE CONNECTS TO THE LEARNING STYLES AND NEEDS OF OTHERS

Learning is the act of taking in and making meaning of new information. By this definition, every time you read an email or dialogue with a colleague you are learning. Learning style refers to the unique preferences of individuals and how each likes to take in and process new information. An important fact for all trainers to understand is that the term "learning style" refers to the part of the learning cycle learners tend to linger in. Regardless of their learning style preference, all learners must move through the complete learning cycle explored in this book. Only when a learner moves through all four steps of the learning cycle are learners fully prepared to implement what they've learned in the real world.

Your own learning preferences naturally influence the training approach you choose. Just as you, as a learner, like to linger in certain parts of the learning cycle, you are just as likely to linger in certain parts of the learning cycle in your trainer role. What this book will help you do is to build skills in each of the four primary parts of the learning (and teaching) cycle and successfully move your learners through the process. You will also learn the favorite questions of each style and how these questions guide your learners' evaluation of learning experiences. In addition, this book will show you what works and what doesn't as you move through the four critical parts of the learning experience and how to simultaneously engage everyone in the room.

STEP 3–BRIDGE THE GAPS BETWEEN YOUR TRAINING STYLE AND LEARNING STYLE AND THOSE OF YOUR LEARNERS

An important mission for this book is to help you explore your own strengths using the Training Style Inventory through an in-depth exploration of the four learning styles and the 4MAT model. After you have discovered your natural strengths, you will get an inside look at what master trainers do well in each of the four parts of the learning cycle through examples taken directly from real-world learning environments. In addition, this book will break down each part of the learning cycle using simple tools and strategies that you can put to use right away to create and deliver effective learning experiences.

Armed with the 4MAT model for designing and delivering training, you will be able to consciously craft and deliver experiences that appeal to all learning styles and move learners toward successful on the job implementation.

HERE'S WHAT WILL BE EXPLORED IN THIS BOOK

Chapter 1: What Are your Natural Training Strengths?

One of the unique features of this book is a companion web site designed to allow you to assess your own strengths in four critical training roles and access support tools (**www.trainers-guide-to-learning-styles.com**). Once you have completed the Training Style Inventory you will receive a comprehensive Training Strengths and Action Guide which details your natural training abilities and strategies for improvement.

Chapter 2: The Four Learning Styles in the Room

You will learn how to recognize and engage every learning style in this chapter. Anyone who has logged time in front of a group of learners knows for a fact that learning style differences exist. The research confirms that there are unique preferences in how we like to take in and process information. In this chapter, you'll learn to recognize each learning style's needs and simultaneously address them as you move through the learning cycle.

Chapter 3: 4MAT: The Four Steps of the Learning Cycle

With a fundamental knowledge of the Four Learning Styles, you will be ready to explore what both the learner and trainer must do to successfully complete each step in the learning cycle. We'll reinforce the importance of completing the cycle by sharing the latest brain research. Understanding what is required in each of the four parts of the cycle and how your training style approach relates to delivering these requirements will help you assess which skills and strategies provided in this book are most important for you to include in your training approach.

Chapter 4: Engage: The Art of Creating Powerful Openings

Creating a compelling opening generates and sustains energy throughout the learning experience. This chapter explores effective approaches for connecting new learning to what the learner already knows. You will explore an inventory of opening approaches designed to encourage personal reflection and dialogue that will enable learners to discover the personal relevance of the content being shared.

Chapter 5: Share: Animating the Learning Content

Learners want information delivery to be informative and entertaining. This chapter explores how to effectively use stories, images, metaphors, and visual imaging exercises to bring any content to life, whether the topic is technical or soft skill related. We will explore how to edit content and effectively use one of the most widely misused visual presentation tools, PowerPoint®.

Chapter 6: Practice: Building Mastery Through Application

Every complete learning experience must include learner practice. You'll focus on improving the learners' ability to make distinctions about the quality of learning implementation using a four-part model for coaching learner performance.

Chapter 7: Perform: Assessing and Impementing

This chapter offers strategies to prepare the learners for successful implementation in the real world. An inventory of practical strategies to push learning beyond the formal learning environment is offered here, including innovative uses of blended and mobile learning.

Chapter 8: Engaging Virtual Training: How to Maximize Online Learning Impact

Designing and delivering learning in a virtual environment requires a different approach. In this chapter, we will explore strategies and activities for engaging all learning styles in the virtual learning environment using the 4MAT model.

Chapter 9: Begin with the End in Mind

Defining what the measure of success is before you begin development or delivery is critical. In this chapter, we'll explore four key learning outcomes that need to be defined before you begin crafting a learning experience. You will find tools you can use to work with stakeholders and subject matter experts to mutually define the desired learning outcomes and accelerate the design process.

Chapter 10: Assessment: Integrating Measurement into Training Design and Delivery

Certain indicators and clues tell us that learners are mastering the content being learned. This chapter explores "on-the-way" assessment strategies to determine how each learner is progressing through the learning cycle. "At-the-gate" assessment strategies are offered to assess learning at completion points in the learning process. You will learn how to integrate these assessments into the design and delivery of learning and to adjust your approach along the way to maximize impact (ROI) of the learning experiences you design and deliver.

WHY SHOULD YOU STRETCH? WHY NOW?

This book will bring together the critical components in effective learning design and delivery. When connected together, you'll see a creative blueprint for designing and delivering learning experiences which are compelling and transformative and create measurable impact.

Why is this important?

- Now, more than ever, learning initiatives must generate a measurable return on investment.
- Participation does not equal engagement. Fun icebreakers and interactive exercises are not enough to engage learners at a deep level. Personal relevance must be generated in a learning experience, and this takes a higher instructional skill set to create and deliver.
- Learning is happening everywhere. If we define learning as the process of taking in and making meaning of new information, the ability to share information in a compelling way that appeals to all learning styles is an essential skill in every role within an organization. 4MAT provides a simple learning language that you can share with learners, front-line managers, and subject matter experts that will influence the ultimate outcome of your training.

Let's begin.

"The moment you start focusing on strengths, you immediately focus on performance."

~ Marcus Buckingham
June 30, 2010, The Society for Human Resource Management's
62nd Annual Conference & Exposition

Your strengths are an expression of who you are. They are connected to the way you think, perceive, and evaluate the world around you. Marcus Buckingham, who is often referred to as the leader of the "strengths revolution," points out that our strengths are a composite of natural talent, skill, and knowledge. In other words, your strengths are directly linked to innate abilities (a talent for reading others or seeing the big picture) and the skills/knowledge (effective coaching skills or strategic planning skills) that you bring to the table.

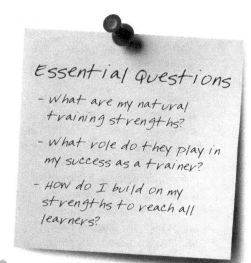

Essential Questions

- What are my natural training strengths?

- What role do they play in my success as a trainer?

- How do I build on my strengths to reach all learners?

For example, I have a friend who is a truly masterful networker. She has used her talent to generate a great deal of knowledge—connections and relationships she can tap into when needed. The skill she has developed is the methodical way she meets, greets, and follows up with her contacts. Taken together my friend's strength has given her a network of valuable contacts. On the other hand, networking is not one of my natural strengths. Yet, I have managed to acquire the needed skills and knowledge to thrive in business through observing and learning from masterful networkers (like my friend) and figuring out what works for me.

The Trainer's Strengths

The ability to effortlessly deliver engaging and transforming learning experiences is a rare gift. Most trainers and instructional designers come to the craft with a natural ability in one or more training approaches (dynamic storytelling or organized delivery, for example). Other approaches require us to build knowledge and skills, just as I had to work on my networking skills.

As we develop skill, we move though a predictable process. The Conscious Competency Spectrum describes the stages we move through as we develop our abilities and build skill and knowledge. Learners begin in a stage of "unconscious incompetence" and move to the final stage of "unconscious competence" (Chapman).

In the unconsciously incompetent stage, we have little to no knowledge of a given subject and are often unaware of what we don't know. When we discover how much we don't know, we become consciously incompetent. We seek out new information and practice new skills, which brings us to the stage of being consciously competent. And if we continue to practice and gain mastery, we move to the stage of unconsciously incompetent.

In this book, you will become aware of skills you are unconsciously competent (even masterful) in because they are an extension of your natural strengths. And you will become aware of skills that, if practiced, can greatly enhance your ability to perform the real job of a trainer, which is to move learners through a complete learning cycle.

The Conscious Competency Spectrum

Job of the Trainer

As a trainer, you move learners through the competence spectrum by creating an opportunity for them to discover what they know, what they don't know, and the value of knowing more. You do this by guiding the learner through a complete learning cycle that includes four essential steps.

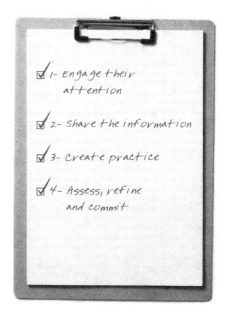

1 You gain the learners' attention and generate interest in the content so that they are aware of the value of the learning and appreciate that there is room for personal growth. If you have ever tried to "teach" people something they believe they already know, you know this is a "not to be missed" step in the learning cycle.

2 Next, you share information that will enable the learner to move into application. One of the most important jobs during this stage is to ensure that the learner is not overwhelmed with information. To accomplish this, the content must be refined to the essential information and delivered with clear and consistent organization.

3 You create an opportunity for learners to practice and build skill. As the learners practice and gain skill in real-world application, the job of the trainer is to coach and assist them as they evaluate their own applications.

4 To ensure performance transfer, you create an opportunity for the learners to assess their applications, refine for implementation, and commit to next steps. In this final step, you prepare the learners to move out into the real world and generate performance results.

Value of This Book

This book will share with you the training skills you need to deliver a complete learning experience that appeals to all learning styles while moving learners through a complete learning cycle. To do this well, you must competently and confidently guide learners through the four unique parts of the learning cycle. You will discover what must happen for real learning transfer to occur. You will learn how to build on your strengths to design and deliver the four critical parts of the learning experience. You will have an opportunity to assess your training strengths using the 4MAT® Training Style Inventory (TRSI). As you move through this book, we'll explore the four critical parts of the learning cycle and show you how to build upon your existing strengths to enable you to be masterful in leading a learning experience that appeals to all learning styles.

Learn·ing cycle, n.

1: the natural process that learners move through when perceiving and processing new information

Let's Get Started: Taking the Training Style Inventory® (TRSI®)

In the companion site to this book, you will access your personal 4MAT Training Style Inventory. The Training Style Inventory will assess your strengths in four critical training approaches. You can access the Training Style Inventory (TRSI) at **www.trainers-guide-to-learning-styles.com**. Use the access code found in the last section of this book.

Once you have completed the Training Style Inventory, you will have access to a comprehensive Training Strengths Report and Action Guide. This guide features an in-depth analysis of your training style strengths and will help you understand how your strengths relate to the diversity of learning style preferences. You'll discover what comes naturally to you and discover the dangers of over-using your natural strengths.

The Action Guide also provides you with skill development strategies identified specifically for your training style strengths and will help you put in place an action plan for developing existing strengths and building new skills. You should carefully read through the results of your assessment and review closely the suggested Action Strategies.

Finally, once you have completed the assessment you'll have the opportunity to connect with other readers through an online forum and explore additional resources to develop your skill and understanding in 4MAT design and delivery.

Take some time now to complete the Training Style Inventory and review your results.

>> **You can access the Training Style Inventory assessment at www.trainers-guide-to-learning-styles.com.**

The Four Training Approaches

After completing your Training Style Inventory, you should know your strength scores in four training styles identified in the 4MAT model: Type One, Type Two, Type Three, and Type Four. Your scores represent the level of focus you have on each of the four training style approaches. The scores do not indicate a level of skill in applying the approaches. We will talk more about assessing your skill in the later chapters of this book. For now, let's explore the focus of each training style and its relation to leading others in the learning process. Here's a quick recap of the focus of each training approach:

Type One Trainer
Focuses on establishing personal meaning by answering the question, "Why?"

Type Two Trainer
Focuses on transmitting knowledge by answering the question, "What?"

Type Three Trainer
Focuses on developing skill by answering the question, "How?"

Type Four Trainer
Focuses on real-world adaptation by answering the question, "If?"

See the table on the opposite page for more detailed information on the favorite question, focus, and approach of each training style. Read through all four descriptions in the chart and notice what applies to you.

TYPE FOUR TRAINER FOCUS AND APPROACH

Favorite Question: If?
Focuses on: Innovation, Synthesis, Possibility

If your preferred training approach is Type Four, you:

- Are interested in enabling learner self-discovery
- Try to help people act on their visions
- Believe training should be geared to learners' interests and inclinations
- See knowledge as necessary for improving the larger system
- Encourage experiential learning
- Like to use a variety of training methods
- Are dramatic and seek to energize learners
- Attempt to create new forms, to stimulate life
- Try to frequently create new boundaries

TYPE ONE TRAINER FOCUS AND APPROACH

Favorite Question: Why?
Focuses on: Relevance, Personal Meaning, Effectiveness

If your preferred training approach is Type One, you:

- Are interested in facilitating individual growth
- Create activities to enhance self-awareness
- Believe training should improve teaming success
- See knowledge as enhancing personal insights
- Encourage authenticity in people
- Use discussion, group work, and feedback about feelings
- Are supportive of others and seek to engage people in cooperative efforts
- Are aware of social forces that affect human development
    - Focus on significant issues in the learning experiences you craft

TYPE THREE TRAINER FOCUS AND APPROACH

Favorite Question: How?
Focuses on: Productivity, Competence, Efficiency

If your preferred training approach is Type Three, you:

- Are interested in productivity and competence
- Try to give people improved skill
- Believe training should be geared to competencies and bottom line pay-offs
- See knowledge as enabling people to be capable of making better decisions
- Encourage practical applications
- Like technical skills and hands-on activities
- Believe the best way is determined scientifically
- Use measured rewards

TYPE TWO TRAINER FOCUS AND APPROACH

Favorite Question: What?
Focuses on: Clarity, Knowledge, Probability

If your preferred training approach is Type Two, you:

- Are interested in transmitting knowledge
- Try to be as accurate and knowledgeable as possible
- Believe training should further understanding of significant information
- See knowledge as deepening personal experience connections
- Encourage sequential thinking
- Like facts and details
- Are a traditional trainer who seeks to imbue a love of precise knowledge
- Believe in the rational use of authority
- Believe training should be presented systematically

4 | 1
3 | 2

Four Trainer Type Assessments

What follows is a reflection exercise to help you further analyze your training style strengths. Review all four training style descriptions and highlight the strengths that apply to you.

TYPE ONE TRAINER

If you a have high preference for the Type One training approach, you have a natural interest in the experiences and perceptions of others. You enter the learning experience with the belief that the learners are able to discover value in the content themselves, and your focus is heavily slanted toward the learner's experience.

Overuse of the Type One strength can lead to spending too much time in reflection and dialogue, which can lead to some learners becoming impatient to move into action.

The Type one trainer focuses on facilitating dialogue to encourage learner self-discovery

TYPE ONE PREFERRED TRAINING APPROACH: FACILITATOR

Your strengths as an instructional designer:

- You focus on the personal relevance of the information being learned.
- You attempt to organize the learning around important concepts.
- You likely rely on personal stories and anecdotes to make the learning come to life.
- You prefer to create an opportunity for the learners to reflect on their own experiences.
- You create situations where the group can discover commonalities of experience through comparison and contrast.
- Dialogue is often used as the means of processing information.

Your strengths as a trainer:

- You attempt to read body language and other cues that learners give you to determine their level of engagement and understanding.
- You adjust your approach, based on your interpretation of the learner's reaction to what is happening in the learning environment.
- You have a strong ability to encourage others to share.
- You are willing to share your own experiences to illustrate the concepts you are sharing.

Areas of opportunity:

- You may not focus enough on practical application.
- You may not spend enough time on organized and structured delivery of the information.
- You may not focus enough on measurable outcomes of the training.
- There may be little emphasis on post-event impact and follow-up.

TYPE TWO TRAINER

If you have a high preference for the Type Two training approach, you are naturally interested in sharing information in an organized, sequential manner. You come into the learning experience with the belief that learners must understand the content before they can apply the content. You always have a plan for what will be shared. You are careful to stay on track. You methodically move through the information, step by step. You make sure the learners understand the knowledge before you ask them to practice applying that knowledge.

Over-use of the Type Two training approach can result in spending too much time in lecture. Some learners may become bored and impatient to "do" something.

The Type Two trainer focuses on delivering content in an organized, sequential manner

PREFERRED TRAINING APPROACH: PRESENTER

Your strengths as an instructional designer:

- You focus on the accuracy of the information being shared.
- You emphasize logical organization of the information.
- You are careful to be accurate in what you share, citing references and sources.

Your strengths as a trainer:

- You prefer to deliver information in a structured manner.
- You likely prefer to use written training materials and visual aids that lead the learner sequentially through the information.
- You emphasize the conceptual coherence of the content.
- You thoroughly cover the content.
- You seek structure and value models and frameworks that help learners make sense of information.

Areas of opportunity:

- There may be too much lecture.
- There may be a tendency to spend too much time on transmitting knowledge and not enough time on practice.
- You may be hesitant to encourage learner dialogue because of concerns about staying "on track."

TYPE THREE TRAINER

If you have a high preference for the Type Three training approach, you see the value in having learners practice applying the information. You likely create opportunities for the learners to practice using the information. You prefer to include real-world examples such as problem-solving scenarios or case studies. You are good at editing content down to the essential and are comfortable answering application-oriented questions.

If you over-use the Type Three training approach, you can lose some learners by rushing too quickly into hands-on practice. Some learners may feel rushed and become overwhelmed.

The Type Three trainer emphasizes hands-on and real-world application

TYPE THREE PREFERRED TRAINING APPROACH: COACH

Your strengths as an instructional designer:	• You focus on the practical. • You bring the real world into the learning environment. • You focus on preparing learners to be successful. • You edit the content down to what is useful.
Your strengths as a trainer:	• You emphasize hands-on practice. • You set up situations for learners to receive feedback. • You create simulated real-world application scenarios. • You focus on usefulness and higher productivity.
Areas of opportunity:	• You may lose some learners in your haste to get to application. • There may be a missed opportunity to engage learners at a deep, personal level.

TYPE FOUR TRAINER

If you have a preference for the Type Four training approach, you see the value in developing the learners' ability to assess their own performance. You recognize the ability to adapt information based on real-world constraints is a critical contributor to successful implementation.

You likely encourage learners to evaluate their own learning applications. You create interaction in partner and group exercises. You allow for peer feedback and use questions to draw the learners' attention to gaps in knowledge.

Over-use of the Type Four training approach can result in learners feeling "overwhelmed" by too many options or confused by a lack of clear guidelines and structure.

The Type Four trainer
encourages self-assessment
and adaptation

TYPE FOUR PREFERRED TRAINING APPROACH: EVALUATOR

Your strengths as an instructional designer:

- You invite big picture thinking through facilitated exercises.
- You create learning projects that encourage self-assessment.
- You prefer to leave room for flexibility in the agenda in order to encourage adaptation.
- You encourage self-assessment.

Your strengths as a trainer:

- You are open to what emerges in the dialogue.
- You are flexible and can adapt to the needs of the learners.
- You weave in seemingly unconnected elements to create a cohesive picture.

Areas of opportunity:

- You may lose some learners who have difficulty following your mental leaps.
- Some learners may perceive the delivery to be disorganized or incomplete.
- There may not be enough emphasis on application and post-event implementation.

Your Learning Style:
What You Look for, You Find

In the introduction of this book, you were asked to think about a particularly transformational learning experience. Let's revisit that experience. Take a few moments and reflect on a powerful learning experience that made an impact on you. How would you describe the experience? What made the experience impactful? What learning elements were present?

What do you notice about the connections between your most powerful learning experience and your Training Style Inventory results?

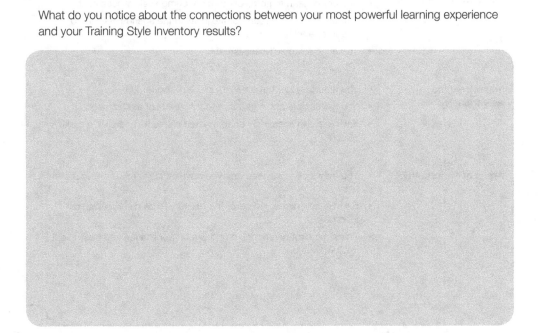

To help illustrate the differences in how each training style values learning experiences, we asked trainers with different training style preferences to share reflections on their favorite learning experiences. Notice how the experiences shared connect to the learning style preferences of each individual.

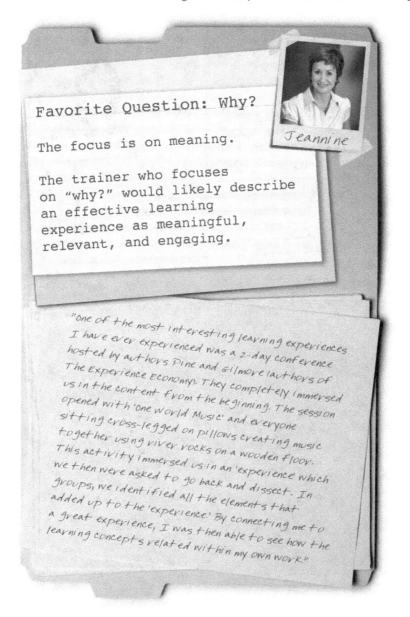

Favorite Question: Why?

The focus is on meaning.

The trainer who focuses on "why?" would likely describe an effective learning experience as meaningful, relevant, and engaging.

Jeannine

"One of the most interesting learning experiences I have ever experienced was a 2-day conference hosted by authors Pine and Gilmore (authors of The Experience Economy). They completely immersed us in the content from the beginning. The session opened with 'One World Music' and everyone sitting cross-legged on pillows creating music together using river rocks on a wooden floor. This activity immersed us in an 'experience' which we then were asked to go back and dissect. In groups, we identified all the elements that added up to the 'experience.' By connecting me to a great experience, I was then able to see how the learning concepts related within my own work."

TYPE TWO TRAINER CASE STUDY: JULIA WATT

Director of Salons and Spas, Dillard's Department Stores

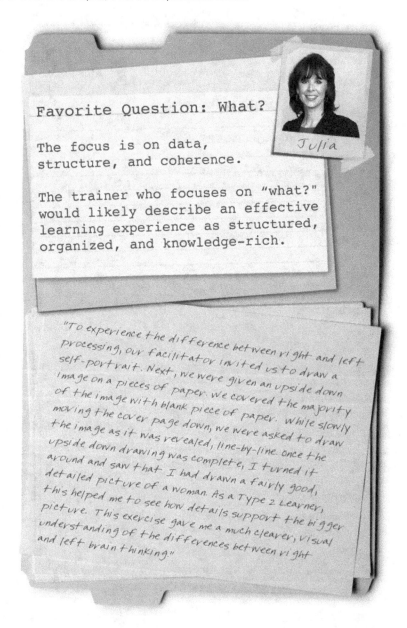

Favorite Question: What?

The focus is on data, structure, and coherence.

The trainer who focuses on "what?" would likely describe an effective learning experience as structured, organized, and knowledge-rich.

"To experience the difference between right and left processing, our facilitator invited us to draw a self-portrait. Next, we were given an upside down image on a pieces of paper. We covered the majority of the image with blank piece of paper. While slowly moving the cover page down, we were asked to draw the image as it was revealed, line-by-line. Once the upside down drawing was complete, I turned it around and saw that I had drawn a fairly good, detailed picture of a woman. As a Type 2 Learner, this helped me to see how details support the bigger picture. This exercise gave me a much clearer, visual understanding of the differences between right and left brain thinking."

Regional Employee Development Supervisor, Grundfos Pumps

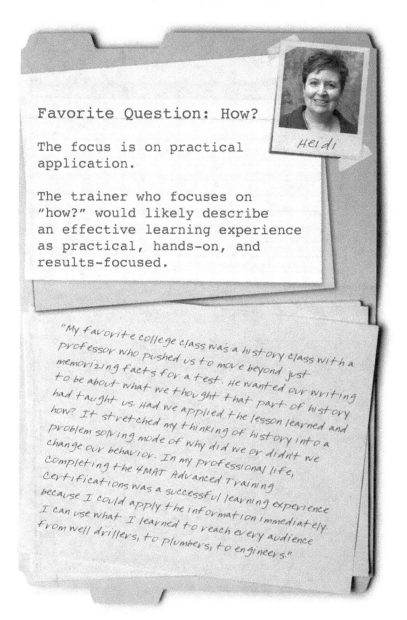

Favorite Question: How?

The focus is on practical
application.

The trainer who focuses on
"how?" would likely describe
an effective learning experience
as practical, hands-on, and
results-focused.

Heidi

"My favorite college class was a history class with a
professor who pushed us to move beyond just
memorizing facts for a test. He wanted our writing
to be about what we thought that part of history
had taught us. Had we applied the lesson learned and
how? It stretched my thinking of history into a
problem solving mode of why did we or didn't we
change our behavior. In my professional life,
completing the 4MAT Advanced Training
certifications was a successful learning experience
because I could apply the information immediately.
I can use what I learned to reach every audience
from well drillers, to plumbers, to engineers."

Founder, Stage Right Organizational Development

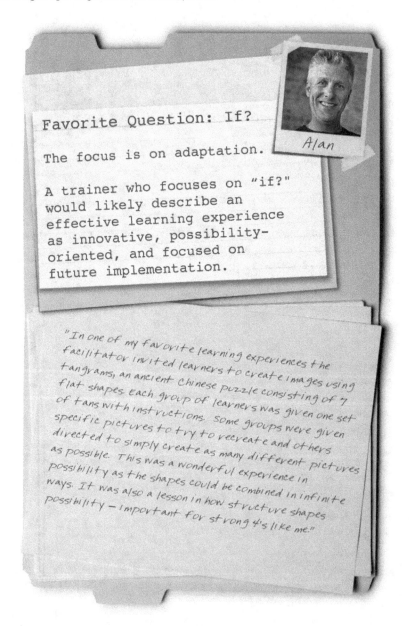

Favorite Question: If?

The focus is on adaptation.

A trainer who focuses on "if?" would likely describe an effective learning experience as innovative, possibility-oriented, and focused on future implementation.

Alan

"In one of my favorite learning experiences the facilitator invited learners to create images using tangrams, an ancient Chinese puzzle consisting of 7 flat shapes. Each group of learners was given one set of tans with instructions. Some groups were given specific pictures to try to recreate and others directed to simply create as many different pictures as possible. This was a wonderful experience in possibility as the shapes could be combined in infinite ways. It was also a lesson in how structure shapes possibility — important for strong 4's like me."

Common Descriptions of Ideal Learning Environments

Over the years, our team has had the opportunity to work with thousands of trainers in our train the trainer and instructional design courses. In an exercise in our 4MAT Advanced Instructional Design course, we ask trainers with different training style results to describe the most important elements that must be included in a learning experience. Not surprisingly, the descriptions vary greatly by training style.

Type One Trainers

Type One trainers emphasize the need for dialogue and group interaction. They tend to evaluate the effectiveness of the learning based on the personal exchange between learners and the depth of sharing.

Type Two Trainers

Type Two trainers emphasize the need for structure and organized delivery of information. They tend to evaluate the effectiveness of the learning based on the information absorbed by the learners.

Type Three Trainers

Type Three trainers emphasize the need for practical application of the information. They tend to evaluate the effectiveness of the learning based on the competencies gained and ultimate productivity of the learner.

Type Four Trainers

Type Four trainers emphasize the need for adaptation of the learning to ensure real-world usefulness. They tend to evaluate the effectiveness of the learning based on the degree of ownership of the information by the learner and the enthusiasm generated for future implementation.

Your Style: The Four Parts of the Learning Cycle

Being aware of your bias can help you develop your skills in all four approaches. Imagine you are a Type One trainer and you are observing a colleague presenting a training course. You notice how she uses an interactive exercise to create a sense of community in the room. Because you value learners getting to know each other and meaningful dialogue, you find this exercise valuable. You might find yourself saying, "Hmmm, I could use that exercise in the class I am teaching next week." You add the exercise to your toolkit and you become even better at the Training Style One approach. Oftentimes, the training strategies we adopt are predominantly focused on appealing to learners who share our learning style preferences. Without conscious intention, we continue to build strength in only one of the four approaches.

It's important to remember that learning style refers to the part of the learning cycle on which a learner tends to invest more time. Regardless of style, each learner must move through all four phases of the learning cycle.

1   In the first step, the learner's attention is gained. Type One trainers have a natural advantage in this step. We call this step "Engage."

2   In the second step, the learner absorbs information and data. The Type Two trainer's focus on organization and structure helps him or her do this step well. We call this step "Share."

3   In the third step, the learner moves into action and applies the information absorbed. The Type Three trainer's focus on real-world skills makes this step easier for learners to accomplish. We call this step "Practice."

4   In the fourth and final step, the learner adapts the information and applies for results. The Type Four trainer's willingness to encourage the learner to adapt information to make it useful is critical to successfully implementing this step. We call this step "Perform."

Learning style refers to the part of the learning cycle in which a learner tends to invest more time. Regardless of style, each learner must move through all four phases of the learning cycle.

In our instructional design programs, we frequently invite trainers to share the factors they believe must be present in an effectively designed and delivered learning experience. Not surprisingly, a trainer's preferred training approach greatly influences his or her description of an ideal learning environment. The learning strategies that one training style emphasizes, another may avoid altogether. In the chart on the next page, you will see examples of what each training style defines as essential elements in the learning experience.

Learn·ing style, n.

1: refers to your preferences related to how you take in and make meaning of new information

Effective Training Strategies as Defined By Each Training Style

TRAINING STYLE 4 RESPONSES

Focus is on If?
- New possibilities realized
- Opportunity to customize
- Big picture thinking
- Adaptive Trainer
- Synthesis

TRAINING STYLE 1 RESPONSES

Focus is on Why?
- Reflection
- Deep insights
- Authentic Facilitator
- Interactive dialogue

4

1

3

2

TRAINING STYLE 3 RESPONSES

Focus is on How?
- Real-world examples
- Practical application
- Experienced Coach
- Hands-on practice
- Immediate results

TRAINING STYLE 2 RESPONSES

Focus is on What?
- Detailed information and data
- Knowledgeable presenter
- Conceptual coherence
- Structured delivery
- Organized information

Summary

Some of us began our careers with the intention of being involved in creating learning experiences. Maybe you are someone who chose to study instructional design. Most trainers share that they landed in the role of trainer through a process of evolution. If this is your experience, you were likely good at a particular skill and you soon found yourself training others in this skill. Eventually, training became more and more of what you do. Either way, you added new tools to your toolkit as you gained more experience. These tools include strategies, models, and techniques.

The variety of learning programs you have experienced and your training style influence the quantity and type of tools you have at your disposal. When we develop or deliver learning experiences, our creativity is limited by the tools available. If all you have is a hammer, everything begins to look like a nail. This book is designed to expand your toolkit using proven strategies and techniques which engage all learning styles.

In this chapter, you discovered your preferred training approach. In the next chapter, you will explore the strengths and needs of each of the four primary learning styles. You will also discover how your natural learning style strengths relate to the needs of each learning style. You will identify the learners you reach easily with your preferred training approach and those who will require you to consciously utilize new training strategies. With this knowledge, you will be prepared to leverage your existing training strengths while building new skills using the tools and strategies shared in the remaining chapters.

At the end of each chapter, you will be invited to "Reflect" and "Act" on the ideas shared. Take a moment to reflect and determine your action steps related to leveraging your training style strengths.

Identifying Areas of Opportunity

Reflect on your training style strengths. Below, you will find suggestions on areas of opportunity for each training style approach. Review the suggestions and highlight areas you would like to focus on as you explore the rest of the book.

TYPE FOUR TRAINER

If you are a Type Four trainer, your training could likely benefit from more structure and practical application.

Your training could benefit from:
- More structured approach to delivering the content
- Being clear in what the learner needs to know
- Giving clear direction and firm standards for performance (more black and white with less gray)
- Clearly defining the desired outcome and staying focused on that outcome throughout the design and delivery of the learning experience

TYPE ONE TRAINER

If you are a Type One trainer, your training could likely benefit from more practical application.

Your training could benefit from:
- More practical application
- Structured approach to delivering content
- Emphasis on results and tracking
- Plan for how you will implement and measure post-training results

TYPE THREE TRAINER

If you are a Type Three trainer, your training could likely benefit from more group dialogue and reflection.

Your training could benefit from:
- More time for interaction and meaningful dialogue
- Focused attention on the step-by-step delivery of the information before the learner applies the information
- Plan for addressing learners' challenges in implementing the information after the learning event is complete

TYPE TWO TRAINER

If you are a Type Two trainer, you likely could benefit from more interaction and flexibility in learning approach.

Your training could benefit from:
- More interaction
- Higher level of learner engagement, at a personal level
- More hands-on
- Greater emphasis on post-learning application and real-world impact

FAQs

Q: Is it possible to be tied in two styles?

Yes. Read the descriptions for each style and see whether if you notice a distinct preference for one approach.

Q: What does it mean if I am a "square" (all four scores are equal)?

When all four scores are equal, it means that you are either fairly balanced in your training approach or unclear about your preferences. It is important to remember that the Training Style Inventory assesses where you focus attention in the design and delivery of learning experiences. It does not measure skill in each approach. While you may have a balance in all four scores, you may find that you are more skilled in one area than others.

Q: I have taken the Learning Type Measure® and the Training Style Inventory. Why is there a difference between my learning style and my training style?

When you take the 4MAT Learning Type Measure, you are assessing the combination of preferences in how you take in new information and how you make meaning of that information. The Training Style Inventory assesses your preferred approach to transferring information to others. It is not uncommon for trainers to adopt a training approach that is different from their preferred learning approach. This may be a product of an awareness of a tendency to lean too heavily on our preferred learning approach at the expense of missing important parts of the learning process.

» You can find the Learning Type Measure at www.trainers-guide-to-learning-styles.com.

If you haven't already completed the Training Style Inventory (TRSI), it is recommended that you do this before continuing further. You will find your unique e-code in the back of this book. Go to **www.trainers-guide-to-learning-styles.com** to access the online assessment.

- Review the results and read through the Action Guide. Highlight insights that resonate with you.
- Visit the Discussion Forum to post any questions or insights that are emerging for you.

Complete the following personal reflection:

How have my training style strengths served me as a trainer? As a leader?

What is the biggest opportunity for growth for me?

If you are reading this book with a group, here are some action items to facilitate deeper conversation:

Create a composite graph of your training team's strengths. You can do this by downloading the Training Style Inventory graph found on the companion site of this book, **www.trainers-guide-to-learning-styles.com**. Mark each team member's scores on the graph, using different colored markers. Your graph should look like this when complete:

After viewing the graph results, reflect on the following questions:

What do you see as your team's composite strengths?

How do our individual strengths show up in our results, as a team?

Which area needs the most attention?

How can my individual strengths support the team in areas of needed attention?

"Knowing others is intelligence;
Knowing yourself is true wisdom.
Mastering others is strength;
Mastering yourself is true power."

~ Lao Tzu
Tao Te Ching

I once consulted on the redesign of the leadership curriculum for the corporate university of a large financial institution. The senior leader in charge of learning and development in the organization told me he could not move past getting buy-in from key stakeholders on what should be included in the curriculum. He had presented the curriculum outline to the stakeholders twice and both times ended up back at the drawing board. He asked for support in implementing a better process for determining what should be included in the course. Jointly, we facilitated an initial in-depth needs analysis process to identify the critical learning outcomes for the course. One of the questions posed to the group of stakeholders was, "What new behaviors will you see exhibited by the participants of this course, as a direct result of this training?"

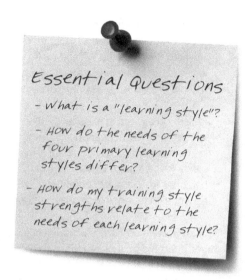

Essential Questions

- What is a "learning style"?

- How do the needs of the four primary learning styles differ?

- How do my training style strengths relate to the needs of each learning style?

A senior leader responsible for branch operations responded that the best possible outcome from the course would be an appreciation for the value of the organization's operational systems. This leader was convinced that if this value was emphasized then the immediate impact would be a solution to consistency issues throughout the organization and would result in much less "reinvention of the wheel."

» View a short video on the "4 Learning Styles" at www.trainers-guide-to-learning-styles.com.

Another senior leader responsible for strategic growth agreed with the learning outcomes expressed by his colleague, but thought it was critical that managers in the company have the ability to "learn on the fly" and make well-thought-out decisions when the situation demanded it. It is clear to see in this example why consensus was so hard to reach. The principal decision-makers did not have a shared expectation of what the curriculum should deliver.

Reflect on a learning experience when you have not been able to meet the expectations of every learner. Your learners are no different than the senior leaders in this story. Learners evaluate a learning experience by comparing their experience against personal expectations, just as the senior leaders approached valuing the content in the curriculum design project based on their particular interests and points of view. The old adage that "the source of all unhappiness is unmet expectations" certainly applies to the evaluation of training experiences.

Most trainers and instructional designers have had the opportunity to review written feedback from learners on their reactions to a specific learning event. It can be surprising to find that learners in the same learning situation could have such different experiences. One learner can find the learning experience to be "powerful," while another can find it "painful." If you want to create satisfied learners, you have to meet their expectations. The challenge, of course, is that sometimes learners cannot articulate that expectation. With an understanding of the expectations of the four primary learning styles, you can craft an experience that appeals to the needs and wants of everyone in the room.

In this chapter, we will explore the four learning style preferences and discover how these preferences relate to your natural training approach. "Learning style" refers to the part of the learning cycle that you prefer and tend to invest more time in. Each learning style has a different definition of "ideal learning" with variations in what they expect. To fully understand learning styles, you must first understand what happens in the learning cycle.

In this chapter, you will explore:

- What is learning?
- The four learning styles
- How your training style relates to the needs of each learning style

What Is Learning?

Two primary actions define learning: perceiving and processing.

- Perceiving refers to the act of taking in information through our senses.
- Processing refers to how we make meaning of that information.

By this definition, when you read an email, sit in a meeting, or talk to a colleague, you are learning.

PERCEIVING: HOW DO YOU PREFER TO TAKE IN INFORMATION?

Some of us prefer to take in information experientially. "Feelers" enjoy being immersed in an experience. Feelers take in information from an "inside" place. They rely heavily on their own experience and intuition. They prefer to be personally involved in a learning experience. You will see these preferences in action in a classroom learning situation. Feelers like to hear and share stories. They enjoy dialogue and group activities. Are you a feeler?

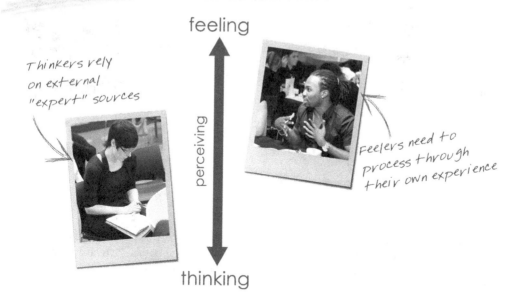

feeling

Thinkers rely on external "expert" sources

perceiving

Feelers need to process through their own experience

thinking

Other learners prefer to take in information intellectually. "Thinkers" prefer to read, research, or learn from an expert source. Thinkers take in information from an "outside" place. They enjoy structured, well-organized presentation of information. You will see these preferences in action in a classroom learning situation. Thinkers prefer well-researched data, concepts, and organized lecture. Are you a thinker?

PROCESSING: HOW DO YOU MAKE MEANING OF NEW INFORMATION?

Once we take in information, we process the information. We make sense of it. Some of us linger in reflection. "Watchers" prefer to reflect before moving into action. Watchers like to understand the information. They want to make sense of what they are experiencing before deciding how to act upon this new information. You will see these preferences in a learning situation. The watchers will hang back and observe. They will ask clarifying questions. They will be more reflective as they approach learning activities. They like to see things unfold before jumping in. Are you a watcher?

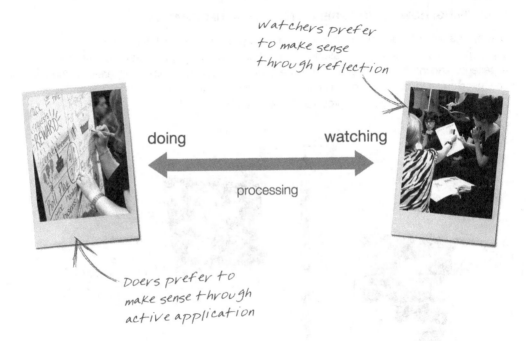

Watchers prefer to make sense through reflection

doing   watching

processing

Doers prefer to make sense through active application

Others prefer to jump into action. "Doers" are imagining how they will use the information you are sharing. They will be quick to move into activity, sometimes disregarding the directions. They will finish quickly. And they will have little interest in content that doesn't seem to be practical. Are you a doer?

Your Learning Style

When you combine the perceiving preference for feeling or thinking with the processing preference for watching or doing, you discover four distinct preference combinations. These four combinations are the foundation of the 4MAT design and delivery model and the 4MAT learning style descriptions:

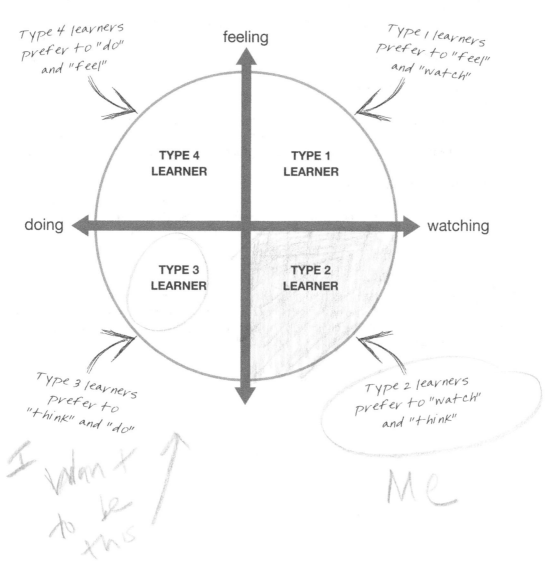

Type 4 learners prefer to "do" and "feel"

Type 1 learners prefer to "feel" and "watch"

feeling

TYPE 4 LEARNER

TYPE 1 LEARNER

doing

watching

TYPE 3 LEARNER

TYPE 2 LEARNER

Type 3 learners prefer to "think" and "do"

Type 2 learners prefer to "watch" and "think"

I want to be this

Me

The 4MAT Learning Styles

Learning style refers to your preference for how you like to take in and make meaning of new information. The combination of different approaches shapes the behaviors of learners:

Type One Learners
Prefer to take in information from a "feeling" perspective and make sense of it by "watching." In a new learning situation, Type One learners will rely on their intuition and gut when deciding on the relevance of information. They will take time to think things through before acting.

Type Two Learners
Prefer to take in information from a "thinking" perspective and make sense of it by "watching." In a new learning situation, Type Two learners will rely on external data and knowledge when deciding on the relevance of information. They will make sense of new information by reflecting and thinking things through before trying out new approaches.

Type Three Learners
Prefer to take in information from a "thinking" perspective and make sense of it by "doing." In a new learning situation, Type Three learners will rely on practicality as a guide in determining relevance. They will figure things out by playing around with new information and experimenting.

Type Four Learners
Prefer to take in information from a "feeling" perspective and make sense of it by "doing." In a new learning situation, Type Four learners will rely on their intuition and sense of what will work. They will try different approaches to determine the usefulness of the information being learned.

Want to be more this

The Four Primary Learning Styles

TYPE FOUR: DOERS/FEELERS

- Seek hidden possibilities
- Need to know what can be done with things
- Learn by trial-and-error, self-discovery
- Enrich reality
- Adaptable to change and relish it
- Enjoy variety and excel in being flexible
- Enjoy taking risks
- Often reach accurate conclusions without logic

Strength: action, carrying out plans

Goals: to make things happen

FAVORITE QUESTION: WHAT IF?

TYPE ONE: FEELER/WATCHERS

- Seek meaning
- Need to be personally involved
- Learn by listening and sharing ideas
- Absorb reality
- Interested in people and culture
- Function through social interaction
- Idea people

Strength: innovating and imagination

Goals: self-involvement in important issues, bringing unity to diversity

FAVORITE QUESTION: WHY?

TYPE THREE: THINKER/DOERS

- Seek usability
- Need to know how things work
- Learn by testing theories using practical methods
- Edit reality
- Use factual data to build concepts
- Enjoy hands-on experiences
- Problem solving
- Need "real-life" correlation

Strength: practical application of ideas

Goals: bringing their view of the present into line with the future

FAVORITE QUESTION: HOW?

TYPE TWO: WATCHER/DOERS

- Seek and examine the facts
- Need to know what the experts think
- Form reality
- Interested in ideas and concepts
- Critique information, collect data
- Thorough and industrious
- Enjoy the traditional classroom
- Function by adapting to experts

Strength: creating concepts and models

Goals: self-satisfaction and intellectual recognition

FAVORITE QUESTION: WHAT?

4 1
3 2

ME

Understanding Your Thinking Map

The 4MAT Learning Type Measure measures the degree of preference for each of the four learning approaches. When you complete the Learning Type Measure, you receive a score in all four learning approaches. Everyone has some level of strength in each of the four approaches. When plotted on a graph, the combined scores create a visual representation of learning and thinking preferences. We call this a "thinking map."

The preferred approach and the least preferred approach of a learner are equally important. We will explore what high strength in each of the four areas looks like. And we will also explore what lack of strength in each area looks like.

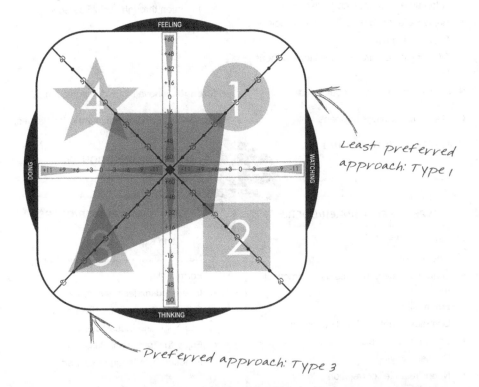

Least preferred approach: Type 1

Preferred approach: Type 3

» Learn more about taking or administering the Learning Type Measure at www.trainers-guide-to-learning-styles.com. Download a free guide to lead an interactive exploration of your team's learning style.

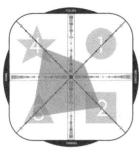

This learner will emphasize objective information including data, expert thinking, and real-world, proven approaches over opinions and anecdotal information.

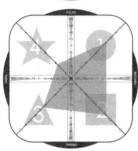

This learner will emphasize learning through doing. He or she may become easily bored with spending too much time in lecture and other instructional methods that "prepare" one to apply versus actually applying.

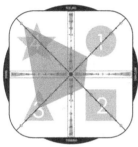

This learner prefers to make sense of information through reflection and will prefer time to "think things through" before moving into action.

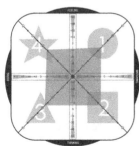

This learner has equal scores in all four approaches. This may be a result of equal preference in all four styles, limited self-awareness, or different learning approaches based on context.

In the next section, we will explore how each learning style strength shows up in different learning situations.

THE TYPE ONE LEARNER

 The Type One learning approach is highly participative and people-oriented. The Type One learning approach emphasizes exploring the relevance of the information being received. With this approach, learners reflect on their own experience and engage in interaction with others to compare and contrast their own experiences with those of others.

As a learner

High 1 ●━━━━━━━━━━━━━━━━━━━━━━━━━━━━━━● **Low 1**

Learners who are high in the Type One learning approach will spend more time reflecting on their own experiences and the experiences of others. They will enjoy interactive partner or group exercises that allow for dialogue and personal sharing.

Learners with a low level preference for the Type One learning approach will prefer to spend less time in interactive activities. They may be uncomfortable or impatient with too much emphasis on group sharing. They can quickly become frustrated with a "touchy-feely" approach to learning.

As a team member

High 1 ●━━━━━━━━━━━━━━━━━━━━━━━━━━━━━━● **Low 1**

The Type One team members need to understand the purpose of the work. They seek to uncover personal relevance. They perform best when they begin a project with a clear idea of the intended outcome. They rely on intuition and peer feedback when making decisions.

Team members with a low level of preference for the Type One learning approach will tend to emphasize objectivity. They will rely on outside sources, such as data, to guide decision making. They may be unaware of the impact of personal actions on others.

As a leader

High 1 ●━━━━━━━━━━━━━━━━━━━━━━━━━━━━━━● **Low 1**

Leaders who are high in the Type One learning approach will emphasize people as central to the success of the organization. They will use values and culture to guide behaviors.

Leaders with a low level of preference for the Type One learning approach will tend to emphasize external sources such as data and results to guide decision making. Their objectivity may result in their being perceived as aloof or uncaring.

Learner Type 1

Favorite question: why?

what's your story?

Date _____

- Seeks meaning
- Needs to be personally involved
- Learns by listening and sharing ideas
- Absorbs reality
- Interested in people and culture
- Functions through social interaction
- Idea people

I'm a **1** Are you ok with that?

The Type Two learning approach is analytical and fact-oriented. With this approach, a learner will place emphasis on exploring ideas and details.

As a learner

High 2 ●————————————————————————————● **Low 2**

All learners look for relevant information that will help them understand. Learners who are high in the Type Two learning approach will spend more time analyzing the information. They will have a higher need to understand the big ideas and details completely before moving into action.

Learners who have a low level of preference for the Type Two learning approach may become bored with too much time spent in information delivery or on the details. They can often miss important information or finer distinctions in their impatience to get to action.

As a team member

High 2 ●————————————————————————————● **Low 2**

The Type Two team members want to understand all the facts before developing an action plan. They will appreciate time for reflection before being asked for feedback or results. In a meeting, a Type Two learner will prefer to know the agenda before the meeting begins to allow for adequate preparation.

Team members who have a low level of preference for the Type Two learning approach may rely more on intuition than data. They may suggest strategies or ideas with no tangible "proof" to back them up. They will tend to invest less time in the details and are less likely to be exact in their work approach.

As a leader

High 2 ●————————————————————————————● **Low 2**

Type Two leaders will rely on data to guide decision making. They will use structure such as policies and procedures to guide behavior.

Leaders who have a low level of preference for the Type Two learning approach may rely on gut instinct or intuition for decision making. They may have a bias for action over reflection.

- Forms reality
- Thorough and industrious
- Seeks and examines the facts
- Interested in ideas and concepts
- Enjoys the traditional classroom
- Functions by adapting to experts
- Critiques information, collects data
- Needs to know what the experts think

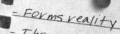

I'm a **2** — I'll send you my spreadsheet on it

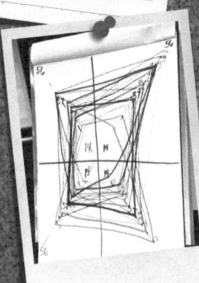

Learner Type 2

Favorite question: what?

THE TYPE THREE LEARNER

 The Type Three learning approach is objective and action-oriented. With this approach, a learner will focus on how things work in the real world.

As a learner

High 3 ●————————————————————● **Low 3**

The learners with a high preference for the Type Three learning approach prefer hands-on activities that focus on real-world issues. They value a practical approach to learning.

Learners who have a low level of preference for the Type Three learning approach may have a higher need for reflection, which will result in a tendency to move slowly into action They may be uncomfortable being "rushed" into practice.

As a team member

High 3 ●————————————————————● **Low 3**

Type Three team members will focus on their personal productivity. They thrive on clear accountability and deadlines. In a meeting, they will emphasize action over

Team members who have a low level of preference for the Type Three learning approach may easily get off-track and lose sight of the desired outcomes of the meeting. They may put little emphasis on defining action items and following up.

As a leader

High 3 ●————————————————————● **Low 3**

Type Three leaders will use results to guide decision making. They will use clear direction and personal accountability to guide behavior.

A leader with a low level of preference for the Type Three learning approach may focus more on the overall strategy, rather than the plan required for successful execution.

Hands On

Learner Type 3
Favorite question: HOW?

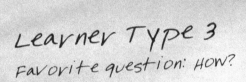

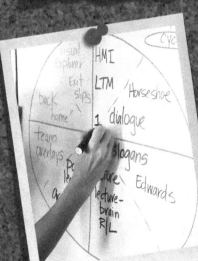

I'm a **3** Are we done yet?

- Seeks usability
- Needs to know how things work
- Learns by testing theories using practical methods
- Edits reality
- Uses factual data to build concepts
- Enjoys hands-on experiences and problem solving
- Needs "real-life" correlation

The Type Four learning approach is intuitive and innovation-oriented. With this approach, the learner will look for patterns, connections, and new adaptations.

As a learner

High 4 ●———————————————————● **Low 4**

Learners who are high in the Type Four learning approach will prefer to have flexibility in the learning environment. They will enjoy open-ended assignments and variety in the delivery approach.

Learners who have a low level of preference for the Type Four learning approach will demonstrate a preference for structure. They may struggle with "making it up" and will benefit from clear direction, guidelines, and structure in learning activities.

As a team member

High 4 ●———————————————————● **Low 4**

Team members with high strength in Type Four will bring creative thinking to the team. They will generate enthusiasm for new ideas. In a meeting, they will emphasize the need for a clear vision on where the team is

Team members who have a low level of preference for the Type Four learning approach will prefer a structured work environment with clear accountabilities.

As a leader

High 4 ●———————————————————● **Low 4**

Type Four leaders will use strategic competitiveness to guide decision making. They will use a shared vision of the future to guide behavior and inspire the team.

Leaders who have a low level of preference for the Type Four learning approach will lead through clear policies and procedures. Leaders who have a low level of preference for the Type Four learning approach may place more value on objective data versus subjective opinions.

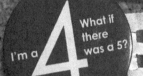

Learner Type 4
Favorite question: If?

I'm a 4 — What if there was a 5?

- seeks hidden possibilities
- Needs to know what can be done with things
- Learns by trial-and-error, self-discovery
- Enriches reality
- Adaptable to change and relishes it
- Enjoys variety and excels in being flexible
- Risk-takers
- often reaches conclusions without logic

Thinking Strengths of Each Style

If you are like most people, you have a certain way that you approach a problem. For example, when I am faced with a challenge to be solved, as a strong Type Four learner, I will first seek to understand the whole picture. I will look for connections, patterns, and themes that are emerging. This type of approach comes naturally to me, and I tend to use it as my default learning and problem-solving approach.

In the chart on the next page, you will see thinking skills aligned with the learning approach of each style. Take a moment to review the thinking skills.

When you are faced with a learning challenge, how do you approach the problem? Imagine a client asks you to look into the problem they are having with customer complaints in their department. Reflect on how you would approach developing a strategy to address the problem and create the desired outcome. What would be your approach? Highlight the thinking skills you would emphasize in your problem-solving process.

Thinking strength,
n., adj.,

1: A preferred approach to reasoning and problem solving which produces desirable outcomes

Thinking Strengths of Each Learning Style

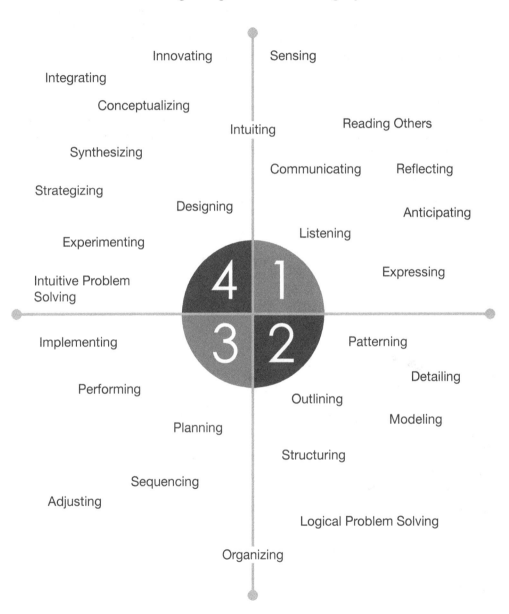

Functional Strengths of Each Style

Your preferred way of taking in and processing information often leads to preferences in the work that you do. Activities that utilize our natural strengths tend to energize us. Activities that require us to work from areas of weakness require more energy and they tend to drain us. We are most successful in the long run when we operate from our strengths, and most of us intuitively recognize this. This is why most people find themselves in careers or roles that play to their strengths.

In the chart on the next page, you will see functional activities overlayed on each of the four learning styles. Think about the type of work that excites you. Review all of the activities and then highlight three to five functions that energize you. It is not uncommon to notice that your preferred work is in alignment with your learning style approach. On the flip side, there are thinking skills that require more energy to engage in for any substantial period of time. Using a different color marker, highlight three to five functions that you find require more energy, or that might even drain you. Pay attention to how frequently you engage in energizing and draining functions in your current role.

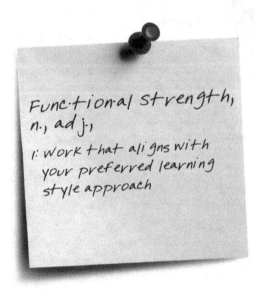

Functional strength,
n., adj.,
1: work that aligns with
your preferred learning
style approach

Functional Strengths of Each Style

Innovating   Engaging   Nurturing

Counseling

Strategizing   Teaching

Including

Leading

Facilitating

Uncovering Needs

Selling

Communicating

Marketing

Sharing Ideas

Designing

Executing   Organizing

Driving for Results

Creating Policies

Logical Problem Solving

Maintaining Systems

Developing Real-world Solutions   Record Keeping

Data Collecting

Coaching

Creating Structure

Supervising   Controlling Resources

ROLE AND LEARNING STYLE CORRELATION

Through our research on learning styles using the Learning Type Measure, we have discovered a correlation between roles and learning style preference. The research indicates strong correlation between learning style preferences and functional role choice. Here is a snapshot of how different roles are positioned on the 4MAT learning styles model:

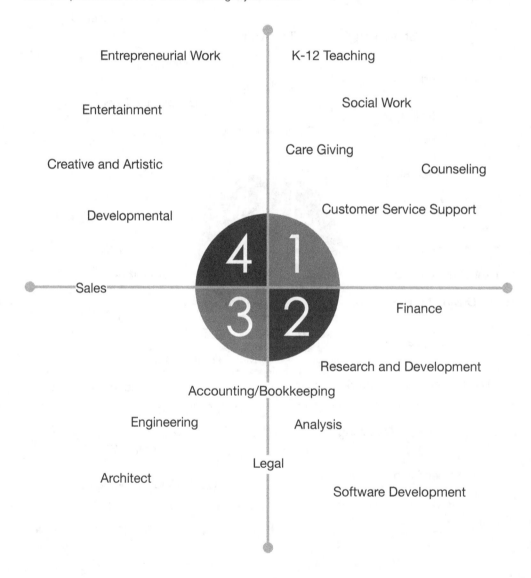

How Your Training Style Relates to the Needs of Each Learning Style

Your training style appeals more to some learning styles than others. When you apply your natural training strengths, you will likely find it easy to fulfill the needs of the learners who share your style preferences. To become conscious of where you need to stretch to reach those learners who have different needs, we will explore how your training style relates to the needs of each learning style. Once you have identified learners you need to stretch to reach, you can begin to expand your toolkit of instructional design and delivery strategies to reach all learners. First, let's review the needs of each learning style and how this might show up in a classroom learning environment. In the illustration below, you will find descriptions of the needs of four learners. In the remainder of this chapter, we will explore how each training style relates to each learning style, along with strategies for "stretching" to engage all learners.

TYPE FOUR: JOHN

John is a dynamic, Type Four learner. He loves spontaneity and the freedom to explore ideas and likes to interject his own insights into the dialogue. He enjoys trainers who create a dynamic learning environment and encourage creative thinking.

TYPE ONE: SAM

Sam is an imaginative, Type One Learner. He prefers to be connected with others. He loves interacting in small groups, discussing meaningful issues. He enjoys stories and meaningful dialogue. He enjoys authentic, personal trainers who he perceives to have high integrity.

TYPE THREE: ANITA

Anita is a hands-on, Type Three learner. She loves solving problems. If she never has to participate in another icebreaker activity again, that would be fine with her. She often prefers to do activities herself, to save time and reduce frustration.

TYPE TWO: GRACE

Grace is an analytic, Type Two learner. She prefers facts and sequential thinking. She loves organized lectures, but sometimes struggles with visionary thinking or random ideas being interjected into the discussion. She prefers to stay on track with the agenda.

Your training approach naturally appeals to some learning styles more than others. Let's explore how each style reacts to each training style approach.

The Type One Training Approach and All Four Styles

Type Four learners focus on doing and feeling

The Type Four learners will enjoy the opportunity to share their own experiences. If the dialogue becomes too "touchy-feely," they will grow frustrated with the lack of focus on real-world application.

Stretch to reach Type Four learners

Think about how personal insights explored will benefit real-world application. When leading dialogue, be careful to balance the exploration of past experiences with the impact on future application.

Type One learners focus on feeling and watching

The Type One learners appreciate your preference for exploring personal experiences. They will enjoy the opportunity for dialogue that your training approach often provides. They will need you to lead them into application of the information.

Stretch to reach Type One learners

It will be easier to engage Type One learners because your preferred training approach matches their learning preferences.

Type Three learners focus on thinking and doing

The Type Three learners have needs that oppose your preference for exploring personal experience and reflecting. Type Threes will quickly become frustrated with a lack of "how to" if you linger too long in feelings and personal experiences.

Stretch to reach Type Three learners

Define clearly the skills the learner will need to practice to be successful. Use dialogue and reflection to the extent it serves to engage and prepare learners for application. Balance learning time between watching and doing. When you are debriefing learner reflections or sharing, be sure to draw attention to how this will be useful in the real world.

Type Two learners focus on watching and thinking

The Type Two learners share your appreciation for reflection. However, they have a strong preference for concrete information over personal anecdotes. They will grow impatient with over- emphasis on personal experiences and opinions.

Stretch to reach Type Two learners

Structure your approach. When facilitating dialogue, be careful to call attention to the themes emerging in the dialogue. Connect the dialogue themes to the expert knowledge that validates the personal experiences of the learners.

The Type Two Training Approach and All Four Styles

Type Four learners focus on doing and feeling

The Type Four learners have needs that oppose your preference for reflection and methodical delivery of information. Type Four learners need to have an opportunity to explore and share their experiences related to the content. They will appreciate the willingness to explore ideas that may not be part of the planned content.

Stretch to reach Type Four learners

Look for opportunities to include interaction in your delivery of information. Create structures that will encourage learner input while maintaining control of the dialogue at the same time.

Type One learners focus on feeling and watching

The Type One learners share your appreciation for reflection. They will value the methodical way that you move through information. If you skip the opportunity for learners to explore the personal relevance of the information, the Type One learners will miss this.

Stretch to reach Type One learners

Allow time for exploration of the meaning of the content. Create a sense of community in the learning environment by allowing time for learners to get to know each other and identify what they find mutually important in the content being explored.

Type Three learners focus on thinking and doing

The Type Three learners share your appreciation for objective data and concrete knowledge. They will enjoy step-by-step delivery of information. Once they understand the steps, they will want to move quickly into action. Type Threes will have little patience for re-presenting or summarizing information, once they believe that they "got it."

Stretch to reach Type Three learners

Edit your content delivery to the essential knowledge needed to successfully apply the information in the real world. Be careful to create interaction during lecture and to look for alternative non-lecture ways of delivering content.

Type Two learners focus on watching and thinking

The Type Two learners appreciate the way you deliver information in an organized, methodical way. The Type Two learners will benefit from your guidance in moving into application.

Stretch to reach Type Two learners

Notice when Type Two learners over-emphasize the need to "know" over the need to "do." Create practice situations that allow all learners to check their understanding before you escalate practice to real-world situations.

The Type Three Training Approach and All Four Styles

Type Four learners focus on doing and feeling

The Type Four learners will enjoy the active learning environment that you create. They are less likely to follow the step-by-step, as you define it. They will want to be able to get creative with the application of the content.

Stretch to reach Type Four learners

Allow time for dialogue and brainstorming. Create opportunities for learners to self-assess their application and adapt for real-world implementation.

Type One learners focus on feeling and watching

The Type One learners have needs that oppose your preference for sharing concrete information and moving quickly into action. If you miss the opportunity to establish personal meaning and connections between the learners, the Type One learners will be impacted the most.

Stretch to reach Type One learners

Slow down and create an opportunity for learners to reflect on the importance of the information. Be willing to invest time in allowing learners to share their feelings and experiences.

Type Three learners focus on thinking and doing

The Type Three learners appreciate the way that you integrate real-world application into the learning environment.

Stretch to reach Type Three learners

Notice when Type Three learners want to move too quickly into action. Create reflection opportunities that appeal to this type of learner by connecting them to real-world skills.

Type Two learners focus on watching and thinking

The Type Two learners share your appreciation for objective data. However, they prefer to make meaning through reflection, rather than action.

Stretch to reach Type Two learners

Slow down and make sure that all learners are clear on the "how to." Create practice activities that enable you to check for understanding before turning learners "loose."

The Type Four Training Approach and All Four Styles

Type Four learners focus on doing and feeling

The Type Four learners share your appreciation for active learning and personal reflection. They will benefit from a balance of thinking and reflection.

Stretch to reach Type Four learners

Create opportunities for reflection. Encourage learners to do it the "expert" way before getting creative.

Type One learners focus on feeling and watching

The Type One learners share your appreciation for personal experience. They will appreciate the dialogue that you create in the learning environment. However, they prefer to make meaning through reflection and may have difficulty moving quickly into active learning application without time for personal reflection.

Stretch to reach Type One learners

Take time to encourage learner reflection. Balance individual, partner, and group reflection. Create learning activities that allow opportunities to reflect, before moving into application.

Type Three learners focus on thinking and doing

The Type Three learners share your preference for action. They will appreciate your emphasis on real-world issues. Type Three learners will appreciate structure and clear standards of performance.

Stretch to reach Type Three learners

Define clearly the skills the learner will need to practice to be successful. Be clear on standards of performance.

Type Two learners focus on watching and thinking

The Type Two learners needs oppose your natural training approach. You will need to be careful to organize your delivery in an easy-to-digest structure and to reference sources and base your assertions on data or expert thinking.

Stretch to reach Type Two learners

Structure your delivery. Create an agenda and stick to it. When leading interactive exercises, be conscious of linking the dialogue back to the established learning objectives. Give clear criteria for application before moving learners into practice.

Summary

In this chapter, we have explored the unique needs of the four primary learning styles. Your training style strengths will enable you to naturally connect with some learning styles more than others. To reach all learning styles, you will consciously include specific strategies that engage each learning style. More importantly, you will lead all learners through a learning cycle that must be completed for true learning to occur.

Your learning style refers to the part of the natural learning cycle that you tend to linger in. In Chapter 3, we will explore what the learner and trainer are doing in each step of this cycle of learning. You will discover that your training approach works in some parts of the cycle more than others. With a strong understanding of what must happen in the learning process to ensure learning transfer, you will be ready to explore and incorporate effective design and delivery strategies for each of the four parts of the cycle.

Q: Is one learning style more effective in a training role than another?

The key to being an effective trainer is the ability to satisfy the needs of all learners while delivering the desired learning transfer. All trainers, regardless of style, can use stretching strategies to reach all learners. The 4MAT Training Style Inventory (TRSI) measures your degree of focus in all four training dimensions.

Q: Is it possible to have preferences in more than one quadrant?

Yes, we all have strengths in each of the four quadrants. When you take the Learning Type Measure, you receive a visual display of your strengths that looks like the graph below.

Notice that the learner has strengths in all four quadrants. You may find that there are two styles that seem to describe your learning approach. Here are some common combination styles:

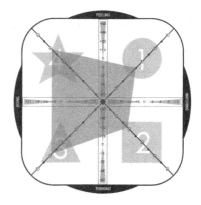

- Type 1-4 learners have high people skills in nurturing and influencing.

- Type 2-3 learners combine theory and application easily.

- Type 3-4 learners generate ideas and ask, "Will this really work?"

Q: Is the goal to be equal in all four learning approaches?

Should you be focused on developing equal skill, or equal scores, in all four learning approaches? The answer to this question is "no." Your natural strengths lead you to the activities that energize you. The goal should be to have the ability to access the learning skills needed in any given situation. For example, I have a natural strength in big picture thinking. I would prefer to spend time in concepts, rather than details. When I find myself in a situation that requires detailed thinking, I have developed strategies that enable me to pay attention to the details while also keeping the bigger picture in mind.

Reflect on the needs of all four learning styles. Which learning styles does your training style naturally engage? Which styles might you be missing?

Reflect on your role. How frequently are you engaged in work that utilizes your natural thinking strengths? How might you operate more frequently from your strengths?

- Identify which learning styles your style naturally engages and which styles you might be missing.
- Focus on leading learners through the four key questions (Why, What, How, and If) when you design and deliver learning experiences.

"Simply notice the order of things.
Work with it rather than against it.
For to try to change what is
only sets up resistance."

~ Lao Tzu
Tao Te Ching

Chapter 3

4MAT: The Four Steps of the Learning Cycle

Our brains receive a constant stream of information as electrical impulses from our senses. The information is transported through electrical connections between brain cells, or neurons. The processing of the information being delivered through electrical impulses is what we call "thought."

Recognizing that thinking (and learning) is the product of physiological connections in the brain is important for trainers. Knowledge of how the brain works gives a trainer important insights into how to design brain-friendly instruction such as:

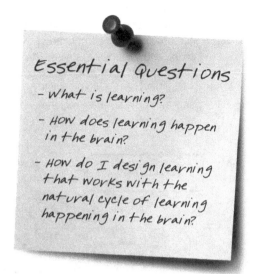

Essential Questions

- What is learning?

- How does learning happen in the brain?

- How do I design learning that works with the natural cycle of learning happening in the brain?

- To gain attention, information must be relevant, interesting, novel, or some combination thereof.

- Thinking and learning are about connections. We learn by connecting to what we already know.

The physiological structure of the brain greatly influences which learning strategies work the best. Understanding the structure of the brain will help you develop learning experiences that work with the natural cycle of learning. In this chapter, we will take a brief tour of the brain and explore what physiologically happens when we learn and how we can use this information to design and deliver impactful learning experiences.

A Brief Tour of the Brain

To better understand how learning happens, let's take a brief tour of the structure of the brain. The human brain is composed of two major components. One is the cerebrum, which is divided into left and right hemispheres. The other component is the cerebellum, located just below the cerebrum. Each of the hemispheres of the cerebrum is divided into four parts: frontal, temporal, parietal, and occipital. In a highly general explanation, each of these four parts of the brain performs some specific, regionalized function. Yet, every part of the brain operates in connection with every other part.

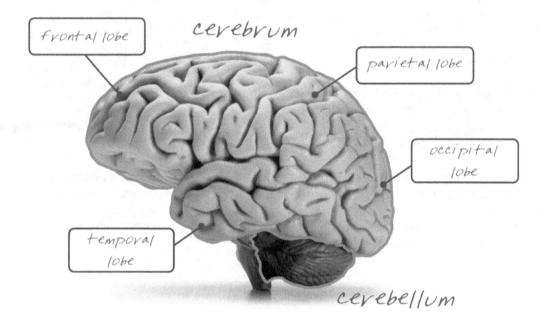

There are more potential connections between the neurons in your brain than there are atoms in the universe. The ability to signal each other through electrical stimulation distinguishes brain cells from any other cell in the body. This transmission of signals between neurons is what we refer to as "thinking."

The surface area of the brain contains layers of nerve cells called neurons. It is estimated that there are over 100 billion neurons in the brain. Neurons send signals to one another through electrical connections. "There are more potential connections between the neurons (in your brain) than there are atoms in the universe" (Carter, Aldridge, Martyn, & Parker, 2009, p. 39). The ability to signal each other through electrical stimulation distinguishes brain cells from any other cell in the body. This transmission of signals between neurons is what we refer to as "thinking."

Some connections between neurons, or synapses, are stronger than others. Or you could say that some connections fire more or less frequently than others. There are two factors that affect the strength of the connections: how much the connections are used and how important the signals are to the learner.

As a trainer, it is important to know that the most effective way to engage a learner is by linking the content you are sharing to something your learners know and/or that is significant to them.

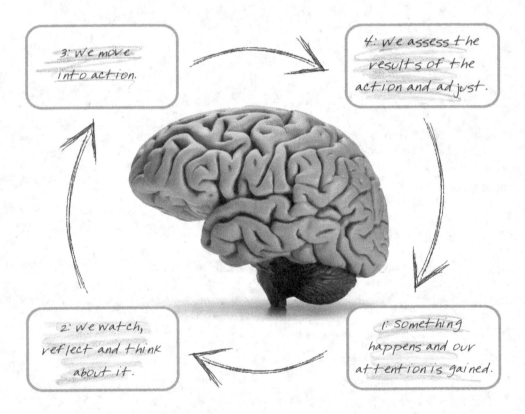

3: We move into action.

4: We assess the results of the action and adjust.

2: We watch, reflect and think about it.

1: Something happens and our attention is gained.

Brain Research on Learning

When we learn something new, our brains move through a four-step cycle. We refer to the four steps of the 4MAT learning cycle as Engage, Share, Practice, and Perform. This chapter explores the four steps of this natural, research-based learning cycle:

4MAT: THE FOUR STEPS

1 **Engage: Something happens and our attention is gained.** The brain takes in a vast amount of information. Only a very small amount of this information is selected for processing to the point at which we become conscious of it. Incoming information that is personally relevant, surprising, or incongruent with what we believe to be true will likely gain our attention. When incoming information is processed and becomes conscious, our attention is gained. We become engaged.

2 **Share: We watch, reflect, and think about it.** We look for what we recognize in the incoming information. We comprehend and make sense of what we are taking in through our senses. We think, judge, and evaluate the incoming information. We begin to plan our movement into action.

3 **Practice: We move into action.** We move into action and apply the information being learned. This new application creates a new experience. Next, we begin to notice what worked and didn't in this new application.

4 **Perform: We assess the results of the action and adjust.** We take notice of the results of our actions. We assess what worked, what didn't, and what could be better. We refine and create our individual adaptation of the information. This new experience begins the cycle again.

The Four Steps

The 4MAT model for instruction mirrors the cycle of learning that occurs naturally in the brain. Let's explore this cycle with a real-world example. Reflect on your own experience of learning to ride a bike. Why did you want to learn to ride a bike? Did you see a cool, new bike in the store? Did your older brother or sister ride a "big kid" bike? Did you want to be able to ride with your friends?

Let's watch as seven-year-old Johnny learns to ride a bike:

1 Engage: Something happens.
Johnny sees his older brother riding his bike to school. Johnny wants to be able to ride to school with his brother. Suddenly, learning to ride a "big kid" bike becomes important to Johnny. Johnny's attention becomes focused on learning to ride the bike.

2 Share: We watch, reflect, and think about it.
Johnny starts to notice how others ride a bike. Johnny watches his brother ride and decides that it doesn't look too difficult. He can imagine himself riding the bike with ease. Johnny decides to ask his dad to teach him to ride. Dad, the "expert," instructs Johnny to pedal fast and keep the handlebars level. Johnny evaluates what his dad says and plans how he will approach the ride.

3 Practice: We move into action.
Johnny begins to practice riding the bike. First, his dad holds the seat of the bike, as Johnny pedals. As Johnny gains more confidence, his dad lets him go.

4 Perform: We assess the results of the action and adjust.
As Johnny rides, he begins to notice what works for him and what doesn't. He does some of what his dad told him to do and begins to come up with his own way of riding the bike. Johnny is having his own experience. He begins to ride his own way. The cycle now begins again.

Johnny begins to ride his own way

Johnny sees his older brother riding his bike to school

4: Perform: we assess the results of the action and adjust

1: Something happens

3: We move into action

2: We watch, reflect, and think about it

Johnny practices with Dad's help

Johnny watches and learns from his Dad

Reflect on something you learned recently and ask yourself how you moved through these four parts of the learning process.

How did you adapt the information to make it useful in your world? How did you know if you were doing it "right"?

What grabbed your attention? Why was learning this information meaningful to you? Why was it worth investing time to learn?

4 1

3 2

How did you put the information to use? Did you have a chance to apply the information to real-world problems?

What information was shared that would prepare you for application? What resources did you use to learn the information? Was there an "expert" who shared information with you?

Using the 4MAT Model to Design Learning

4MAT is a straightforward adaptation of what we know about how people learn. When you follow the four steps of the 4MAT Cycle and lead the learner to ask and answer the four key questions (Why?, What?, How? and If?), you will deliver brain-friendly learning that mirrors how learning happens in the brain.

In each step of the 4MAT cycle, both the learner and the trainer have a specific focus. In the table below, you will find an overview of what is happening in each step of the learning cycle. The skills needed to successfully deliver all four parts of the cycle differ. Your Training Style Inventory results will give you a good idea of which part of the cycle you are inclined to deliver with greater ease. Here is an overview of the different focus of each step and the skills needed to deliver each step well:

STEP IN THE CYCLE	WHAT THE LEARNER IS DOING	WHAT THE TRAINER IS DOING
Engage	Establishing a relationship between the content and his or her personal life.	Constructing/facilitating an experience that connects the learners personally to the information being shared. Guiding reflection and using dialogue to generate insights and build community. **Trainer Role: Facilitator**
Share	Seeing how the information fits together. Receiving information, evaluating and making sense. Connecting the dots.	Sharing information and knowledge needed to support the desired behavior shift. **Trainer Role: Presenter**
Practice	Moving into action. Applying the information learned. Gaining skill.	Leading practice activities to encourage skill development. Coaching performance. **Trainer Role: Coach**
Perform	Taking ownership of the information and assessing performance. Implementing in the real world.	Encouraging learners to evaluate their own application. Giving feedback and equipping learners with the ability to assess their own performance. Gaining commitment on future performance. **Trainer Role: Supportive Evaluator**

In this rest of this chapter, we will explore what the trainer is doing in each of the four parts of the learning cycle. In Chapters 5 through 8, we will dive deeper into the strategies, techniques, and tools you can use to design and deliver the desired learning outcome for each part of the cycle.

The First Step: Engage

In the first step of the learning cycle the learner's attention is gained. The trainer leads the learner through this part of the cycle by exploring the question, "Why?"

- Why is this content meaningful?
- Why is this content relevant?
- Why should I pay attention to and apply this information?

Personal stories, individual and group sharing, dialogue and reflection are all fundamental elements of this part of the learning cycle. Strong facilitation skills are needed to deliver this part of the learning experience successfully. The trainer connects the content to the learners' lives by establishing personal relevance and encouraging reflective dialogue.

ESTABLISHING PERSONAL RELEVANCE

The challenge with most training or learning experiences is that the experience leads with data, facts, and logic. The difference between the impact of logic and the impact of emotion is huge. We rarely act on logic alone. Although logic is an important part of the decision-making process, more often than not, it is emotion that moves us out of inertia into action. For example, 1 in 5 people in the US smoke despite the data, facts, and logic that would suggest that quitting would be a wise choice. It often takes a health crisis to encourage a smoker to stop smoking (American Cancer Society, 2011).

ENCOURAGE REFLECTIVE DIALOGUE

If you want to grab attention, engage, and inspire, you have to tap into the learner's personal beliefs, motivations, dreams, desires, and existing paradigms. You must ask "What does the learner want?" and connect the content to this desire. This doesn't mean that every set of training materials should come with a box of Kleenex®. It does mean that authentic, real conversations have to be invited into the learning process. All learning is the product of asking and answering questions. In the first part of the learning cycle, the ability to uncover the questions the learners are asking themselves and to frame the learning around these questions is essential to tapping into the intrinsic motivations of the learner.

The opening of the learning experience is critical. In those first moments of a learning experience, learners evaluate the experience and determine the level of attention they will invest. In Chapter 4, we will explore how to create openings that engage the learner immediately. You will also find examples of activities that work well in this step of the learning experience.

Handwritten margin notes:
The Question is: Why?
Personal Relevance not facts + data
Let them share their thinking + ideas.
Invite authentic real conversations reflect real life.

The Second Step: Share

In the second part of the learning cycle, Share, the learner begins to explore and understand the content. The trainer leads the learner through this part of the cycle by exploring and answering the question, "What?" What information should be explored around this content? What data exist? What do the experts have to say? What does the learner need to know to be able to apply this information in the real world? Lecture, video, demonstrations, and presentations are all standard fare for this part of the learning cycle. Strong presentation skills are needed to deliver this part of the learning experience successfully. When stories, images, and metaphors are included, the content is brought to life.

The question is: What?

THE POWER OF STORIES

From the beginning of time, humans have shared meaning through stories. Stories are powerful because they illustrate the impact of choices and actions of others.

Whats important to know to apply this

When we share the right story, we wrap up all the information we need to get across in a package that the learner can't wait to open. We are born hard-wired to learn through stories. When we elicit stories from the learners, we create an opportunity to discover their previous experiences and existing paradigms around the content being shared.

THE POWER OF IMAGES

Elicit stories from the learners — their experiences

Not straight lecture ↓ Bring content to life through — stories — metaphor — images

In this part of the learning cycle, the trainer shares knowledge, generally through lecture, demonstration, and media such as PowerPoint®. The use of well-chosen, relevant images has the power to exponentially increase learning transfer. In Chapter 5, we will explore how to maximize the impact of visual tools including how to use flipcharts, visual organizers, and PowerPoint to reinforce your message.

All learning comes from asking + answering questions

Each piece of info is a thread. Weave them together. = Cohesive whole

Each new thread must connect to the others.

What metaphor will best guide them?

THE POWER OF METAPHORS

Learners with different levels of competency will "see" the content being learned differently. A fourth-grader has a different perspective of biology than a college professor with a PhD in biology. The metaphor is a powerful tool for a trainer to use to understand how the learner sees the content and for changing that view by introducing a new metaphor. If we want to shift behavior toward a desired outcome, we must identify what metaphor will best guide the thinking and action of the learner.

WEAVING IT ALL TOGETHER

When sharing information in a learning experience, it is helpful to think of each piece of information as an individual thread. Each thread has to be connected to and woven together with all the other threads to form a cohesive learning experience. When this is done well, the threads come together to form a cohesive whole, not unlike a tapestry. When sharing lecture, think of yourself as the weaver working the loom. Each new thread of information has to connect to all the others.

The ability to structure the content so that the learners can make sense of the parts and the whole is critical in this part of the learning cycle. In Chapter 5, we will explore how to maximize the use of images, stories, and metaphors in your lecture and how to weave it all together into a cohesive whole. You will also find examples of activities that work well in this part of the learning experience.

The Third Step: Practice

In the third part of the learning cycle the learner moves into application. The trainer leads the learner through this part of the cycle by exploring and answering the question, "How?"

- How is this information useful?
- How might I use this in the real world?
- How might this information help me solve real-world problems?

The question is:

HOW?

In this part of the learning cycle, the learners take ownership and begin to explore how they will make use of the information in their world. In this step, the trainer moves "off-stage" and focuses on giving valuable feedback. Strong coaching skills are necessary to deliver this part of the learning experience successfully. Case studies, role plays, simulations, and hands-on application are some of the types of activities that make up essential elements of this part of the learning cycle.

MOVING OFF-STAGE

In the beginning of the learning cycle, you are doing the heavy lifting. You get the conversation going and you lead the learners through exploring the content they will need to understand to be able to apply the information. When you move into Practice, the learner takes over. You move off-stage and begin to play the role of observer and coach.

The ability to listen, observe, ask questions, and give direct feedback is critical to your success in this part of the learning cycle.

GIVING VALUABLE FEEDBACK

The trainer's role in Practice is that of the coach. To do this well requires active listening and keen observation. To be an effective coach, a trainer also has to be curious about the process the learner is moving through. Coaches have to suspend judgment in order to truly listen and really see what is going on, both on and under the surface. In Chapter 6, we will explore a four-part model for offering coaching. You will also find examples of activities that work well in this part of the learning experience.

The Fourth Step: Perform

In the fourth part of the learning cycle the learner adapts and refines the information for successful implementation in the real world. The trainer leads the learner through this part of the cycle by exploring and answering the question, "If?"

- If this information is to be applied, what adaptations will I have to make?
- If I were to combine this with existing knowledge or systems in my world, what might this create?

Self-assessment, peer feedback sessions, and action planning are appropriate activities for this part of the learning experience. Assessing performance, gaining commitments and measuring success are key focus areas for the trainer during this step of the cycle. Strong evaluation and feedback skills are necessary for successful delivery of this part of the learning experience.

ASSESSING PERFORMANCE

Learners are equipped with a critical skill—the ability to assess their own progress and anticipate barriers to implementation in this step. This involves creating an opportunity for the learners to figure out what they did well and where they see areas of improvement. Self-assessment, performance standards, and peer feedback are all examples of approaches that work well in this part of the learning cycle. Here the trainer focuses on gaining commitment on future implementation and measuring success.

GAINING COMMITMENT

Designing a mechanism to ensure that the learner applies the information outside the learning event is a critical part of the final piece of the learning design. Learner commitment forms, follow-up sessions, and in-field observation all fit well in this part of the learning cycle.

MEASURING SUCCESS

Assessing how you measure success is an important first step in the design process. In Chapter 10, we will explore further how to define the measure of success before you begin designing your training. You will craft four learning outcomes which will help guide you in your activity choice for each part of the cycle.

Summary

The 4MAT model provides a four-step framework for delivering brain-friendly instruction: Engage, Share, Practice, and Perform. Your training style preferences may influence in which parts of this model you are strongest. The remainder of this book focuses on how to build strength in all four parts of the learning cycle. In the next four chapters, we will explore how to effectively design and deliver instruction in each part of the cycle.

REFLECT

Reflect on a recent learning experience. Determine which parts of the learning cycle were addressed in the learning process.

How did the trainer connect you to the meaning and personal relevance of the content?

How was the delivery of the information structured? Was it easy to grasp? Were stories and images used to animate the content?

Did you have an opportunity to apply the information?

Were you encouraged to be creative with the information? Was there a standard provided that allowed you to judge your own application?

Were there some parts of the learning process you enjoyed more than others?

Revisit a recent training or presentation that you delivered and ask yourself the following:

Were all four parts of the learning cycle present?

Did you emphasize some more than others?

How would your design or delivery benefit from a different balance of focus?

Identify which of the four steps you most need to focus on.

What strategies do you use that might enhance your weaker training approaches?

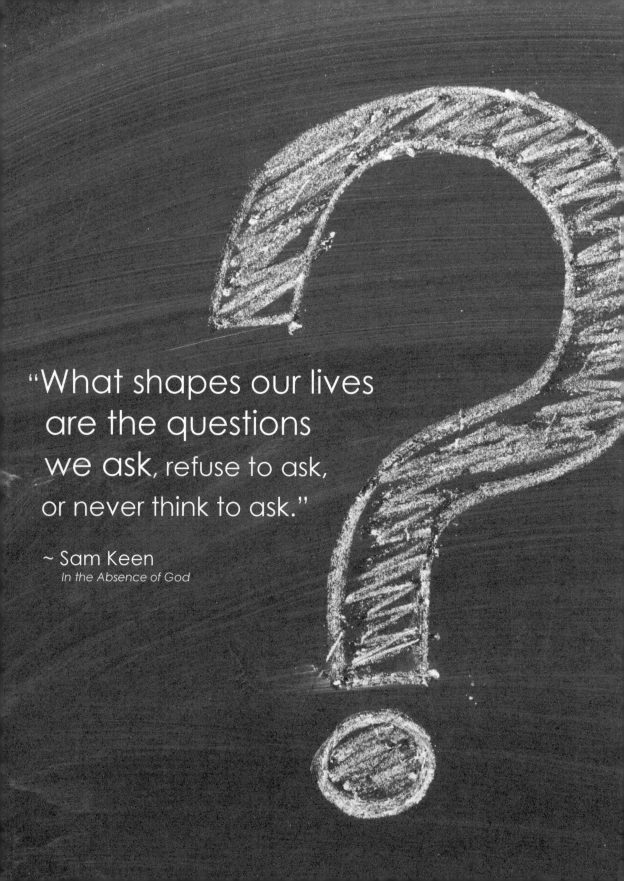

"What shapes our lives
are the questions
we ask, refuse to ask,
or never think to ask."

~ Sam Keen
In the Absence of God

Chapter 4

Engage: The Art of Creating Powerful Openings

David gets to work early to finish up some emails, grabs a cup of coffee, and rushes to the training class. He finds his assigned seating, puts on his name badge and waits for the session to begin. The facilitator walks to the front of the room and invites people to share their names and the departments in which they work.

After 35 minutes of introductions, the facilitator begins the program by telling them what they will learn and why it will be important to them. David begins to think that this course sounds an awful lot like the course he attended last year. The facilitator begins lecturing using PowerPoint and invites everyone to follow along in their workbooks. The day proceeds with the learners listening (a lot) and the facilitator inviting groups to periodically come together to "process" their insights and ask questions.

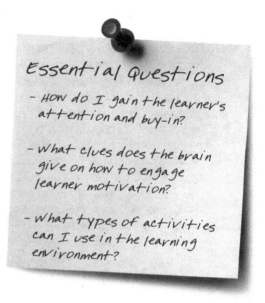

Essential Questions

- How do I gain the learner's attention and buy-in?

- What clues does the brain give on how to engage learner motivation?

- What types of activities can I use in the learning environment?

Across town, Jennifer gets to work early to drop off some presentation materials to a colleague and then rushes over to her training class. As she arrives at the door, she is welcomed by a poster with a thought-provoking question. The facilitator arrives at the door and greets her. The facilitator explains that she will be shaping the "conversation" today around the interests of the group. The facilitator hands Jennifer a sticky note. On the note Jennifer reads: "Reflect on the biggest question you have on the topic today. If you could have one question explored and answered, what would it be? Write your question on this sticky note and post it on the 'Wonder Wall.'"

As Jennifer enters the room, she notices the energizing music and flipcharts with visuals posted throughout the room. A PowerPoint slide displays a quote related to the topic of the day on a screen at the front of the room. Jennifer chooses her seat, reflects, writes her question, and posts in on the colorful flip chart labeled "Wonder?" She takes a moment and reviews questions posted by other learners in the room. The facilitator opens the session by quickly orienting everyone to the course materials, class structure, and objectives of the day. Learners are invited to complete a reflection exercise which elicits issues learners deal with related to the content being explored. The facilitator uses questions on the "wonder wall" to initiate a dialogue on why the content being learned is significant and how the exploration of the content will address the learners' questions. The sense of community established during the sharing process carries forward throughout the rest of the program. Which session would you rather attend?

Creating engaging learning sessions begins with focusing on the interests of the learners. Gaining the learners' attention by connecting to what they already know about and are interested in related to the content will increase learner engagement. The ability to facilitate meaningful dialogue is critical to leading this part of the learning cycle, Engage.

In the first part of the 4MAT cycle, Engage, the learner is focused on discovering the personal relevance of the content being shared. The learner asks the question, "Why?" The types of activities included in this step are designed to encourage learners to reflect upon experiences and knowledge related to the concept being explored. The goal in Engage is to establish personal relevance and meaning.

Before we explore what effective facilitators do, it is important to note what effective facilitators believe that enable them to facilitate masterfully. There are two beliefs that will support you in maximizing your impact in the facilitation role:

- Belief 1: The wisdom lives in the room.
- Belief 2: By giving up control, you enable the learning process.

BELIEF 1: THE WISDOM LIVES IN THE ROOM

Socrates was a 5th century B.C. Greek philosopher credited as one of the founders of Western philosophy. He believed that each person was born with full knowledge and it was the responsibility of an educator to tap into that knowledge. He used a method of questioning students to lead them to self-discovery, which is referred to as the "Socratic Method." The Socratic Method can be seen as the basis for the facilitation or dialogue method that is effectively used by trainers in the learning environment. Using the Socratic Method, the facilitator uncovers the wisdom in the room by:

- Creating opportunities for the learners to reflect on their experiences related to the content.
- Asking questions that encourage reflection and self-awareness.
- Creating safety in the room by honoring all responses as valuable.

Think like socrates.

BELIEF 2: BY GIVING UP CONTROL, YOU ENABLE THE LEARNING PROCESS

I was lucky enough to work with a mentor who taught me a great deal about the power of perspective. Regardless of his official role in any situation, he always showed up as an influential leader. In meetings, he would often say little. Then there would be a moment when he would pose a question, summarize the dialogue, and frequently stun the rest of us with his insights. He seemed to have a magical ability to harness the focus of the group. I remember remarking on this once to him and asking him how he did this. He shared, "Too many people are focused on being in control when their focus should be on generating influence. To gain influence, you need perspective. People who can be objective and who can distance themselves from their own opinions can see what is really going on and have the greatest perspective. When you have the broadest perspective, you always have the most influence."

The questions are more important than the answers

If you want to be an effective facilitator, focus on cultivating perspective. The right questions will allow you to uncover the learners' experiences and beliefs connected to the content. Trust that the patterns and themes that emerge in the dialogue will give you a critical connection point to motivate learning.

Now, let's look at what a trainer does to effectively facilitate learning.

What Happens in Engage

In Engage, the trainer plays the role of "facilitator," creating an opportunity for the learner to explore questions and generate possible answers by encouraging personal reflection and dialogue. To play the role of facilitator effectively, you focus on three things:

Focus 1: Gaining the attention of the learner by linking the content to what they already know.

Focus 2: Using questions to encourage reflection, generate dialogue, and guide the movement of the group.

Focus 3: Creating a safe environment which encourages sharing. We will explore strategies for each focus in this chapter. The methods shared in this chapter can be applied in any learning situation including meetings, keynote sessions, one-hour programs, and multi-day programs. You will also find activities that work for this part of the cycle shared in the context of how they might be used in real-world training situations.

Focus 1: Gaining Attention by Linking to What Learners Already Know

We can think of "attention" as energy that we budget with great care. We are bombarded on a daily basis with sights, sounds, aromas, and other sensations. Our brains filter out the vast majority of this while paying conscious attention to only a small portion of it. If you want to engage the learner, you have to capture the attention of the learner. A good facilitator gains attention by tapping into what the learner already knows about the content while focusing on what is significant to the learner.

ALL LEARNERS COME TO THE LEARNING EXPERIENCE WITH SOME PRIOR KNOWLEDGE

The brain is made up of cells called "neurons" and the connections between these cells are called "neuronal connections." Knowledge is stored in the neuronal connection pathways. Any change in knowledge comes from changes in the neuronal connections. Each new experience creates new connections. The strength of these connections varies based on the frequency of use (how often we think a thought) and the relative importance to the learner. If you want to connect to what the learner already knows, one of the easiest ways to do this is to explore the learner's experiences related to the content you are teaching and the larger concepts associated with it.

More relevance and repetition lock experiences into long-term memory. Knowing this, trainers can connect new information to existing connections by tapping into the learner's previous experiences with the content and repeatedly referencing these connections throughout delivery of the information. In The *Art of Changing the Brain*, Dr. James Zull shares three things that every presenter, leader, coach, and trainer needs to know about the existing knowledge of learners (Zull, 2002):

- All learners come to the learning experience with some prior knowledge.
- Existing knowledge does not go away or change without some new experience.
- All new knowledge is built upon existing knowledge.

To change the beliefs, attitude, and perception of the learner, you have to create a new experience that forms new connections in the brain.

EXISTING KNOWLEDGE DOES NOT GO AWAY WITHOUT A NEW EXPERIENCE

What we believe influences the way we behave. To change behaviors, we must change beliefs. Beliefs are always rooted in past experience. To create a new way of thinking, you must create a new experience.

ALL NEW KNOWLEDGE IS BUILT UPON EXISTING KNOWLEDGE

Reflect back on learning something that had little personal relevance or no concrete experience associated with it. Was it difficult to learn?

Without an existing concrete experience of the concept being explored, learners struggle with making meaning of new information. When you point the learners toward what is familiar and known about the content, they recognize an existing neuronal connection or pathway. This existing pathway of understanding enables learners to make meaning of the new information being shared.

For many of us, learning algebra is a great example of how much effort has to be exerted when we have no existing concept of what is being taught. Learning quadratic equations, for example, can be a struggle for learners who have no concept of how this relates to their world. Connecting the content to familiar concepts helps learners establish personal relevance. A group of math teachers worked with Dr. Bernice McCarthy to develop 4MAT 4Algebra, an ingenious way of teaching algebra using ten over-arching concepts that are familiar to grade-school-level students. The first concept introduced is the concept of "Communication." Students experience a variety of exercises that tap into their experiences of understanding through language. When algebra is introduced as a "language" that enables students to mathematically describe events that happen in the real world, the content immediately becomes more familiar and learning is enhanced. A study of the impact of this curriculum was conducted in an inner city school setting comparing a group of students being taught algebra using the 4MAT method versus students being taught using traditional teaching methods. Algebra students in the 4MAT–based teaching group passed at a rate of 80.4 percent versus a comparable pass rate of 42.7 percent of students taught using traditional teaching methods. The 4MAT model's emphasis on connecting to what learners already know resulted in nearly twice as many students grasping the concept of algebra.

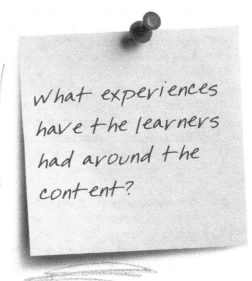

What experiences have the learners had around the content?

CONNECTING TO WHAT THE LEARNER ALREADY KNOWS

You might ask, "How do I begin with what they know if the reason I am there is to teach them what they don't know?" You do this by tapping into what the learner already knows by inviting in previous experiences. The more significant the experience and/or the more ingrained the thoughts you evoke, the more relevance the learner attaches to the experience. Personal relevance is the source of learner motivation and inspiration.

Think about your audience. Get into their mindset. Ask yourself:

- What experiences have these learners had around this content?
- What concerns them?
- What do they talk about?
- What stories might I elicit?
- What keeps them up at night?
- What is holding them back?
- What do they want?

The process of connecting learners to the content being learned can begin before learners arrive in the formal learning environment.

ENGAGING LEARNERS BEFORE FORMAL LEARNING BEGINS

Learners come to a formal learning experience with some pre-determined level of engagement. The feedback from colleagues who previously attended the program, the information they received on the course (or didn't), and the tantrum their three-year-old exhibited at daycare drop-off are all examples of factors that influence engagement. There are some we can control and others we cannot.

Reflect on something you have recently learned. What question were you trying to answer? We become actively engaged in the learning process when we have a question we want answered. A learner's question such as, "How can I stop bringing home work on the weekend so that I can have more time with my family?" can become the source of motivation to learn more about effective time management.

Think about how you can engage learners before the formal learning event begins. Focus on how you can encourage learners to identify and explore the questions they want to answer around the content to be explored. Personal reflection, storytelling, journaling, and group dialogue are examples of the types of activities that work well in this step. In the next section of this chapter, we will explore effective Engage strategies you can use before and during the formal learning experience.

When you point the learners toward what is familiar around the content and what they already know, they recognize an existing pathway. This pathway of understanding leads them to making meaning of the new information being shared. They can learn with much less effort.

STRATEGIES TO ENGAGE LEARNERS BEFORE FORMAL LEARNING BEGINS

To optimize engagement, learners must identify the questions they want to explore in the learning experience. In the table below you will find examples of methods you can use to engage learners before formal learning begins.

Engaging Invitations and Sign-In Materials	Make the invitation to the training program compelling. Think about incorporating visuals, pictures of past participants, or testimonials on the course. Choosing a theme for the event can often serve as inspiration for the invitation and sign-in materials. Example: For a course on managing cost reduction, a group of trainers developed a theme of "Hidden Treasure." The invitations to mid-level managers were packaged like a scroll with a "treasure map" outlining the key learning outcomes of the course.
Choose a Theme	A theme can convey the tone of the learning experience, creating positive expectations before learners arrive. Example: For a personal development course on goal setting, the theme of the event was "Dream Trippin'." The training room incorporated 70's style images and the metaphor of a road trip (in a 70's VW wagon) was used to illustrate the goal setting "journey."
Book or Article with a Companion "Study Guide"	Pre-reading assignments can help prepare learners and lessen lecture time. Identify what you want learners to gain from the reading and design "book study" questions to focus the learners' attention. Example: In a leadership journey focused on exploring the concept of "strengths," participants were invited to read the *Harvard Business Review* article by Peter Drucker, "Managing Oneself" (Goldstein, 2011). A series of questions encouraged learners to reflect on personal relevance of the concepts to be explored in the course.
Self-Assessment Tool	We are activated to learn new behaviors when we recognize there is a gap between our current reality and our desired reality. Self-assessment tools can lead learners to recognize performance gaps that provoke new questions that will be addressed through the course content. Example: In a time management workshop, learners are invited to complete a self-assessment questionnaire which invites reflection on personal values (what learners say is most important) and where they actually invest their time.
Podcast, Video, or Recorded Webinar	Record a welcome message to create a sense of community and preview the content. A powerful pre-session message can create an opportunity for learners to connect with the larger purpose of the training. Example: To launch a company-wide training initiative, a podcast featuring the CEO sharing a welcome message highlighting the value of the content to each team member is shared.

Reflections

Creating an opportunity for learners to reflect on their own experiences related to the content can begin prior to the learning event.

Example: Learners are invited to share reflections on "My favorite learning experience" in an online course forum, prior to the beginning of the first classroom session. The stories shared are incorporated by the facilitator into the Engage portion of the course.

Quotes

Share a quote and invite learners to reflect on the meaning of the quote. Or share a series of quotes and invite learners to choose one that best illustrates their beliefs around the content being explored. You can also invite learners to bring a favorite quote to the course.

Example: In a Six Sigma course, learners are sent three quotes related to the concept of "perspective." Learners are invited to choose one of the quotes which best represents how they view their role in leading quality. The facilitator opens the session by leading dialogue focused on the concept that "what I see determines what I do." The Six Sigma tools are introduced as a way of seeing differently to produce different outcomes.

Visual Organizers

You can create a visual organizer of the content being shared, which links the content to common learner issues related to the content. This can serve as a preview of content being explored, as well as a note-taking tool throughout delivery.

Example: In a product knowledge course, participants are provided a mindmap linking questions salespeople often hear from customers with the content that will be explored in the course.

Metaphors

Metaphors are powerful tools for understanding. Invite learners to identify a metaphor related to the concept you will be exploring.

Example: In a workshop focused on leading change, the question, "Why is change an essential part of growth?" is posed. Learners are asked to bring an "element of nature" that represents how they view change to the learning session. The facilitator opens the session by leading a dialogue on learners' experiences of the "cycle of change" by inviting learners to share the items they chose.

Interviews

You can involve learners in exploring real-world issues related to the content to establish relevance. Invite learners to conduct interviews prior to the workshop using provided interview questions.

Example: In a customer service workshop, participants are asked to interview three customers using the questions provided. When learners enter the learning environment, they are asked to write their findings on large paper charts labeled with each question.

Online Class Forum

Invite learners to join the online class forum for the program. Personal storytelling, reflection, partner and group sharing can all occur in this online environment.

Example: For a leadership development course for first-time managers, participants are invited to post reflections in response to the question "What leader has most influenced your approach to leading others? Why?"

ENGAGING OPENINGS

In Engage, the learners reflect on their own experience and establishes a relationship between the content being explored and their lives. Trainers lead the engagement process by beginning with what is familiar, creating a simulation, or capturing the learners' attention by focusing on real-world issues. Keep in mind that the focus is on the learners reflecting and sharing. This is not where lecture happens.

Here are some examples of strategies you might use to encourage reflection and sharing to connect the learner to the content being explored:

INVITE LEARNERS TO REFLECT ON A PREVIOUS EXPERIENCE

In an "Effective Project Management" course, learners are invited to individually reflect on a successful project they have completed. Individually, learners identify three to five factors that contributed to the successful delivery of the project and write each factor on a sticky note. Learners form groups of five and share their factors, as they post them on a group paper chart. As a group, learners cluster the factors into "themes." Each group shares the common themes of effective project management.

SHARE THOUGHT-PROVOKING QUOTES

In a workshop on conflict resolution skills, learners are asked to reflect on three quotes and choose one that represents their approach to conflict situations. Learners generate a personal example of how the concept shared in the quote was illustrated in how they handled conflict in a real-world situation. In small teams, learners share their quote choice along with their conflict experience. Learners are asked to identify common themes or "barriers" to effective conflict resolution.

Which quote represents your approach to conflict?

"Don't be afraid of opposition. Remember, a kite rises against, not with, the wind."
~ Hamilton Mabie

"A pessimist sees difficulty in every opportunity; an optimist sees opportunity in every difficulty."
~ Winston Churchill

"Every conflict we face in life is rich with positive and negative potential. It can be a source of inspiration, enlightenment, learning, transformation, and growth—or rage, fear, shame, entrapment, and resistance. The choice is not up to our opponents, but to us, and our willingness to face and work through them."
~ Kenneth Cloke and Joan Goldsmith

"What we see depends mainly on what we look for."
~ Sir John Lubbock

BEGIN WITH AN INTRIGUING STATEMENT OR PROVOCATIVE QUESTION

Learners become engaged in the learning process when the questions being explored are relevant to their real-world issues. You invite learners to identify the key questions they would like to explore. For example, as learners enter the learning environment, they are invited to identify the "one big question" they would like to explore related to the course topic. Learners write their questions on sticky notes and place them on a large piece of art paper labeled with "Wonder?" Learners are invited to review the sticky notes. In small groups, learners reflect upon the question themes and identify the most pressing issues that should be explored in the learning experience.

Example:

IF THE CONCEPT YOU ARE EXPLORING IS:	A POSSIBLE QUESTION MIGHT BE:
Leadership	Reflect on a leader who positively influenced your perception of what it means to be a leader. What made this individual so influential?
Quality	Reflect on instances when you have happily paid more for something that it is tangibly worth. What determines value?
Effectiveness vs. Efficiency	If you were to illustrate the difference between "doing the right thing" and "doing the thing right," what personal examples come to mind?

SHOW A COMPELLING VIDEO TO ENCOURAGE REFLECTION

Opening a learning session with a compelling video can provide a launchpad for reflection and dialogue. There are many videos available under a creative commons license which grants permission to show the videos with certain guidelines. TED.com is an excellent resource for inspiring talks on a variety of topics.

For example, in a course on "Leading Change," learners view a video of Martin Luther King, Jr.'s famous speech, "I Have a Dream." The facilitator invites learners to identify a leader they have worked with who shared a vision powerful enough to move others into action. In small groups, learners identify the common themes in their experiences by identifying what must be present to rally others to a possible vision of the future.

SIMULATE AN EXPERIENCE

Sometimes, learners may not have an experience of the content being shared, or the individual experiences may vary greatly. In this situation, creating a shared experience through a simulation or game can enable group reflection. For example, in a "Decision Making Under Pressure" course learners participate in a "Survival" game which simulates a plane crash in arctic conditions. As a team, the group must rank items found in the plane in order of importance to their survival. The facilitator debriefs by encouraging group reflection on the decision-making dynamics of the group.

» To watch a video on "Defining the Concept: How to Create a Powerful Opening" check out www.trainers-guide-to-learning-styles.com.

ENCOURAGE SELF-ASSESSMENT

An assessment tool can be provided to allow learners to identify potential performance gaps that will motivate the desire to learn. For example, as a pre-session exercise for a "Leading from Strengths" workshop, learners are asked to invite colleagues and friends to share feedback on their experiences related to the strengths of the learner. The facilitator provides instructions and copy for learners to email ten friends. Learners bring the reflections on their strengths to the session to initiate a dialogue on awareness of personal strengths and the value others receive when we operate from our strengths.

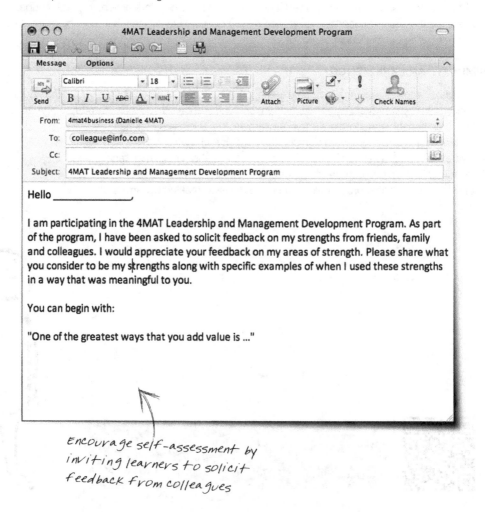

Encourage self-assessment by inviting learners to solicit feedback from colleagues

You can use many different strategies to connect learners to the content while developing a common commitment to the learning process. Notice that all of the examples provided focus the learners' attention on their personal experiences. In this part of the cycle, the learners' attention is first focused internally in order to reflect upon what they already know about the content. This is not where lecture happens. Whatever activity approach you choose, invite learners to share their experiences in such a way that they uncover the importance of the content.

As learners share their reflections, focus on uncovering the themes emerging in the conversations. You can facilitate the debriefing of reflections by asking questions and recording individual and group insights. You will find more examples of activities that work in this part of the learning cycle at the back of this chapter.

SHARE AND COMPARE: PAYING ATTENTION TO OUR EXPERIENCES

Learners will begin to notice the similarities and differences in their experiences by discussing and analyzing what happened. This is an important step in the learning cycle which allows learners to examine their own experiences and the experiences of others related to the concept being explored.

After learners connect to their previous experiences, invite them to share and compare experiences. There are many ways you can focus the learners' attention on their beliefs, perceptions, and insights generated from their experience(s):

- Invite learners to partner up and share their reflections and insights.
- Ask the groups to record the themes showing up in their experiences. What are the common themes or issues? Most significant questions being raised?
- Make the conversation visible. Invite the groups to create and share paper charts that capture the big ideas emerging in their conversation.

The goal is to create a community focused on exploring the content, at hand. You may find that a combination of these elements will create the movement needed to gain the learners' attention and create a unified focus on the learning outcome.

Focus 2: Using Questions to Provoke Reflection, Generate Dialogue, and Guide the Movement of the Group

In Engage, your most powerful teaching tool is the question. The right question will direct the learners' attention and move the group in the direction you needed. Let's look at how questions create movement.

In the learning cycle, learning begins with personal experience. This experience can be real or simulated. After the learners tap into their experience, the trainer invites the learners to step back and examine their experience. The right questions will encourage the learner to gain perspective on their own experiences and invite comparison with the experiences of others. You create this movement from personal reflection to group experience by asking the right questions.

What Doesn't Work in Engage

HOW QUESTIONS CREATE "MOVEMENT"

A masterful facilitator appears to guide the group effortlessly toward the desired insight or outcome. He or she creates movement in the group by asking the questions that guide the thinking of the group. In Engage, the training method used is dialogue. Questions are the primary tool used to guide learners through this part of the learning cycle.

The way the facilitator phrases or "frames" a question will determine the possible set of answers that might emerge from that question. For example, the closed-ended question, "Do you like the color blue?" opens up two possibilities: yes or no. The open-ended question, "What is your favorite shade of blue?" opens up many possible answers, including sky blue, baby blue, neon blue, cobalt blue, etc.

Comparing Lines of Questioning

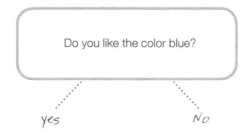

VS.

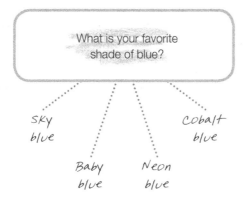

COMPARING LINES OF QUESTIONING

Imagine you are observing Ingrid, a trainer, asking a group of learners the question, "What do you hope to learn from this course?" Use the questions below to reflect on the impact of Ingrid's question on the group of learners:

- Is the question broad or narrow?
- What assumptions are embedded in the framing of this question?
- What purpose does this question serve?
- What learning climate will this question generate?
- Will this question generate new possibilities and/or deeper questions?

If learners are clear on the relevance of the course, Ingrid can expect feedback. If learners have no expectations or see no relevance to the content, there will likely be little to no energy generated from this question. Ingrid's question may invite total silence (with one lone cricket chirping in the background).

COMPARING LINES OF QUESTIONING OR CREATING MOVEMENT WITH QUESTIONS

A question is an invitation to explore, to move in a new direction. A "good" question is one that moves the conversation in a productive direction. Well-chosen questions have the power to provoke insight, to initiate dialogue, to challenge, to generate a new way of thinking about a situation.

All learning begins with what the learner already knows. In the beginning of the learning experience, you ask questions that tap into the individual's experience. You invite reflection to establish relevance and personal meaning. Ask yourself, "What experiences do the learners already have that connect to the content you are about to share with them?" Think about the question you can use to move the learners forward in the learning cycle, creating an opportunity for them to compare and contrast their own experiences with those of others.

Through your questions, you continue to invite learners to establish what they want to create as a result of the learning experience. The questions you use will lead the learners to uncover the importance and relevance of the content.

Let's go back to the question Ingrid posed earlier and compare it to a different question:

Compare Ingrid's question, "What do you hope to learn from this cou   th a different
question such as, "If you could only solve one problem related to time   ment today, what
would be the most important problem to solve?"

Comparing Lines of Questioning

What do you hope to learn
from this course?

*I'm not sure
what this
course is about...*

Hmmm ...

VS.

If you could solve only one problem related
to time management today, what would be
the most important problem to solve?

*HOW can I
stop bringing
work home?*

*HOW can I deal
with constant
interruptions?*

*HOW do I
get out of
time-wasting
meetings?*

*Note:
That's
how someone
talks.
Imagine
them
frustrated.
overwhelmed.
What words
they use,*

What do you notice about the two questions? Where would the learners go in response to these
two questions? With the first question, the learners are likely to begin thinking about all kinds of
topics they might be interested in exploring. With the second question, the learners are likely to
focus on the real-world problems they are dealing with that must be solved related to the training
topic of time management. The intentional framing of the question will determine where the
learners' attention will go and enables the trainer to guide the conversation and keep the learning
on-track.

HOW QUESTIONS CREATE MOVEMENT

Well-framed questions have the power to move the learner forward in the learning cycle. When framing a question, think about what movement you want to create. Notice how each question influences the learner's focus:

What are you feeling?

Movement created:
Notice how this is different from "how" you are feeling. By asking "what," you encourage the learner to name the emotion, which creates distance.

What insights are emerging?

Movement created:
Notice how this question encourages the learners to step out of the experience and pay attention to how their thinking has shifted.

What do you want to create through this learning experience? What is the ideal outcome?

Movement created:
This question creates tension between where the learners are now and where the learners would like to be. The learners move into action to resolve the tension.

What new behavior, if consistently executed, would produce a different outcome?

Movement created:
This question moves the learners forward to think about how they will apply the information.

HANDLING "NEGATIVE" DIALOGUE

Trainers often share that one of the greatest fears in encouraging dialogue is maintaining focus on the content being explored. Trainers often ask, "What if it goes off-track? What if they start to complain about things I can't do anything about?"

The only way we can tap into the learners' commitment to the content is to welcome the dialogue. The dialogue will tell you what the learners are committed to. In *Seven Languages for Transformation: How the Way We Talk Can Change the Way We Work*, authors Kegan and Lahey share, "…people only complain about something because they are committed to the value or importance of something else" (Kegan and Lahey, 2001, p. 30). When a learner says he is upset about one thing, what he is really telling you is that he is committed to something else. It's your job to figure out what that is. Rather than thinking about how you address the complaint, focus on the bigger message being delivered. The opposite of what we complain about is what we want. With each complaint, the learner is giving us the key to engagement—what it is he truly wants to create.

My manager doesn't bring the team together to plan. So, I don't see how team planning skills are going to work for me.

Do we all agree that there is value in aligning our individual planning? What are some ways individual team members can plan together without a manager leading the process?

...people only complain about something because they are committed to the value or importance of something else. Thus in avoiding the energy and language of complaint, or regarding it as a force that needs to be expunged, we are also losing the chance to bring vitalizing energy of commitment into the workplace.

~ Kegan and Lahey, 2001, p. 30

The amygdala is the part of the brain that regulates the fight or flight response. When threatened, it can shut down the areas of the brain responsible for higher level reasoning. The amygdala triggers the release of a rush of stress hormones before the prefrontal lobes (regulating executive function) can mediate this reaction. Any strong emotion, such as anxiety, anger, joy, or betrayal, trips off the amygdala and impairs the prefrontal cortex's working memory. The power of emotions overwhelms rationality. That is why when we are emotionally upset or stressed we can't think straight. Daniel Goleman, author of *Emotional Intelligence* refers to this as an "amygdala hijack" (Goleman, 1996, p. 18).

The amygdala plays an integral part in regulating response to emotional triggers. In a learning environment, it is important to regulate stress and perceived threats that can effectively shut down the parts of the brain that must be accessible for higher learning to take place. When fear shows up, learning shuts down. What does "learner safety" mean, really? In a typical learning situation, we aren't talking about physical safety. What are some of the fears that you observe or have experienced in a learning situation?

In Engage, you set the tone for the learning experience. By encouraging learners to share and explore their experiences and relevant issues, you develop "common unity" or "community" around the learning focus. We need to engage the emotional part of the brain to gain the learners' attention and create investment in the learning process. And we need to manage stress and perceived threats in order to keep the learning pathways open. How does a trainer do this? We turn up the "heat" slowly.

THE PARABLE OF THE BOILED FROG

There is a popular anecdote related to change that you may have heard at some point in your career, the "Parable of the Boiled Frog." In this story, there was a group of scientists who conducted a series of experiments focused on sensitivity to change. The scientist designed the experiment using a pot of water and a frog. For the first round of the experiment, the scientists heated a pot of water to near boiling temperature. They then placed a frog in the water and observed what would happen. (Obviously, cruelty to amphibians was not an issue for these scientists.) As you might expect, the frog swiftly jumped out of the pot. Next, the scientists placed the frog in a lukewarm pot of water. The frog sat in the water with no movement. The scientists began to gradually heat the water. The frog did not sense the minute changes in temperature and remained in the pot. Eventually, the poor frog boiled to death.

In this story, the frog immediately sensed a drastic change in the environment. The subtle changes produced by slowly turning up the heat went unnoticed and the frog remained in the pot. How does this idea of "turning up the heat slowly" apply to designing and delivering a learning experience? Start with an activity in which learners can comfortably participate. Slowly, turn up the "heat" and take some learners out of their comfort zones.

To prevent an amygdala hijack and the likelihood of learners "jumping out of the pot," trainers must turn up the heat slowly. Think about the comfort level of your learners and ask yourself how you can push the engagement envelope without losing them in the process.

ACTIVITY HEAT INDEX

Some activities have the potential to create anxiety for learners. Be conscious of "turning the heat up" at a pace that keeps your audience engaged.

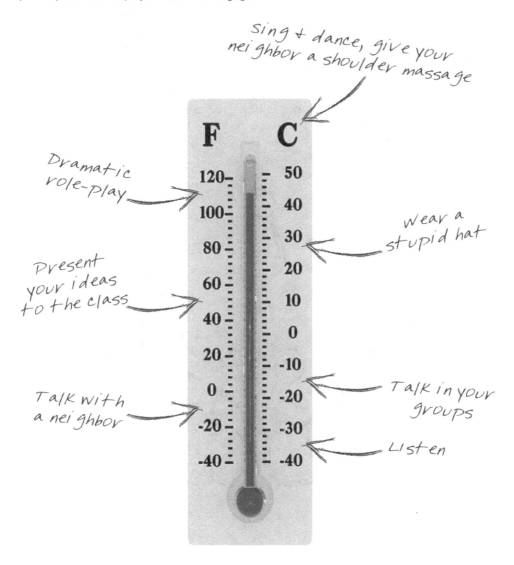

Five Ways to Enhance Learner Safety While Building a Sense of Community

INDIVIDUAL-PARTNER-GROUP REFLECTION

Reflection and dialogue are a critical component of the learning process. Some learners are uncomfortable with sharing out loud in a learning environment. Structure activities in a way that all learners can share and there is also an option for volunteers to share out loud with the larger group. For example, when you assign a reflection exercise, encourage all learners to reflect on their own. This takes care of the learners who prefer more time for reflection before they formulate ideas to share in a dialogue. Next, invite individuals to partner and share their individual reflections. Next, invite table groups to share the interesting insights from their partner conversations. Finally, ask for a few volunteers to share from the tables with the larger group. This movement from individual to partner to table to larger group allows everyone to contribute and benefit from the dialogue. At the same time, it ups the safety factor. All learners have a choice related to their level of sharing.

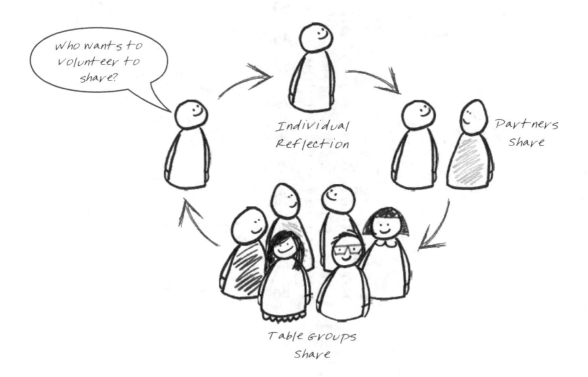

ASK FOR VOLUNTEERS WHEN INVITING SHARING

The way you frame invitations to share can help prepare reflective learners:

- "Who would like to share an insight around this?"
- "At this point, I imagine there are questions emerging around this…."
- "In your table groups, share your experiences. In a few moments, we will explore this as a group."
- "Let's have three table groups volunteer to share the themes showing up in their conversations."
- "Does anyone feel compelled to share an experience?"
- "Who has an 'aha' you would like to share?"
- "In a few minutes, I am going to invite a volunteer from each table to share your group's poster chart. Be thinking of who will represent your table."

CLEARLY DEFINE EXPECTATIONS

There are two ways we define expectations: in what we do and what we say.

- At the beginning of a session, review the defined outcomes for the course and the agenda.
- Before a break, preview what the group will be doing when they return.
- When sharing directions for activities, be clear around the process and the final product of the activity.
- When asking learners to share, you can also define expectations through what you do. For example, if you want learners to raise their hands when they agree, you can raise your hand, as you pose a question.
- When giving directions for an activity, offer an example of what you are looking for by sharing a personal response or asking the group to do the first round of the activity together.

ALLOW LEARNER RESPONSES TO GUIDE THE PROCESS

Connect back to the comments learners provided earlier in the learning session. Here's what that might sound like:

- "Earlier in our dialogue, we decided that the biggest obstacle to raising issues with a colleague is often how to start the conversation in a non-confrontational way. We are about to explore how to introduce an issue in a neutral way."

- "John just made a great observation. How does this observation shift your approach to the exercise?"

USE LANGUAGE THAT AFFIRMS THE LEARNER'S EFFORTS AND REINFORCES DESIRED BEHAVIORS

- "Great point."
- "I love that you are challenging this line of thought … let's explore this more."
- "Dave just raised a great question…."

In the final part of this chapter, you will find examples of Engage strategies used in real-world training situations. You will also find facilitator instructions for adapting these activities to your own content.

Summary

In this chapter, we have explored the importance of connecting new learning to the previous experience, knowledge, and interests of the learners. Reflection through journaling, personal storytelling, simulations, and exploration of shared experiences are some of the types of activities that work well in this part of the learning cycle.

As you design for and lead the Engage step, focus on creating a dialogue centered around the learners' experiences, rather than telling. Your questioning skills will help guide learner discovery of the relevance of the content being shared.

Step in the Cycle: Engage

What the learners are doing:
Establishing a relationship between the content and their personal lives. Paying attention to similarities and differences in learners' experiences.

What the trainer is doing:
- Constructing/facilitating a learning experience that connects the learner personally to the content
- Guiding the reflection, encouraging sharing of personal perceptions and beliefs, connecting the learners

Activities that work well:
- Personal storytelling
- Simulations
- Scenarios that really take place
- Reflections on past experiences
- Interactive dialogue
- Sharing stories and insights in pairs or groups
- Creating mindmaps of common and different elements
- Choosing images that represent perceptions of the content

After the "Reflect" and "Act" sections of this chapter, you will find examples of activities that work well in the Engage part of the learning cycle. Review "Your Training Style in Engage" and reflect on your training style strengths related to this part of the learning cycle.

YOUR TRAINING STYLE IN ENGAGE

To generate the reflection and dialogue needed to allow learners to discover their personal connection to the content requires effective facilitation skills. If you have a natural strength in the Type One training approach, it is likely that you already rely on facilitation skills in your training delivery. If your area of strength lies in one of the other three approaches, be aware of what you will need to focus on to be successful in this step.

	HIGH STRENGTH IN TYPE ONE TRAINING APPROACH	HIGH STRENGTH IN TYPE TWO TRAINING APPROACH	HIGH STRENGTH IN TYPE THREE TRAINING APPROACH	HIGH STRENGTH IN TYPE FOUR TRAINING APPROACH
	Be aware of the potential over-use of this strength.	Balance your natural thinking approach by honoring the feeling approach. Rather than telling, let the learners generate their own insights.	Slow down and take the necessary time to allow learners to come to their own conclusions around the value of the content.	Be careful to stay on track in the dialogue. Rather than contributing your own insights, focus on what is emerging for the group and guide the dialogue using questions.
	Type One Trainer comment: "I equate effective learning with deep sharing. I have to be careful to not spend too much time here or to lose the focus of the content in all the group conversations."	Type Two Trainer comment: "I get concerned with open dialogue because the conversation can so easily get off-track. Oftentimes, my challenge lies in figuring out how to get them back on track with the content we need to cover."	Type Three Trainer comment: "I struggle with spending too much time exploring personal experiences, feelings, and stories. I get impatient when the sharing seems repetitive."	Type Four Trainer comment: "I have to be careful to not get swept up in all the possibilities. I find it helpful to ask the learners to generate a record of their conversation. I also use a paper chart to visualize the connections and keep the whole group on track."

Think about the conversations that are happening in your work world.

To what extent do leaders and trainers invite in and work with the real-world conversations that are occurring? When have you seen this done effectively?

How would valuing the impact of conversation as a learning tool influence your approach to creating learning experiences? What might you do differently?

Reflect on an example of a process or training activity you have experienced that invited in the knowledge and experience of everyone in the room. What worked about the process?

What are some of the most effective ways you have seen dialogue captured and displayed visually? What can be learned from this?

ACT

In the next training you design or deliver, which strategies will you include?

	YES	NO
• Personal reflection	✓	
• Simulation		
• Personal storytelling		
• Journaling		
• Partner sharing		
• Groups identifying common themes in their experiences		
• Other ideas I will try…		

Examples of Engage Activities

In this section, you will find examples of activities that work well in Engage. The activities are presented within the context of a training course. The directions related to leading each activity are presented in a generic format that can be adapted to work with any type of content.

ENGAGE ACTIVITY EXAMPLE: LEADERSHIP COURSE ON "ALIGNING TEAMS"

In a leadership development course, the trainer chooses to focus on the concept of "alignment" to explore the topic of "Improving Productivity." The trainer invites learners to reflect on experiences of being part of an aligned team. Learners journal their responses and share their experiences with partners.

In table groups, partners share their experiences and define common elements that are present in aligned teams. Next, learners reflect on and share the level of alignment within their own team using the "Arrow Exercise" shared below.

ARROW EXERCISE FACILITATION INSTRUCTIONS

Focus: Visual activity which illustrates the concept of alignment while encouraging personal reflection.

Resources Needed
- Paper
- Markers

Description
1. Draw an image of a large arrow with many small arrows within it on a flip chart paper. The small arrows should be pointed in the same general direction as the larger arrow.
2. Explain that effective teams have a strong overall sense of direction (large arrow) with individuals (small arrows) aligning their actions to move in the same direction.
3. Ask learners to draw a large arrow. Next, draw individual arrows which represent the degree of alignment of their team (or organization).
4. Invite learners to share their visuals with partners.

Trainer Script
"Within an effective team, there is an overall sense of direction. (Draw large arrow.) The individuals working within that team (draw small arrow inside the large arrow, moving in the same direction as the larger arrow), align their actions to move the team forward in that direction. Sometimes, alignment is not present. (Draw a second larger arrow. Draw smaller arrows within moving in different directions.) Reflect on the degree of alignment within your team (or organization). Draw a visual using both large and small arrows, to illustrate the degree of alignment within your team. Share a personal experience of how this level of alignment has affected your team's performance."

ENGAGE ACTIVITY EXAMPLE: SYNCHRONOUS WEB COURSE ON "SOCIAL MEDIA MARKETING"

The facilitator for this course chose to use the concept of "tribes" to explore the power of social media marketing. Prior to the first online session, the facilitator sends an invitation to learners introducing the concept of "tribes" and how they play an integral role in social media marketing. Learners are invited to send the web address for online communities, or "tribes," they belong to or find attractive. The facilitator begins the live online session by inviting partners to chat with each other about what attracts them to the examples shared.

BEST SURFING SPOTS (E-LEARNING) FACILITATION INSTRUCTIONS

Focus: Individual reflection exercise which explores preferences and interests related to the content being explored.

Resources Needed
- Online class forum to accompany the course

Description
1. Prior to the beginning of the learning session, invite learners to post websites of personal interest on the online class forum.

2. Choose a post from each individual or a sample of individuals to share with the class. You can take screenshots of the home page of each submitted site and copy into your PowerPoint for quick transitions.

3. If you are not sharing a site example from each individual, you may choose to partner learners.

4. Ask each pair to chat with their assigned partners about the sites they shared. It is helpful to pre-assign partner groups. You can do this by placing partner names in a table labeled "Partner A" and "Partner B." Display the table on a slide or whiteboard.

Trainer Script
"The groups we belong to and the things we find of interest offer an insight into who we are. In this exercise, we will explore what makes an online community attractive while also learning about each other. On the screen, you will find your partner's name. In the chat, you will share the websites and/or online communities you chose in our pre-session reflection. Chat with your partner and explain what you find interesting about these communities. Partner A will share first for 2 minutes. I will signal time to switch and Partner B will share for 2 minutes."

Notes:

_____

_____

_____

ENGAGE ACTIVITY EXAMPLE: A CREATIVITY WORKSHOP

Using the concept of "circles and lines," the facilitator explores the differences in how learners view the world. Learners are invited to reflect on the differences between viewing the world as a "circle" versus viewing the world as a "line." Learners will identify examples of when they have looked at a life situation from the lens of "life as a circle" and "life as a line." Learners are then introduced to the 4MAT Hemispheric Mode Indicator to assess their thinking strengths in right-mode (circle) and left-mode (line) thinking. In the remainder of the session, learners explore how to build skill in each way of thinking using thinking strategies and team process tools.

CIRCLES AND LINES FACILITATION INSTRUCTIONS

Focus: Group reflection exercise which explores the differences in the way we view the world.

Resources Needed
- Lengths of string long enough for members or each table group to hold the string simultaneously

Description
1. Share the facilitator script below.
2. Ask participants to individually reflect on an example of when they have viewed the world as a "circle" and when they have viewed the world as a "line".
3. Give each table group a length of string.
4. Ask learners to hold the string in a line, with each member touching the string. Invite learners to share their example of thinking from the perspective that "life is a line."
5. Ask learners to hold the string in a circle, with each member touching the string. Invite learners to share their example of thinking from the perspective that "life is a circle."
6. Ask each group to develop a list of the characteristics of both ways of viewing the world to present to the larger group.
7. Debrief.

Trainer Script
"Richard Nisbett is a social psychologist at the University of Michigan who leads research studying how humans think about the world. In his book, *The Geography of Thought: How Asians and Westerners Think Differently...and Why*, Nisbett shares a story of a conversation with his student from China. The student told him, 'You know, the difference between you and me is that I think the world is a circle, and you think it's a line' (Nisbett, 2003, p. xiii). I invite you to reflect on the difference between circle and line thinking. Reflect on an experience which illustrates when you have approached a situation from a 'circle' point of view and a 'line' point of view."

Additional facilitator notes: In his book, Nisbett shares how the student elaborated on the differences between these two ways of viewing the world (Nisbett, 2003, p. xiii):

The World Is a Circle	The World Is a Line
• Constant change • Things always moving back to some prior state • Paying attention to many things • Information comes from many sources • You can't understand the part without understanding the whole	• Simpler world view • Focus on objects or people versus the larger view • Knowing the rules will help you control the outcomes • Some sources of information are more valuable than others • Believe understanding the parts will lead to an understanding of the whole

ENGAGE ACTIVITY EXAMPLE: HIGHS AND LOWS

In a workshop on "Leading Through Difficult Times," learners are invited to reflect on the "highs" and "lows" of their careers. Learners draw a horizontal (horizon) line on a paper chart and indicate the highs and lows by graphing them above and below the horizon. Next, learners label what was happening at each peak and dip. In partners, learners share their stories. The facilitator leads a dialogue that focuses on the interrelationship between events culminating in group awareness that each "high" is typically preceded by a "low" that motivates new action.

TIMELINES

Focus: Reflection exercise which explores connections between "high" and "low" career and life points

Resources Needed
- Paper charts
- Tape
- Markers
- Workbook page with timeline (alternative to wall chart)

Description
Using a visual timeline, learners plot experiences that have shaped their perceptions or current understanding of the content being shared.
1. Create a visual timeline on a large paper chart. You can do this by taping together paper charts along a wall and drawing a timeline down the horizontal length of the paper.
2. Ask learners to reflect on experiences that have shaped their perceptions and understanding related to the topic. Ask learners to plot "high" experiences above the horizon line and "low" experiences below. Encourage learners to incorporate visual imagery.

Trainer Script
"Our experiences shape our perceptions and current understanding of any given subject. To begin our conversation today on leadership (or other topic) we are going to reflect on your experiences around this topic. On the timeline on the wall (or workbook or table), make note of what has happened in your life and career that has shaped your approach to leadership (or other topic). Plot the 'high points' above the horizon line while plotting the 'low points' below the line. Think about the people, events and experiences that have defined your definition of effective leadership. On the timeline (in your workbook, on the wall, or at your table) make note of what has happened in your life that has shaped your definition of leadership. Once you have completed your timeline, share your timeline with your table group."

Notes:

_____

_____

_____

_____

ENGAGE ACTIVITY EXAMPLE: ONLINE MESSAGE BOARD REFLECTIONS

In an online course on "Understanding Learning Styles," learners are invited to reflect on what they already know about learning styles. The facilitator invites learners to post messages in the online class forum in response to the questions, "What types of learners do you work with most successfully? What types of learners are most difficult for you to engage?" The facilitator begins the online class by revisiting the comments shared by the learners in the forum.

ONLINE MESSAGE BOARD REFLECTIONS

Focus: Reflection exercise to identify experiences related to the content being discussed.

Description
1. Post a question on an online message board which will encourage reflection around what the learner already knows about the content.
2. Monitor posts and share results in the online delivery of the course. Optionally, you may capture comments and post into a slide deck for presentation during the synchronous portion of an online course.

Trainer Script
Email participants or share the following in the online forum: "To encourage reflection and to tap into the knowledge of our group, I would like to invite you to think about what you already know about learning styles. Before our first session, take a few moments to post your response to the questions: What types of learners do you engage most successfully? What types of learners are most challenging for you to engage?"

Notes:

ENGAGE ACTIVITY EXAMPLE: WORKSHOP ON COACHING PERFORMANCE

In a workshop focused on coaching skills for new managers, the trainer invites learners to reflect on a mentor or coach who had a positive impact on their development. The facilitator invites the learners to reflect on their coaching relationship with this individual using a collection of images.

IMAGE CARDS

Focus: Reflection exercise using visual images to elicit insights.

Resources Needed
- Image cards or clipped magazine images

Description

In this exercise, you will provide the learner with a collection of images. Learners will choose an image or series of images to use as visual prompts to share their responses to a reflection question or assignment.

1. Display the collection of images on a table or on the floor of the room.

2. Clarify the focus of the activity. Ask learners to choose an image that represents their response to the question you pose or task you present.

Trainer Script

"Reflect on your experiences of working with a coach that had a powerful impact on you. What qualities did this coach embody that enabled him or her to make such an impact on your life? Choose an image that conveys this quality (or qualities) and be prepared to share with a partner."

Notes:

_____

_____

_____

_____

_____

_____

_____

_____

_____

_____

ENGAGE ACTIVITY EXAMPLE: TEAM VISIONING SESSION

A departmental team begins an annual strategic planning session by completing a "Team Visioning" session. Team members are invited to reflect on how they can contribute fully to the vision process by completing a series of three statements:

- The value of my perspective lies in…

- My vision is…

- My biggest hope for this process is...

Each team member then creates a visual collage which represents his or her responses to the statements. The group begins the planning session with each team member explaining his or her collage.

PERSONAL VISUAL COLLAGE

Focus: Visual processing exercise designed to encourage personal reflection and elicit sharing in partner and group exercises

Resources Needed
- Magazines with colorful images and interesting headlines
- Poster boards or personal journals
- Scissors
- Glue sticks

Description
1. Develop the statements to be completed by learners as they develop their collage. See examples of prompt statements mentioned earlier.
2. Instruct learners to use the materials provided to create visual representations of their personal responses to the prompt.
3. Invite learners to form small groups to share their collages.

Trainer Script
"To encourage reflection, I am going to invite you to reflect upon the following: <share question or prompt>. On the table in the back of the room, you will find images and the necessary tools needed to create a visual representation of your reflections. Your task is to create a visual collage that you will use to share your insights with the group."

Notes:

_____

_____

_____

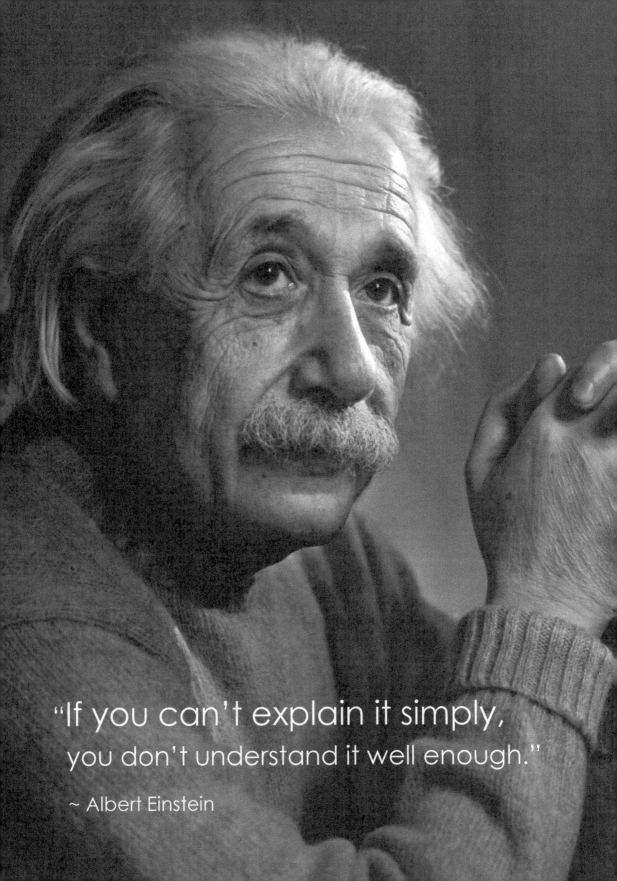

"If you can't explain it simply,
you don't understand it well enough."

~ Albert Einstein

Chapter 5

Share: Animating the Learning Content

On the morning of December 10, 1996, a blood vessel exploded in the left half of Dr. Jill Bolte Taylor's brain. Over the course of the next four hours, she watched as her brain lost its ability to process information. As a brain scientist, Taylor was having a firsthand experience of the brain processes she had studied over the lifetime of her career.

Taylor survived to share her story in a riveting TED conference presentation. During her presentation, Taylor pauses to put on a pair of latex gloves before picking up a human brain. As Taylor shares that this is indeed a real human brain, the loud gasp of the audience affirms that this will be one of the most memorable moments of a highly engaging presentation.

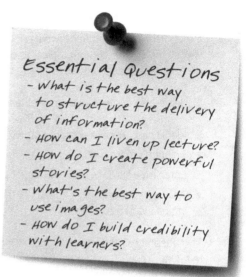

Essential Questions
- What is the best way to structure the delivery of information?
- How can I liven up lecture?
- How do I create powerful stories?
- What's the best way to use images?
- How do I build credibility with learners?

WHAT HAPPENS IN SHARE

In the second part of the 4MAT learning cycle, Share, the learner is focused on understanding what is known about the topic being explored. The learner asks the question, "What?" Some activities which work well here include imaging exercises, stories, lecture, visual organizers, and demonstrations. The goal in Share is to transfer understanding of the essential knowledge related to the content being explored.

During this step in the learning cycle, the learner takes in information in order to gain understanding of the information needed to successfully produce the desired learning results. The learner takes in this information through two channels: verbal and visual. In the verbal channel, the learner receives the content you share through your lecture, the reinforcing text in your PowerPoint slides, workbook, or flipcharts. In the visual channel, the learner takes in the images shared in your PowerPoint, flipcharts, and workbooks, along with the mental images created through the stories, metaphors, and examples you share. Often, it is the visual elements that learners recall most readily.

In this part of the 4MAT cycle, the trainer plays the role of "Presenter." You focus on organizing the content in a way that allows the learners to easily understand both the larger concepts, as well as the smaller content topics, to equip learners with the knowledge needed to deliver the desired performance outcome.

To deliver this content in a way that learners will retain the information, you must be able to:

- Identify appropriate content that will deliver on the desired knowledge outcome
- Edit and organize content into manageable "chunks"
- Establish a balance between visual and verbal delivery strategies
- Animate your carefully chosen content with brain-friendly delivery strategies such as stories, images, and metaphors

This chapter will show you how to structure and animate your content to maximize learning retention. You will also find activities appropriate for this part of the cycle as well as examples of their use in real-world learning environments.

Two Channels of Delivery:
Visual and Verbal

In *Slideology*, author Nancy Duarte shares that an audience tunes into two channels when you are presenting information to them: visual and verbal (Duarte, 2008). When the visual and verbal align, attention is focused and retention increases. When the visual and verbal connection is not clear to the learner, attention suffers and retention decreases. One of the most widely used visual training tools is PowerPoint. PowerPoint offers a great example of the need to align text (verbal) and images (visual). If the visual and verbal messages are not congruent, the learner's attention is distracted. For example, I observed a sales training presentation on how to generate more leads. The image on the accompanying PowerPoint slide had a spider web and a very large spider. I found my attention wandering from the lecture as I pondered how many sales people in the room would leave thinking the concept was to lure customers into a trap. In my experience, choosing the right image can be more challenging and time-consuming than choosing the right words. In this chapter, we will explore how to choose the right image strategy to reinforce learning.

The audience will either read your slides or listen to you. They will not do both. So, ask yourself this: is it more important that they listen, or more effective if they read?

~ Duarte, 2008, p. 6

The Verbal Channel:
How to Organize Your Lecture

Humans have both a limited attention span and a limited ability to keep large amounts of information in working memory. It's important to keep this in mind as you determine how much content you will include and how it will be delivered. To overcome these natural barriers to learning, let's explore how to organize your lecture for maximum learning impact.

THE LIMITS OF HUMAN ATTENTION

In a learning experience, we naturally tune in at two points in the delivery: the beginning and the end. We tune in at the beginning to determine whether the content is relevant, whether the presenter is engaging, and whether the information is of interest. We tune in at the end to determine whether anything important is being summarized and to see what we need to do next.

In the middle of the experience, our attention usually slumps. John Medina, a developmental molecular biologist and author of *Brain Rules*, shares that "The brain seems to be making choices according to some stubborn timing pattern, undoubtedly influenced by both culture and gene" (Medina, 2008, p. 74). To avoid or minimize this natural slump, you should make a shift in your delivery roughly every ten minutes or you risk losing the learners' attention. You can accomplish this shift by animating your lecture with a variety of delivery mechanisms such as analogies, illustrations, metaphors, stories, and images. My experience is that overall attention of the learners increases when we include these mechanisms.

LIMITS OF WORKING MEMORY

In 1981, the musical group Tommy Tutone released the hit song called "867-5309/Jenny." The song made the phone number, 867-5309, the most popular number in the 80's. Given a recent eBay bid of $350,000 for the phone number, it still seems to be quite popular (Duke, 2009). What if Tommy Tutone had added the area code to the song? Besides making the lyrics harder to rhyme, the extra three digits would have made the number much harder to remember—and likely far less worthy of a $350,000 price tag.

Our working memory is only capable of holding seven new (and previously unassociated) bits of information at one time; thus the problem with the area code. As a trainer or instructional designer, you should organize content so that working memory can handle the information load. You do this by "chunking" information, organizing the information into connected clusters so that the learners can easily assimilate the information. In the next section of this chapter, we will explore how to address the limits of attention and working memory by effectively structuring your lecture.

THREE STEPS TO ORGANIZING LECTURE

The goal in step 2 of the 4MAT model, Share, is to deliver the knowledge the learner needs to understand so that performance of the desired behaviors takes place; this, of course. has the added benefit of achieving the intended results of the training program. As you explore possible content to include in the Share portion of your course or presentation, keep your focus on the essential knowledge required to deliver the desired performance outcome.

Here are some simple steps to follow:

- **Step 1:** Identify possible content and filter against the knowledge outcome.
- **Step 2:** "Chunk" the content until you are left with a maximum of five key messages. This doesn't necessarily mean you have to cut content. It simply means you must figure out how to categorize the information into five or fewer "chunks" of information.
- **Step 3:** Under each chunk, use learning devices to animate your message: stories, data, examples, metaphors, analogies, and images.

ORGANIZING LECTURE STEP 1: IDENTIFY POSSIBLE CONTENT AND FILTER

Begin by researching possible content for the course. In Chapter 9, we explore how to conduct stakeholder and subject matter expert interviews. The knowledge outcome defined during your interviews will serve as your guide to researching and choosing content to include in your course. Ask yourself, "What does the learner need to know and understand to perform the necessary skills to deliver the desired result?" The content for the Share portion may come from a variety of sources, including company policies or procedures, articles, videos, product knowledge manuals, books, journals, blogs, and more. Use the knowledge outcome as a filter to decide which content should be included. Ask yourself, "Will understanding of this content lead to successful delivery of the performance outcome?"

Once you have identified possible content, arrange it in a visual format that allows you to see how the content might be organized for the learner. Mindmapping is an excellent way to visually organize all of the possible content. Many trainers find that using a visual technique to organize content, such as mindmapping, does not come naturally and find themselves eager to skip this part of the process and go straight into a linear approach such as listing or outlining the content. Seeing the content mapped out enables you to see how the bigger ideas and topics are connected. In this step, you begin to see how to best organize the information for the learner. While this exercise take time in the front end, discovering the natural connections in the content will save you time in the long run.

HOW TO MINDMAP

Here is a simple overview of how to develop your own mindmap. You will also find additional recommended resources in the back of this chapter.

1. Start at the center of the page in landscape position. Label your mindmap and, ideally, include a visual image.

2. Branch out from the center of the image with key topics. Include images to represent the words.

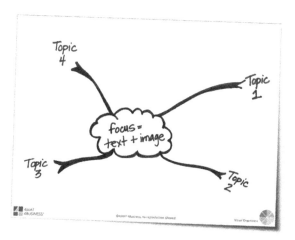

3. Add additional lines for each word. The lines should connect to associated words/concepts. Typically, the lines curve and are thicker at the center of the mindmap and narrower as you extend outward.

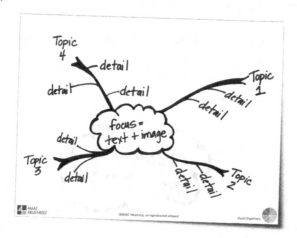

4. The organizing structure that will emerge will illustrate the connections in a radiant fashion. This structure enables the trainer to see how the content fits together. Usually, the main ideas and supporting topic hierarchy will be immediately visible.

MY APPROACH TO DEVELOPING CONTENT

I am often asked to explain my approach to developing content. I integrate several different strategies into my design approach. Some of you may find it helpful to see this process, so I will share:

- **Learning journal:** I keep two learning journals going at any given time. The first one is an artist board that allows me to create mindmaps of content I am exploring. For example, when I read a new book of interest I create a mindmap in my learning journal. I include the author's name and the title of the book. I mindmap out anything of interest that I might be able to use in a future course, a blog post, a facebook post or newsletter article. I reference the page number of any ideas or quotes I make note of to help me find the information later.

- **Story journal:** My second journal is a slim Moleskine®. When something interesting happens, I make a note of it in my story journal. For example, if I have an interesting customer service experience at Starbucks or a participant in one of our courses shares a great insight, I make a note of it in this journal. This journal is solely focused on tracking ideas for stories, analogies, and metaphors that I might use in delivery. The key is to write it down, even when you don't yet know how you will use it. Trust me, you will use it later.

- **Mindmap the content:** When I am ready to create something new, I start mindmapping possible content. I go back to my journals to get ideas, I scan the web, and I look through reference materials. All of this is integrated into a mindmap that allows me to begin to see how it might come together into a cohesive learning experience.

- **Storyboard using index cards:** When I am ready to build my lecture, my left brain kicks in and I start focusing on the organization of the content. I write the ideas for the lecture on index cards—one idea per card. The ideas could be talking points, stories, case studies, etc. I then storyboard the lecture out.

ORGANIZING LECTURE STEP 2: CHUNK THE CONTENT

"Well-organized" is the key criteria in evaluating lectures. Learners describe painful lectures as "wandering," "disorganized," and "all over the place." Once you have the content visually displayed, you can begin to identify the themes or categories of the content. The most obvious way to organize delivery of content in Share is by topics. For example, if you were teaching a product knowledge course, an obvious way to organize lecture would be by product categories, but clearly there are many alternative approaches.

Here are some other ways you might organize the lecture:

- **Topics:** organize the content by categories or subjects.
- **Problem and solution:** organize the content around common problems the learners face and how the content being explored provides a solution.
- **Cause and effect:** organize the content around how specific actions create different results.
- **Pros and cons:** organize the content by comparing and contrasting the advantages and disadvantages of one over another.
- **Acronym:** create acronyms to help the learners understand the structure of the delivery and to improve retention of the information.
- **Timelines:** organize the content based on the past or future.
- **Visual icons:** organize the content using a visual organizing structure.

ORGANIZING LECTURE STEP 3: BALANCING VERBAL WITH VISUAL

In the next section of this chapter, we will explore how to animate content through metaphors, stories, visual data, and images in your delivery. These "animation" strategies will help the learners "see" the content by reinforcing the verbal with images, both real and mental.

Let's look at how the different structures of delivery might work to teach a product knowledge delivery course on haircare products, as an example:

Topics
Organize by the type of products. Here the content is organized by categories such as shampoos, conditioners, and styling aids.

Problem and Solution
Organize by the problem the hair care client wants to address. Here the content is organized by client needs such as "volume," "shine," or "curly."

Cause and Effect
Organize by the root cause of the issues. Using this method, product knowledge might be organized around issues (causes) that affect hair performance such as "dealing with humidity."

Pros and Cons
Organize by comparing and contrasting products. Using this method, product knowledge might be delivered by comparing each product to a competitive offering.

Acronym
Organize delivery using an acronym that helps learners remember the product recommendation steps.

Timelines
Organize chronologically based on each product's launch date.

Visual Icons
Organize by using visual cues that relate to main categories.

The Visual Channel: Animating Lecture Using Visual Strategies

In Engage, you invited the learners to reflect and dialogue to discover the personal relevance of the content being explored. When you transition from Engage to Share, it is helpful for learners to "see" how the content relates to what they already know. It is also essential that you provide a "meta-view" or broader perspective on what is being covered and how the content is organized. Exploring the metaphors that learners already use to understand the content and providing learners with a new metaphor for understanding will greatly enhance the learning transfer in Share.

ANIMATING LECTURE USING METAPHORS

First, let's begin with defining "metaphor." A metaphor is a word or phrase that transfers the meaning of one thing to another.

Here are some examples of metaphors:

- This room is an icebox.
- Hang on, this is going to be a wild ride.
- Life is a journey.
- Our company is a family.

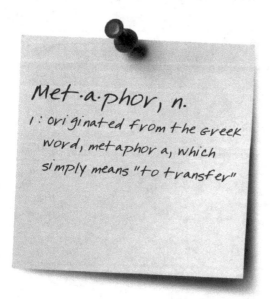

Met·a·phor, n.
1: originated from the Greek word, metaphora, which simply means "to transfer"

WE THINK IN METAPHORS

For most people, metaphors are seen as a device to creatively articulate some idea. Poets, musicians, and creative storytellers are often perceived to be the masters of metaphor. On the contrary, we are all quite masterful at applying metaphors to generate understanding.

The value of metaphors in learning lies in their ability to compare a new concept to a familiar one. Metaphors create a visual image of how one thing is similar to another. The power of metaphors stems from the physical relationship of the neuronal connections in our brains. The connections in our brain generate meaning. Any concrete example a trainer provides taps into the existing neuronal connections in the learner's brain. Metaphors are existing "maps of understanding" that can be used as a foundation to lead the learner to new understanding. When choosing metaphors, think about how you might accelerate learning by linking the new ideas you are sharing to a familiar one.

In *Metaphors We Live By*, authors George Lakoff and Mark Johnson share, "…metaphor is pervasive in everyday life, not just in language but in thought and action. Our ordinary conceptual system, in terms of which we both think and act, is fundamentally metaphorical in nature" (Lakoff and Johnson, 1980, p. 3). We think in metaphors. Lakoff and Johnson illustrate brilliantly the many ways we think in terms of metaphors.

We think of time as money (Lakoff and Johnson, 1980, p. 7):

- "How did you *spend* your *time* today?"
- "There was just not enough *ROI* on my *time* on that project."
- "You need to *budget* your *time* wisely."

We think of an argument as a container (Lakoff and Johnson, 1980, p. 92):

- "That argument has *holes* in it."
- "Your argument *won't hold water*."

Trainers need to understand that a difference in metaphor will create a difference in understanding and approach.

For example, many people perceive conflict as a "battle" to be won:

- "I'm prepared for *battle*."
- "I'm going to *take him down*."
- "He won't know what *hit him*."

What if that metaphor were shifted? What if conflict were viewed as a creative process? As a collaboration? As a dance with each party taking turns leading? How might a shift in metaphor shift the way we prepare for, approach, and resolve conflict? A shift in the metaphor we use to understand shifts the way we think and the way we act. The metaphor is a powerful tool for understanding the concepts that guide the learners' understanding and approach. If you want to shift behavior toward a desired outcome, you can begin by understanding the metaphors which learners use to understand a concept. You can then provide learners with a new metaphor to encourage a new way of seeing the information being presented.

IMAGINE IF YOU WILL...

For example, imagine that you are leading a workshop for department managers on how to implement the strategic planning tools used to develop annual budgets. Which of the following visual metaphors would you use to create a shared understanding of the process you are leading the group through?

Telescoping spyglass: illustrating how the individual, team, department, and division objectives must fit within the long-range vision.

Mason jar with rocks, pebbles, and sand: illustrating how we must allocate space for the big initiatives (rocks), then secondary initiatives (pebbles). Otherwise, all of our resources (the space in the jar) are consumed with low impact initiatives that generate minimal return (sand).

Pie: illustrating that there is a limited budget and limited resources (pie). Each department's allocation of budget (slice of the pie) will be determined based on the merits of plans submitted.

Metaphors are powerful because they generate mental images through words. We invited trainers to share metaphors they use to describe the process of leading learning for others. Here are a few examples:

- **Planting a seed:** "A seed of knowledge being planted that is nurtured to grow and develop."
- **Peeling an onion:** "We begin with the basics and then make finer and finer distinctions, revealing greater and greater depth—layer by layer."
- **Light bulb going off:** "When the light bulb goes off, everything begins to make sense. The personal 'aha' sheds light on all kinds of new possibilities."
- **Adventure:** "Learning is a journey. You begin where the learners live and move them down a path to new lands they haven't traveled."
- **Sustenance:** "Learning is the fuel that keeps me going."

What metaphor would you use to describe "learning"? How does the metaphor you use to understand affect the way you approach training?

At the end of this chapter, you will find examples of metaphor activities you can use to determine both the learner's current understanding of the content and how to guide the learner to a new way of seeing the content.

ANIMATING LECTURE USING STORIES

Because we understand in the context of human experience, stories are a powerful delivery tool. They greatly enhance the retention of the information being shared. Many different types of stories work well in a learning context. Let's look at four examples of story structures that are effective at engaging an audience while enhancing learning:

- **Children's stories.** Children's stories can be used to illustrate a point in an entertaining way. For example, I observed a trainer in an innovation workshop begin a session with a dramatic reading of Dr. Seuss', *"Oh! The Places You'll Go!"* At the end of the passage below, the trainer invited the learners to reflect and share the beliefs that support innovation in the workplace.

> "…You have brains in your head.
> You have feet in your shoes.
> You can steer yourself any direction you choose.
> You're on your own. And you know what you know.
> And YOU are the guy who'll decide where to go." (Seuss, 1990, p. 2)

- **Fables or historical stories.** Fables and historical stories illustrate lessons learned through the experience of others. In the opening of his TED presentation on "The Battle Between Your Present and Future Self," Daniel Goldstein opens with the story of Odysseus. Goldstein entertainingly illustrates how Odysseus' tying of himself to the mast of his ship to avoid the siren's song parallels the "commitment devices" many people use to control their financial behaviors.

- **Stories of others.** You have many sources to uncover the stories of others, including books you've read, television shows or movies you've watched, or even other training sessions you've attended. It's a good idea to keep a story journal and make notes of story techniques you observe other presenters using. In a course on "Win Win Thinking," a colleague's story of a high-stakes negotiation or a child's story about compromise on the playground are both examples of how stories of others might be used to illustrate the concept being explored.

- **Before and after story: "the big why."** "Before and After" stories can provide the crucial "why" that sparks a learner's interest in the "what." For example, our company offers an online 4MAT training design tool called 4MATion®. In a course teaching a new user how to use the tool, I would not begin by clicking on every button while describing *what* it does. Instead I might describe the process of 4MAT training design "before and after" by telling the story of how one of our clients achieved powerful results with the tool's introduction, emphasizing the time-saving benefits. The before and after story reinforces the "*Why*" and the learner is likely to be more interested in hearing about the functionality of the design tool.

DEVELOPING YOUR OWN STORIES

If someone were to ask you if storytelling was a gift or a skill, what would your answer be? I frequently ask this question in workshops, and most people believe that both answers are correct. Some of us are born storytellers, and the rest of us can develop the skill with effort. If you are one of those gifted storytellers, feel free to skip this section. If you want to get better at identifying and structuring stories to animate your lecture, let's first explore what we can learn from moviemakers, who are the masters of modern day storytelling.

ELEMENTS OF A GREAT STORY

In *Resonate*, Nancy Duarte shares how powerful stories have a common structure. Understanding this predictable structure will help you develop an engaging story. You are already familiar with this structure, as you have seen it in just about every movie you have ever watched. The three-part structure looks like this (Duarte, 2010, pp. 28-29):

1 You are introduced to a character(s). You get a feel for what is going on in the character's world and what new possibilities might exist. In most cases, the character is likable and you become interested in what's about to happen to him or her.

2 Something is at stake. There is some crisis or obstacle to overcome. Tension is created between "what is" and "what could be." The bigger the crisis, the more engaged we become.

3 The character resolves the tension. In the end, the character(s) figure out how to overcome the challenge.

Take a look at how some popular movies fit into this structure in the table below (Duarte, 2008, p. 29). See whether you can identify the structure in one of your favorite movies.

EXAMPLE	YOU MEET THE CHARACTER(S)	SOMETHING IS AT STAKE—TENSION IS CREATED	THE TENSION IS RESOLVED
Finding Nemo	Marlin is a clown fish and single parent of Nemo. Marlin views the Great Barrier Reef as a dangerous place after experiencing loss.	Nemo swims off "the drop off" and is captured by a scuba-diving dentist. Marlin must find Nemo, despite his anxiety about risk, before the dentist gives Nemo to his soon-to-be-arriving, destructive niece.	Marlin meets Dory and swims to Sydney Harbour, where he rescues Nemo and all is well in the Great Barrier Reef again.
Jaws	Police chief Brody escapes life as a NYC police officer. He and his family arrive in the quiet beach community of Amity.	Giant Great White shark begins eating beachgoers just as the town's profitable sunbathing season approaches. Brody is committed to "protect and serve" while the mayor instructs Brody to keep things quiet.	Brody heads out into the ocean with marine biologist Matt and hardened fisherman Quint in pursuit of the Great White. Things don't turn out well for Quint. In the end, the shark dies and Brody survives for the sequel.
Titanic	In the early 1900s, upper-class Rose boards the *Titanic* with her steel tycoon fiancé, Cal, and her destitute mother. Jack Dawson, a poor artist, wins a free ticket to travel on *Titanic*.	Not wanting to marry her fiancé and feeling the pressure to preserve her mother's lifestyle, Rose contemplates suicide and meets Jack. Rose and Jack become romantically involved and Rose begins to dream of a different life. Just as things begin to heat up, *Titanic* hits an iceberg and begins to sink.	Cal arranges a lifeboat for himself, Rose, her mother, and Jack. At the last moment, Cal double-crosses Jack. Rose jumps from the lifeboat and remains on *Titanic* with Jack. Jack doesn't survive the frigid waters, but Rose does. She takes on the identity of Rose Dawson and goes on to live the type of life she imagined she might have with Jack.
My favorite movie:	Who are the characters?	What crisis or conflict were they faced with? What was at stake?	How did the story end?

To share compelling stories with your audience, simply follow the three-part story structure.

You can use stories to reinforce the key concepts you are sharing. Begin to pay attention to the experiences you encounter that may provide content for a great story. I highly recommend you explore Duarte's *Resonate* to go deeper into the art of creating stories that resonate with your audience.

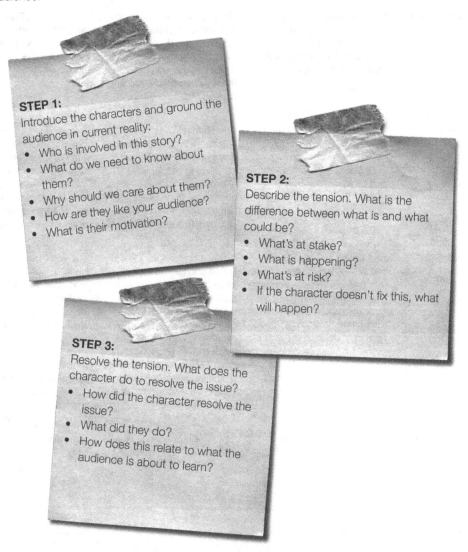

STEP 1:
Introduce the characters and ground the audience in current reality:
- Who is involved in this story?
- What do we need to know about them?
- Why should we care about them?
- How are they like your audience?
- What is their motivation?

STEP 2:
Describe the tension. What is the difference between what is and what could be?
- What's at stake?
- What is happening?
- What's at risk?
- If the character doesn't fix this, what will happen?

STEP 3:
Resolve the tension. What does the character do to resolve the issue?
- How did the character resolve the issue?
- What did they do?
- How does this relate to what the audience is about to learn?

ANIMATING LECTURE USING VISUAL DATA

Research and data are often part of the information delivered in Share. The Type Two learner particularly enjoys seeing the research that validates the information you are sharing. For data to have meaning, learners must be able to visualize the data in context.

- **Choose to Be Precise or "Round Off"?** When presenting data, be precise to cultivate credibility. For example, the statement "82 percent of respondents said..." builds credibility. Round off to focus on comprehension, "80 percent of results are determined by..." Be aware that lack of precision can translate into low credibility with some learners, especially the Type Two learning style. Comments such as these can detract from credibility:

  > "*Many* experts say..."
  > "I read *somewhere* that..."
  > "If I had to *guess*..."
  > "It's *somewhere* in the *neighborhood* of about..."

- **Create context:** Put the data into context to help learners grasp meaning. For example, when Steve Jobs, CEO of Apple, shared sales data on the initial launch of the iPhone® he said, "We have sold four million iPhones to date. If you divide four million by 200 days, that's 20,000 iPhones every day on average" (Gallo, 2010, p.105).

- **Illustrate the data in the mind's eye of the learner:** Whenever possible, convert numerical data into visual data. For example, "The 440-yard relay is roughly the length of 4 and a half football fields."

QUESTIONS TO ASK YOURSELF WHEN PRESENTING VISUAL DATA

1. **Begin by asking the question**, "What question am I answering with this visual?" Articulate the question before you seek to find the right visual answer.

2. **Answer the question**, "What relationship am I trying to illustrate?" Is the relationship of the data spatial? Chronological? Conceptual? Qualitative? Should I use a diagram? Chart? Map? Relationship web? Is the interface static? Interactive? Animated?

"Very often, learning is about forming the right images when we hear or read language. And the right images can be precise. As we become expert in some subject, our images become more and more exact and complex. A freshman in chemistry may think of an electron as a negative particle, but a more advanced student will think of it as the region in space where negative charge is most likely to be found. A novice may think of a poem as a limerick or a nursery rhyme, while a poet will think of a Shakespearean sonnet or T.S. Eliot's *The Wasteland*.

When we show that we have a precise and complex image for a word, we demonstrate deep learning. We demonstrate comprehension of the language of our field." (Zull, 2002, p. 170)

THE VISUAL CHANNEL

My daughter, Mackensie, is an avid reader. When she was ten years old, I asked her what it is about reading that she loves so much. She responded with, "I would rather read a story than watch the movie [version] because when I read, I get to choose how I see it." Imaging is a central part of the comprehension process. When we read or hear words, a mental image is created.

Providing a visual image of the key concept being taught ensures that the mental image being created leads the learners to deeper understanding and, ultimately, successful application. Asking learners to choose or create an image enables you to check the level of understanding.

CHOOSING THE RIGHT IMAGE

Because you are focused on helping learners see something in a new way, choosing the right image is important. The image must generate deeper understanding. When designing PowerPoints, this is especially important. If the image does not align with the verbal message, the learner is distracted into figuring out what the connection might be. Be especially careful with clip art. Clip art images are often too generic to create a meaningful reinforcement.

To choose the right images:

1 **Begin by asking the question, "What question am I answering with this visual?"** Articulate the question before you seek to find the right visual answer.

2 **Ask yourself, "What do I want the learner to see in her mind's eye?"** The answer to this question should be directly connected to what high producers or masterful individuals see. For example, if a master negotiator sees the negotiation process as a "dance," you might invite novice learners to answer the question, "If your last negotiation were a dance, what tune was playing?" You could share several songs and invite learners to choose one and explain their choices to a partner or group.

3 **Look for ways to convey the image.** You can incorporate visual elements into many dimensions of your presentation: flipcharts, PowerPoints, visual processing activities, visual organizers, and peripherals. Get creative.

With enough leverage, you can change your company, your industry, your world.

~ *Brand Hijack: Marketing Without Marketing*, Alex Wipperfürth

No bullet points found on this slide

ANIMATING LECTURE WITH CARTOON IMAGES

Imagine you are visiting a local elementary school and you walk past a classroom which has taped the work of the students on the wall outside of the room. Take a look at the self-portraits created on this page. If you didn't know what grade level of students created these portraits, what grade would you guess?

At one point in time, we all loved to draw. Over the years, many of us decided that we weren't very good at it and stopped drawing. When participants in our courses are asked whether they draw well, typically under 20 percent will raise their hands.

The self-portraits on this page were created by participants in our trainer programs-all of them well into their adult years. When I asked these "artists" what grade level they would assign to their skill level, the most common answer was "third- and fourth-grade levels." Why does our drawing ability seem to peak at the third- and fourth-grade levels? Some might argue that this may have a great deal to do with the emphasis on left-brain learning that kicks in at this grade level. Reading, writing, and math are all left-dominant brain processes while drawing is a right-dominant brain processing activity. Others might suggest that many of us give up at this point because we realize that our images are not "real" enough.

Drawing is not really very difficult. Seeing is the problem, or, to be more specific, shifting to a particular way of seeing.

~ Edwards, 1989, p. 4

BASIC CARTOONS—MADE FROM BASIC SHAPES

Images do not have to be realistic to be powerful. In fact, most popular cartoonists tend to create characters that are far from realistic. A third- or fourth-grade-level drawing competency is all you need to incorporate images into your training. If you can draw a simple, basic shape, you can create all kinds of characters from that shape by adding "accessories." Below and on the next page, you will see how easy it is to create basic cartoon people. I would like to acknowledge Mike Artell, a cartoonist, trainer, author, and illustrator, who shared this technique with me.

step 1

Draw a circle for the head.

step 2

Draw the body by coming out from the head with a curved line. (Necks complicate things unnecessarily. Go straight from the head).

step 3

Draw a slightly curved line between the two sides of the body.

step 4

Draw the arms, as shown.

step 5

Draw the hands as "mittens." Forget about fingers.

step 6

Draw the legs with a line that moves out and then inward, as shown.

step 7

Draw the feet as a flat oval that extends outward from the leg. The angle of the feet gives depth to the character.

step 8

Add eyes and mouth. Leave the nose off, to make things easier.

step 9

Add hair, clothes, and accessories.

Cartoon people can be used on flipcharts and PowerPoint slides. Here are some of the ways you can incorporate characters into your sessions:

- **Reflection Exercises:** Draw a cartoon character in the center of the paper with a thinking bubble over the head. Put a big "?" in the thinking bubble. Invite learners to record their reflections on the paper chart.
- **In a PowerPoint:** You can create your own collection of cartoon people and scan them. You can then use your own "clip art" in your PowerPoint designs.

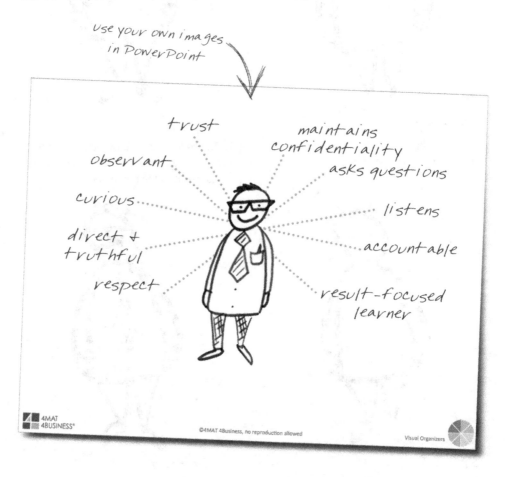

ANIMATING LECTURE WITH VISUALLY APPEALING FLIPCHARTS

With the technology now available to trainers, flipcharts might be considered a bit "old school." However, flipcharts are one of the most versatile and engaging tools available to trainers. Flipcharts involve the learner in lecture, reinforce key ideas, link images and concepts, and provide a visual record of the key ideas being shared. Here are some tips to maximize the impact of flipcharts:

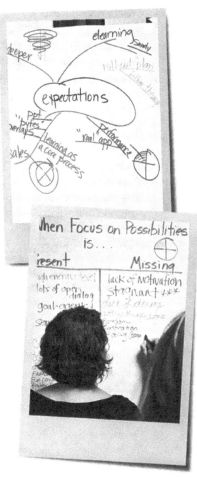

- **Write BIG.** If the person in the back of the room can easily read the chart, you are writing large enough. Use large-tipped markers—chisel point is the best.
- **Focus on the big ideas.** Rather than writing out lists or lots of text, share one idea per page.
- **Include words and images.** Choose visuals that reinforce the big idea. Simple images, cartoon characters, and diagrams work well.
- **Use upper- and lower-case letters.** This will make reading the charts much easier for the learners.
- **Add color.** You should have a minimum of four colors to work with—red, green, black, and blue work well. Be careful of yellow, pink, and orange, which can be difficult to read from a distance.
- **Write, then recite.** When writing an idea on the chart, finish writing the word or phrase before you share with the audience. If you share something like, "The three elements are a, b, and c," and then proceed to write each on the chart, the audience will lose interest. However, if you share, "The three elements you need to be aware of are…," then begin writing, the audience will tune in to resolve the tension of not knowing what the three things are.
- **Talk to the audience, not the paper chart.** Write, then turn to the audience and talk about what you have just written. By the time you have finished recording the idea, the audience has already processed it. Rather than reading what you wrote, use the message on the chart as a cue to elaborate further.

- **Create a visual story.** Tape the key charts on the wall as you go. Think about the flipchart serving as a visual reinforcer of the key ideas being shared in the session. You can reference the ideas on the walls and also use the charts for group review. Paint tape, which can be found at most hardware stores, will adhere to walls without damaging the paint.

- **Add characters.** You can add characters to your flipcharts to add more interest. Think about adding talking and thinking bubbles that encourage the learners to reflect and reprocess the key information.

- **Create a visual record.** When you have completed the session, take photos of the charts to create a visual record of the session. During training sessions I lead, I often invite the learners to take a stroll with their camera phones and take photos of any ideas they want to capture. You would be surprised at how many people will do this when given the invitation. You can also use the images as follow-up to the session. Think about emailing the image with a key message or posting the image in a post-class online forum for group discussion.

TRICKS FOR THE DRAWING-PHOBIC

- **Pre-prepare your charts.** If you are uncomfortable with drawing "on the fly," you can pre-prepare your charts. Use a light pencil to sketch out your charts in advance. The audience will not be able to see the faint lines and you can trace over them easily with your markers.

- **Attach visual props.** You can easily attach printed visual images to your flipcharts. Create an inventory of images that work to support the key ideas of your training content. You can attach the images to your chart using tape. For example, if you are teaching a course on "Work and Life Balance," you might print an image of a see-saw to place in the middle of a flipchart you are using to record learner responses on "Things we need to balance..." Place the images on a table near the flipchart. Adhere tape to the back of the images prior to your session.

SYMBOLS YOU CAN EASILY DRAW

Basic symbols can add interest to your flipchart papers. Here are some symbols you can include on a flipchart to create visual interest:

Tension

Ideas

Movement

Processing

Emotion

Animating Lecture with Visual Organizers

Visual organizers are frameworks for illustrating the relationships between information.

You can use visual organizers to:

- Record ideas being generated by learners
- Present information in PowerPoint, on flipcharts or whiteboards (web environment)
- Structure the format of group debriefing of exercises
- Encourage learners to take notes during lecture

Here are some examples of visual organizers:

MINDMAPS

Learners can be asked to mindmap the key ideas being shared. Alternatively, you can also provide a "starter" mindmap handout with the big ideas illustrated. Learners can be asked to add details as you lecture. A more linear approach to mindmapping can be found in the fishbone diagram.

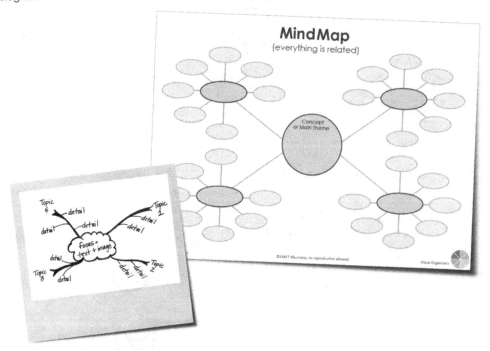

FISHBONE DIAGRAM

A fishbone diagram, or cause and effect diagram, allows for the analysis of the causes of a particular result or problem. Label the issue as the head of the "fish." The branches represent major contributors to the issue. Frame up the diagram by posing a question to the learner, e.g., "Why is our new client retention low?" It is helpful to provide the categories to help learners see the organizing structure of the information you are delivering.

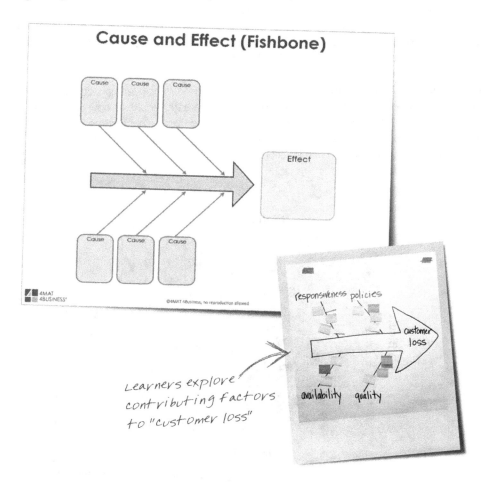

Learners explore contributing factors to "customer loss"

FOUR SQUARE FRAMES

Four square frames allow the trainer to share the various relationships between two variables. This is illustrated as a box with four "panes." Here are several examples:

Four Frame for Assessing: In Share, you are helping learners make new distinctions among good, better, and best application of the content being shared. You can use a four frame to visually organize these distinctions. For example, in a course on developing engaging presentations, a four frame can be used to show how entertainment value and information value combine to create different levels of impact in presentations. Presentations that represent each combination can be shared by the trainer or learners.

Four Frame for Diagnosing: A four-frame box can be used to help learners connect real-world experiences to the content being shared. For example, as a trainer shares how to diagnose causes of low employee performance, a four frame can be used to connect performance issues to combinations of high or low skill and high or low willingness to perform. The trainer might share video vignettes illustrating each combination.

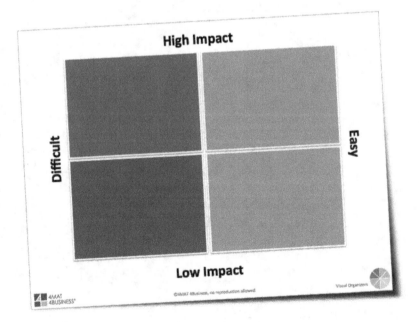

SCALES

Scales can be represented on a vertical or horizontal line. Typically, they include some description of different levels of measurement. In a lecture, you might use a scale to assess learner reaction. As learners break after a lecture, learners can post colored sticky dots on a scale to indicate their current level of comfort with the information shared.

COMPARE AND CONTRAST—VENN

Venn diagrams are simply two overlapping circles. They are used to compare differences and similarities between two elements. In each circle, the unique characteristics of each item being compared and contrasted are recorded. In the overlapping part of the two circles, the common elements are recorded.

Venn diagrams can be used many ways, such as to compare and contrast models, distinguish responsibilities of different teams, or illustrate mutual and distinct interests.

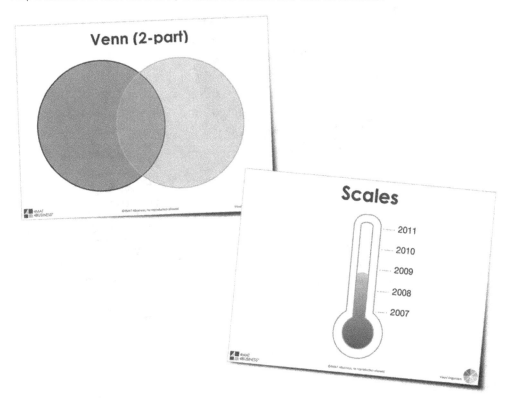

CONCENTRIC CIRCLES

Concentric circles offer an effective way to illustrate the "ripple effect." The central circle represents the "core." Each extending circle represents a degree of separation from the core. For example, a trainer might write a corporate value in the center circle. In the next circle, learners are invited to identify and record behaviors that illustrate this value in action. In the next circle, learners identify and record the value created for customers as a result of the behavior.

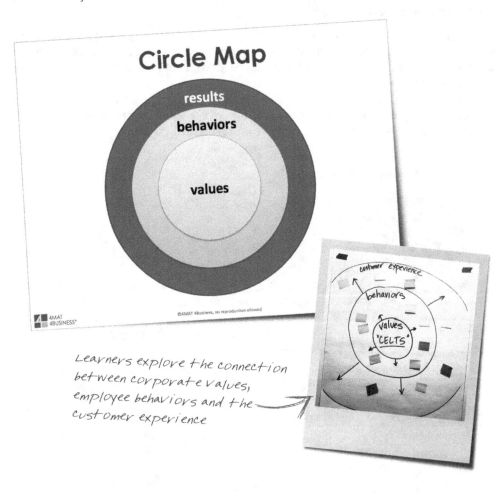

Learners explore the connection between corporate values, employee behaviors and the customer experience

BRACE MAP

A brace map helps learners see the relationship between a whole and its parts. Typically, brace maps can be illustrated left to right or top to bottom. On the first level, the "whole" is defined. In the next level (or brace), the major parts of the whole are defined. In the next level, the sub-parts are defined.

Brace maps can be provided in advance of a lecture for note taking. In a product knowledge lecture, for example, a brace map can be provided that visually illustrates major product domains with sub-categories of related products within each domain.

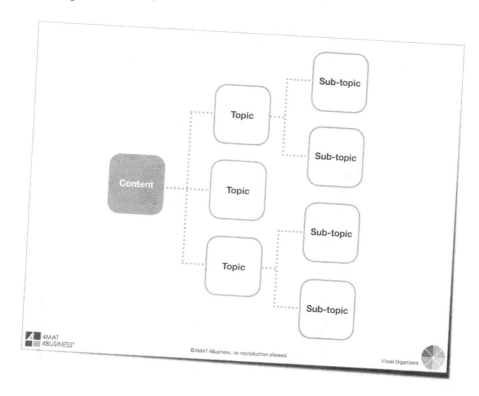

HUMAN GRAPHS

Human graphs are a way to kinesthetically involve learners. The trainer orients the learners to the dimensions being graphed. Learners are then invited to position themselves accordingly in the physical space of the learning environment. By asking learners to position themselves physically in the room, you can create a visual image of the factor(s) being discussed.

For example, in one of our 4MAT courses, we invite participants to position themselves on an imaginary "horseshoe" based on their Hemispheric Mode Indicator® (right and left brain processing preferences) score. We then ask the learners to raise their hands in response to questions such as "Who here prefers to initially work alone? Who would prefer to talk things through with someone else before you start? Who here likes things to be 'black and white'? Who prefers some 'shades of gray'?" This exercise promotes lively dialogue on how differences in our preferences for right- or left-mode processing show up in learning and work situations.

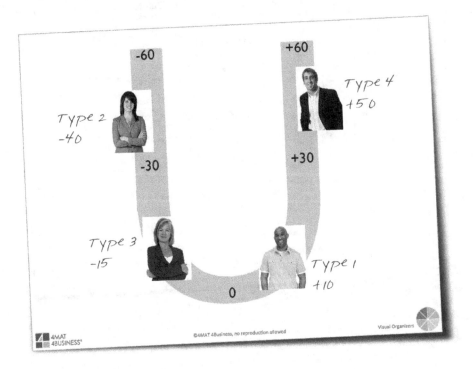

STORYBOARDING

Storyboarding is a visual organizing process that typically shows a series of illustrations or images displayed in sequence. Storyboards were originally created by The Walt Disney Company to plan animations. Trainers can use storyboards to share information or to encourage learners to process information.

For example, in a technical skills course you might include a large blank storyboard at each table. In table groups, learners can process the information being shared by writing key ideas on sticky notes. Sticky notes are then arranged and rearranged by the group using the storyboard structure.

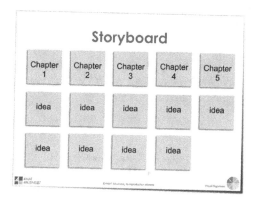

COLLAGES

Collages are typically created by cutting images and pasting them together. Collages are a free-form way of organizing ideas. You can use collages to elicit what learners already know about the subject being explored. They are particularly powerful at eliciting the beliefs and metaphors learners use to understand information.

For example, I once observed a trainer leading a workshop on branding who invited learners to create a collage with images that represented their take on the company's "brand story." The exercise elicited lively dialogue that was woven into the ensuing lecture.

IMAGE CARDS

Image cards are a collection of images used to process information visually. In the previous chapter, we talked about using image cards to encourage reflection. There are many ways you can also use images in the Share portion of the learning experience you are creating.

Think about how you might invite learners to re-process what you are sharing.

For example, you might encourage learners to choose an image card in response to any of the following questions:

- "What is your biggest insight?"

- "What do you see as the biggest problem?"

- "If you had to sum up everything we have explored, what would you define as the overarching concept?"

learners choose an image in response to a reflective question

CONTENT TEMPLATES

Content templates are simply fill-in-the-blank visual organizers. You can create your own visual organizer framework, which you can invite learners to complete throughout the learning session. For example, a brace map with images and text boxes for learners to complete can easily be printed on an 11x17-inch sheet of paper and presented as a "placemat."

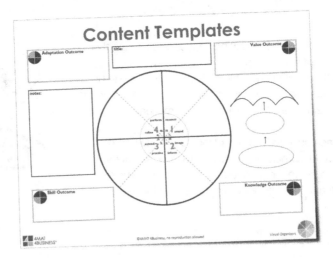

TIMELINES

A timeline is usually presented as a horizontal line that learners record events upon. Timelines can be used many ways. To encourage reflection, you might invite learners to reflect on their experiences related to the content over time. For a product launch, you might review each step of the launch in chronological order. In a workbook, you might include blank text boxes for learners to fill out. Other examples of timelines in Share:

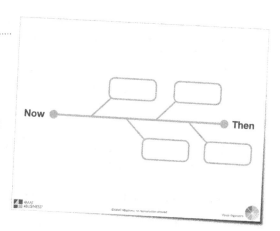

- As a group exercise, invite learners to record important events that shaped their experiences around the content being shared.
- As you share the steps in a process, invite learners to plot the steps on a timeline.

THE 4MAT WHEEL

The 4MAT wheel is a visual organizer that illustrates the process we move through when we learn and act upon new information. You can encourage learners to use this framework when processing new information.

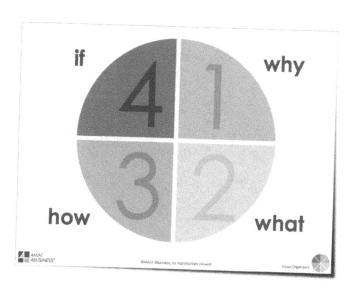

Animating Lecture with PowerPoint

PowerPoint is one of the most widely used tools by trainers. Unfortunately, it is also one of the most widely *mis*used tools. When all of the information the trainer is sharing in the lecture is recorded in PowerPoint, it's easy for the slides to serve as a teleprompter for the presenter. This becomes particularly painful for learners when the presenter insists on reading the information on the slides. Because we can read twice as fast as we can talk, learners are done reviewing the slide just as the trainer gets halfway through reading the slide.

Instead of including bulleted text, think about the slide as a way to visually reinforce your message. Each slide should share one key message. If the slide includes visual and verbal messages, make sure that both messages align.

HOW TO MAP OUT YOUR POWERPOINT

First, it is important to note that the design of the PowerPoint comes after you have organized your lecture. You must first organize the lecture and get clear on the key messages. Earlier in this chapter, we discussed the importance of defining a maximum of five key messages. These messages will serve as the organizing framework for your lecture.

We will use a brace map to illustrate how to effectively structure your PowerPoint.

1 Begin with the Title Slide

2 Introduce the key messages. Think about the visual and verbal message on each slide. I have seen visual icons used as a powerful way to organize a lecture.

3 Define the sub-topics for each key message.

4 Summarize.

Keep in mind that there are two channels you are communicating through—visual and verbal. The words and images should be aligned and chosen to reinforce the key ideas that you are sharing.

THINGS TO AVOID IN POWERPOINT

1 **Bullet points:** Besides being predictable, bullet points are also an indicator that the presenter is likely to use the slide as a teleprompter. Choose one message that sums up the bullet points. Use this message as a cue to share the content you would have included in the PowerPoint.

2 **Multiple themes on one slide:** Be careful to have one message per slide. Your message will be clear and the audience will be engaged.

3 **Unappealing slides:** Designing visually appealing slides is a topic beyond the scope of this book. There are many great books out there that can help you build your "eye" in assessing the visual appeal of your slides. I highly recommend Nancy Duarte's *Slideology* and Garr Reynolds' *Presentation Zen*.

4 **Images that don't align with the message:** Our brains pay attention to incongruency and this can distract from the learning process. An image that does not reinforce the text will deplete the most valuable commodity in the learning experience—the learner's attention.

Think about the slide as a way to visually reinforce your message

Summary

In this chapter, we have explored the importance of creating an opportunity for learners to visualize the content. As you transition learners from Engage to Share, it is important that you create an opportunity for learners to "see" the content. You can do this by using a non-verbal strategy to process what learners know through their own experience. This might involve metaphors—"Choose an image that represents how you view a leader's role in change." It might involve a song—"If the change leader had a theme song, what would it be?" There are many non-verbal methods you can use to encourage processing of experience.

As you move into lecture, keep in mind that you want to shift the delivery method every ten minutes or so. You can incorporate a story, use a visual processing tool, show a video, or use another strategy that engages the learner through multi-modal delivery.

In the next chapter, we will explore how to move the learner into applying the information learned in Share. After the Reflect and Act sections of this chapter, you will find examples of activities that work well in the Share part of the learning cycle. Review "Your Training Style in Share" and reflect on your training style strengths related to this part of the learning cycle.

Step in the Cycle: Share

What the learner is doing:
- Seeing the bigger picture of the content about to be delivered
- Visualizing the desired outcome
- Gaining understanding of expert knowledge
- Grasping the larger concepts and detailed topics

What the trainer is doing:
- Using another medium (neither reading nor writing) to connect the learners to the concept (visual arts, music, movement, etc.)
- Transforming the concept to be taught into an image or experience—a "sneak preview" for the learners
- Creating an opportunity for the learners to see the bigger picture of the concept
- Organizing the content to clearly deliver key information and ideas

Activities that work well:
- Visual metaphor exercises
- Imaging exercises
- Storytelling
- Visual data representation
- Multi-media presentations
- Lecture
- Demonstration

YOUR TRAINING STYLE IN SHARE

If you have a natural strength in the Type Two training approach, it is likely that you already rely on presentation skills in your training delivery. If your area of strength lies in one of the other three approaches, be aware of what you will need to focus on to be successful in this step.

	HIGH STRENGTH IN TYPE ONE TRAINING APPROACH	HIGH STRENGTH IN TYPE TWO TRAINING APPROACH	HIGH STRENGTH IN TYPE THREE TRAINING APPROACH	HIGH STRENGTH IN TYPE FOUR TRAINING APPROACH
	Be comfortable with the idea of sharing "expert knowledge."	Be aware of the potential over-use of this strength. Be sure to include visual strategies that balance "telling."	Slow down and take the necessary time to allow learners to fully understand what they need to know before moving into application.	Be careful to stay on track in your delivery. Focus on the key ideas and build your lecture around those ideas, keeping the big ideas and details tightly woven together.
	Type One Trainer comment: "I sometimes struggle with 'being the expert.' I would rather facilitate a conversation than present."	Type Two Trainer comment: "I have a tendency to over-share. I include more information than they really need. Editing content is a big opportunity for me."	Type Three Trainer comment: "I tend to get frustrated with learners who ask too many clarifying questions. I know they will figure it out as soon as they get their hands in it. I have to remind myself that some learners aren't comfortable moving into hands-on without full knowledge."	Type Four Trainer comment: "I have to be careful to stay on track. There are so many things you can bring into a lecture. I remind myself to 'Keep the main thing the main thing.'"

Journal to capture stories, metaphors, images, and interesting ways to share data.

Pay attention to how stories are structured in movies.

Make note of how other trainers use images effectively.

Take the time to reflect on the organization of the content before you start building the lecture.

Ask yourself, "What does the learner need to understand to perform at a higher level?" Focus on editing your content to the essential information.

In the next training you design and/or deliver, which strategies will you include?

	YES	NO
• Mindmapping	✓	
• Visual organizers to help learners see the organizing structure of the information being delivered such as brace maps, Venn diagrams, and four frames		
• More images and less text in my PowerPoint slides		
• A well-crafted story		
• Visual processing activities such as a visual collage or metaphor activity		

Examples of Share Activities

In this section, you will find examples of activities to engage learners during information delivery. You will also find activities to encourage learners to process their understanding of the information in a non-verbal format.

EXAMPLE SHARE ACTIVITY: CONTENT "PLACEMATS"

In a customer service skills course, learners are provided with a visual organizer that conveys the organizing structure of the content being covered in the lecture. Learners are encouraged to take notes using colorful markers.

VISUAL ORGANIZER: PLACEMATS

Focus: Reprocessing activity that summarizes key learning points using a visual organizer.

Resources Needed
- 11x17 printed visual organizer for each participant
- Colorful markers (optional)

Description

1. Identify the visual organizer structure that best illustrates the content organization, e.g., mindmap, brace map, storyboard, or metaphor.

2. Create an organizer with ample room for taking notes. (Printing on 11x17 size paper is optimal.)

3. Hand out organizers to learners or position as "placemats" in front of the learners before the beginning of the session.

4. Encourage learners to take notes by completing the note-taking fields.

5. Allow time for learners to partner or form small groups of three to share their notes. Encourage learners to add ideas gained from the notes of others.

Facilitator Script

"To help you identify and retain the critical information you will need to apply this in the real world, I invite you to take notes using the placemat in front of you. You can use the markers on the table to make your notes more colorful or to color-code for organization. Periodically, we will pause to share your notes with others in small groups."

Notes:

_____

_____

_____

EXAMPLE SHARE ACTIVITY: FLIPCHART REVIEW IN A MULTI-DAY COURSE

In a multi-day program, the presenter creates a colorful flip chart for each key idea shared. At the beginning of Day 2 of the course, learners form small groups and select one of the paper charts. Each group is tasked with re-presenting the key idea to the rest of the group.

BIG IDEA FLIPCHART REVIEW

Focus: Lecture reprocessing activity with learners re-teaching content to fellow learners.

Resources Needed
- Paper charts
- Sticky notes reviewed

Description

1. Facilitator creates one flip chart per key idea presented. This can be created throughout delivery of the content.

2. Facilitator identifies the charts which will be reviewed by placing a large sticky note on each chart. The number of charts should equal the number of groups that will be formed.

3. Learners form small groups. Each group chooses a chart to review.

4. Learners prepare to re-teach the content in a rapid fashion.

5. Each group re-presents the key ideas shared.

Facilitator Script

"Before we explore this topic further, we are going to take some time to review the content explored yesterday. On the walls, you will find six charts with neon pink sticky notes on them. Each chart summarizes a key learning idea from yesterday's session. Each of the six table groups in the room will choose one of the charts to re-present to the rest of us. You will have 15 minutes to prepare your presentation and five minutes to present to the larger group. You may use the paper chart on the wall to present, create a new chart, or to come up with another creative way to share the idea."

Notes:

_____

_____

_____

_____

_____

_____

SHARE ACTIVITY EXAMPLE: STICKY DOT VOTING IN A LEADERSHIP COURSE

In a "Leadership Development" course, the presenter shares mini-lectures alternating with associated practice activities. After the first Share portion of the training design, the presenter invites participants to generate questions. Learners write their questions on sticky notes and place them on a large paper chart in the front of the room. As learners post questions, the presenter clusters related questions into question "themes." Using colored sticky dots, learners prioritize the questions they would like to explore further.

STICKY DOT VOTING EXERCISE

Focus: Kinesthetic polling technique that can be used in many ways, including prioritizing information.

Resources Needed
- Three colored sticky dots per participant

Description
1. Before, during, or after a lecture, invite learners to generate questions they would like to explore related to the topic being discussed.
2. Write the questions on a flipchart(s) in the front of the room. If questions are redundant, group them into themes.
3. Ask participants to vote on the questions they most want to explore. Give each participant a green, red, and yellow sticky dot. Have participants place their dots next to the questions which most interests them. Green = highest interest, Yellow = moderate interest, Red = least interest.
4. Begin the QA session by answering the questions with the highest number of green sticky dots. As time permits, continue by moving on to yellow and red.

Trainer Script
"Review the questions shared by your fellow participants. Choose three questions that you are most interested in exploring in this session. Place a green sticky dot next to your first choice, a yellow dot next to your second choice, and a red dot next to your third choice. We will revisit the lecture part of our session by exploring the three most popular questions."

Notes:

_____

_____

_____

_____

_____

EXAMPLE SHARE ACTIVITY: STORYTELLING IN A TECHNICAL PRODUCT KNOWLEDGE COURSE

In a product knowledge course on water pumps, participants are invited to re-process the lecture by developing a recap of the product features shared in a storytelling or newscast format. The learners are divided into two groups with one sharing a "60 Minutes"–style presentation on the products and the other sharing a "Once upon a time…" tale that links features to fulfillment of client "wishes."

CRAFT A STORY VS REPORT A STORY

Focus: Lecture reprocessing activity that requires learners to develop a story around the information shared.

Resources Needed
- Optional: Physical props such as wands, fairy wings, play microphones, reporter hat, "Press" badge

Description
1. Divide learners into groups of four to six.
2. Give half of the learner groups the assignment to reprocess and share the information learned in a creative storytelling form. Give the remaining half the assignment to reprocess and share the information in a newscast reporting style.
3. Invite groups to share their presentations with the larger audience.

Trainer Script
"Your groups will be given fifteen minutes to reprocess the information we have learned in either a 'Creative Storytelling' format or a 'Newscast' format. For the creative format, think about visual storytelling or fairy tales. For the newscast format, think about creating an evening news–style report. I will assign each group their story type. Each group will have five minutes to present their story to the larger group."

Note: In a class of ten or fewer, divide into two groups. In larger groups, create multiple groups with an equal number of "reporting" and "storytelling" teams. Invite groups to partner with an opposite reporting style team to share their presentations.

Notes:
_____
_____
_____
_____
_____

SHARE ACTIVITY EXAMPLE: "COMPANY VALUES INTERVIEWS"

As part of a new-hire orientation program, participants are asked to conduct interviews with team members in various departments within the organization over a one-week period. Using provided questions, learners conduct interviews and bring their findings to the second session of the orientation program. Learners share their discoveries in small group dialogue.

On a large paper chart on the wall, the organizational chart is illustrated. Groups are asked to write interesting things they uncovered about each department interviewed.

IN-FIELD INTERVIEWS

Focus: Learners facilitate in-field interviews to discover information.

Resources Needed
- Interview question guide

Description

1. Develop a series of interview questions learners may use to discover essential information related to course content.
2. Provide learners with instructions for conducting interviews, including who to interview, how to use the questions provided, and what information they should bring back to the formal learning session.
3. Send learners into the "field" to conduct interviews.
4. Invite learners to share their findings in small groups.

Trainer Script

"To encourage you to learn more about <insert topic>, I am going to ask that you conduct three interviews between now and the next session of our program. In your workbook, you will find three questions you will use in your interviews. You may choose to ask any additional questions, if you like. You may also choose to interview any person, as long as he or she fits the criteria listed in your workbook. Be prepared to share your findings in the next session of our program."

Notes:

SHARE ACTIVITY EXAMPLE: LECTURE TRANSLATION
IN A HIGH-TECH PRODUCT KNOWLEDGE COURSE

LECTURE TRANSLATOR

Focus: Reprocessing of lecture by inviting learners to translate lecture into their own words (and images) to reinforce key concepts.

Resources Needed
• None

Description
1. Share with participants that you will randomly choose "translators" to interpret what you have shared in lecture.

2. Lecture for about five to ten minutes. Pause and allow participants to reflect on what you have shared. Encourage learners to share their insights in small teams of three or four.

3. Invite a group to nominate a "translator" to share their interpretation. Invite the larger group to add any additional ideas.

4. Repeat the process throughout your lecture.

Trainer Script
"During my lecture, I will stop periodically and give you a chance to think about what we are exploring. I'll invite one of you to translate what I said into your own words or your own example. When we pause to translate, you will have time to reflect on your own and then share your insights with your group. I will invite one group to nominate a 'translator' to reinforce the lecture I have just shared by putting it into their own words."

Notes:

_____

_____

_____

_____

_____

_____

_____

_____

_____

_____

SHARE ACTIVITY EXAMPLE: VISUAL ORGANIZER DEBRIEF OF TECHNICAL LECTURE

In a highly technical product knowledge course on pump machinery, the presenter pauses to invite small groups to process what they have learned. Each group is given one product and asked to share the most important information learned using their choice of visual organizers provided.

VISUAL ORGANIZER LECTURE DEBRIEF

Focus: Group visual activity that can be used to re-process lecture using visual organizer tools.

Resources Needed
- Visual organizer examples
- Flipcharts
- Markers

Description
1. Provide learners with examples of visual organizers such as Venn diagrams, fishbone diagrams, flow charts, pie charts, pyramids, and mindmaps.
2. Post four to six flipcharts on the walls around the room. Divide groups evenly amongs the flipchart papers. Ask each group to choose a visual organizer format and re-process the key content shared using that organizer.

Trainer Script
"On the screen, you will see examples of visual organizers. Each tool illustrates different relationships. Venn diagrams illustrate differences and commonalities. Fishbone diagrams illustrate cause and effect. Pyramids illustrate hierarchy of meaning or importance. Pie charts illustrate proportion. Mindmaps show connections between big and small ideas. Your task is to select a visual organizer tool to illustrate the key points shared in our lecture. Create a recap of the lecture by using the visual organizer format you chose to share the big ideas on a paper chart. Once you have finished, post your paper chart on the wall."

Notes:

_____

_____

_____

_____

_____

_____

SHARE ACTIVITY EXAMPLE: METAPHORS IN A NEGOTIATION SKILLS COURSE

In a negotiation skills workshop, the facilitator invites participants to choose a metaphor which represents how they view the process of negotiating. Learners explore how their choice of metaphor influences their approach to negotiations.

Examples of metaphors provided by learners include:

- "Negotiating is a battle because the element of surprise works in your favor."
- "Negotiating is a poker game because sometimes you have to bluff if you're only holding a pair of deuces."

SHARE ACTIVITY EXAMPLE: VISUAL METAPHOR EXERCISE

Focus: Learners process understanding of the overarching concept of the content being explored by completing a metaphor exercise.

Description
1. Facilitator invites learners to choose a metaphor that best represents their understanding of the topic being explored. The metaphor can be a visual image, a physical object, or any other example.
2. Facilitator shares the following statement for completion by the learner:
3. ___(content being explored)___ is ___(the metaphor)___ because ____(reason I chose this metaphor)_.
4. Learners choose their metaphors and share with partners and/or small groups.
5. Facilitator leads a dialogue on the different ways that learners view the content.

Throughout the lecture, the metaphors are woven into the delivery of the content.

Note: In Chapter 5, we discuss the important role that metaphors play in understanding. You may determine that the learners need a new metaphor to help them better understand the content. If this is the case, think about how you can create an opportunity for the learners to "image" this new metaphor.

"Even those who will someday overthrow conventional ways of thinking or doing **need to know what it is they are overthrowing.**"

~ George Leonard
Mastery

Chapter 6

Practice: Building Mastery Through Application

In the third part of the 4MAT learning cycle (Practice) the learner asks the question, "How?" The learner is engaged in taking in the required information in order to gain the understanding necessary to produce the desired learning results. In this step, the learner explores the content using hands-on application techniques such as role plays, simulations, projects, and field work.

The types of activities included in this part of the learning cycle experience encourage learners to experiment with new skills, build competence, figure out how things work, and generate application-related questions. In Practice, the focus is on building skill through application.

Essential Questions

- How do I choose the right activities?
- How do I engage learners in practicing new skills?
- What's the best way to coach learners?

RESULTS HAPPEN IN PRACTICE

Learners solve problems, try out new ideas, innovate, and produce during Practice; it's where the real work gets done and the learners' focus shifts from exploration of ideas to application. For training professionals, practice is where the training payoff begins.

STEP: PRACTICE	
Learners are ...	Practicing skills learned in Inform, hands-on use of the information.
Trainer is ...	Coaching practice activities; providing projects, scenarios, or worksheets. Setting up situations in which the learners use the information being learned.
Examples of Activities	• Role plays • Worksheets • Field work • Simulations • Game show-style reviews • Problem-solving situations • In-field work

You play the role of "Coach" in this part of the 4MAT cycle and focus on creating hands-on application opportunities for the learners. As the trainer, you move "off stage" and allow the learner to take the lead in the learning process.

An effective coach helps the learners come up with their own questions and answers so that they identify how to improve their own performance. Coaches create an opportunity for learners to gain confidence in their knowledge and practice skills to gain mastery.

To effectively create and coach practice, you must be able to:

1. Design outcome-based practice activities
2. Facilitate activities effectively
3. Observe application
4. Coach and debrief

This chapter explores strategies on how to do each of these four activities well. At the end of this chapter, you will find appropriate activities for this part of the cycle, along with examples of their use in real-world learning environments.

The learner takes the lead in Practice. You move "off stage" and play the role of Coach.

Designing Outcome-Based Practice Activities

Reflection without action is not learning. The first two parts of the 4MAT cycle, Engage and Share, emphasize the importance of reflection. In Practice, the learner moves into action.

Effective practice activities emphasize the development of the skills the learners will need to successfully apply the information in the real world. To determine the most effective activities to include in your training design, focus on the skills required to deliver the desired performance. Ask yourself: What behaviors must be executed consistently to deliver the desired results? What skills must the learner possess to competently execute these behaviors?

For example, if you are designing a product education course, the activities chosen should directly link to the desired outcome. In the left-hand column of the table below, you will find three variations of a skills outcome statement for a product education course. On the right, you will find a practice training activity that aligns with each outcome. Notice how the activity links to the outcome focus.

SKILL-FOCUSED LEARNING OUTCOME EXAMPLE FOR A PRODUCT KNOWLEDGE COURSE	TRAINING ACTIVITY EXAMPLE THAT ALIGNS WITH THE DESIRED OUTCOME
Skill outcome: Learners will *recall* key product information.	Product knowledge quiz
Skill outcome: Learners will *recognize* common client issues and *recommend* appropriate product solutions.	Matching exercise focused on connecting common client issues with product benefits
Skill outcome: Learners will *apply* the consultative selling process to customize product solutions.	Role playing the consultative selling conversation

If the desired skill outcome defined for the course requires that learners adapt the information shared, learners should have an opportunity to practice adaptation. You will want to check the learners' fundamental understanding of the content before creating an opportunity for creative adaptation.

For example, take a look at the 4MAT-based training design on "Consultative Selling Skills" below. The desired skills outcome for this course focuses on application of questioning skills in the sales process. In the Practice step of this design, notice how the trainer checks to make sure that the learners understand the steps of the consultative selling process before moving learners into a role-play activity that requires learners to apply the questions in a real-world situation.

 ENGAGE Learners explore experiences of how products fulfill real and perceived needs. In an interactive exercise, the learners dialogue and define the need categories that products fulfill.

 SHARE Learning teams each create a metaphorical visual representation which illustrates the process that a sales person uses to connect clients' needs to the product benefit. The facilitator shares the consultative selling skills process, continually referencing the visual metaphors provided by the learners.

 PRACTICE The first practice activity checks for understanding of the sales skills process. In a game board format, learning teams check their understanding of the consultative selling skills process. The facilitator revisits any content that needs clarification. Once the facilitator is assured that the learners understand the content in theory, the facilitator moves on to real-world application.

In a second Practice activity, learners form teams of three and role play the consultative selling process. Each learner has a chance to play three roles: seller, client, and observer. Sellers must identify the client's primary need through questioning in order to link the need to the product benefit. Clients respond based on the assumptions provided in a "Get in Character" card that outlines the role of the client. Observers watch the role play and offer feedback using an "Observation Assessment" tool.

 PERFORM Learners share self-assessment results of their role plays. Learners complete a "2+2" reflection in which they identify two strengths they will focus on maximizing and two weak areas they will develop further. Learners commit to an action plan to implement what they have learned, which includes a two-week and four-week review of results with their team leader.

In the Practice step of this design, the trainer assesses for understanding before moving into the real-world simulations. If the trainer had moved directly into simulations without checking for knowledge, she could easily have found that the learners were confused on the different product offerings.

When designing Practice, think about how you can check for learner understanding before moving into creative application of the content being learned.

Facilitating (Setting Up) Activities Effectively

Certain aspects of setting up activities may seem obvious, such as the need for giving clear directions. Other factors may not be as obvious but are nonetheless just as important to address.

These factors include:

- **Connecting the activity to the learning experience and previous dialogue.** It is important to set up the activity by connecting it to what has already happened in the learning experience. For example, the trainer might introduce an activity with, "In our earlier conversation, you identified the biggest challenge in customer service is figuring out where the real issue lies. In this next exercise, you will have a chance to apply the questioning framework to identifying real-world customer issues."

- **Clearly defining the criteria that will be used to evaluate the application.** Many learners, especially Type Two learners, want a clearly defined learning objective. It is often beneficial to develop an assessment tool which illustrates the differences among a "good," "better," and "best" practice application. The criteria is ideally introduced during lecture and given to learners before they jump into hands-on practice.

- **Establishing time limits.** When setting up the activity, share how much time learners will have to complete the exercise. Because learners can easily lose track of time, it is beneficial to give periodic timing updates, e.g., "You have five minutes remaining."

- **Allowing time for learners to assess their own application.** If you provide an example of "good," "better," and "best" application criteria before learners begin an activity, they can use these criteria to assess their own application. For example, you might ask learners, "Using the scaling criteria, assess and score your application. In 5 minutes, I will ask you to share your scores along with the 'Why?' behind your scoring."

- **Gaining commitment on how the learners will apply the insights gained.** After assessing and debriefing a practice activity, it is important to weave the insights gained into the next part of the learning cycle.

4MAT provides an easy-to-remember framework for setting up Practice activities:

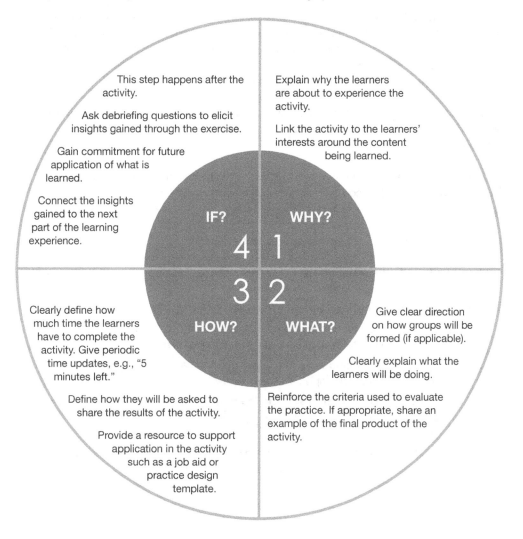

This step happens after the activity.

Ask debriefing questions to elicit insights gained through the exercise.

Gain commitment for future application of what is learned.

Connect the insights gained to the next part of the learning experience.

IF?

4

Explain why the learners are about to experience the activity.

Link the activity to the learners' interests around the content being learned.

WHY?

1

3

HOW?

2

WHAT?

Clearly define how much time the learners have to complete the activity. Give periodic time updates, e.g., "5 minutes left."

Define how they will be asked to share the results of the activity.

Provide a resource to support application in the activity such as a job aid or practice design template.

Give clear direction on how groups will be formed (if applicable).

Clearly explain what the learners will be doing.

Reinforce the criteria used to evaluate the practice. If appropriate, share an example of the final product of the activity.

CREATING JOB AIDS

Do you remember the quick reference guides (also known as "cheat sheets") that some learners used in high school to get through physics? Job aids are basically cheat sheets that share the most important information one needs to know to perform a task or activity. Just as that high school cheat sheet only included the essential information needed to pass the test, a job aid provides only the essential information needed to perform.

In addition to being useful on the job, job aids are helpful in hands-on practice activities. Think about isolating the most essential information needed for a learner to execute the desired behaviors when creating job aids.

In our office, we have a "job aid" that was quickly created by one of our team members to empower anyone to make good coffee. Let's look at what to consider when creating a job aid and see how this "create your own coffee" job aid stacks up:

What to consider when creating an effective job aid:

- **Focus on how the information will be used.** The coffee job aids delivers the information in the order one might need the information.
- **Provide the instructions step-by-step.** The coffee job aid is outlined in seven simple steps.
- **Only include the essential information.** The coffee job aid only includes what you need to know to make the coffee. No history on coffee beans found here.
- **Develop in user-friendly language.** The coffee pot manufacturer refers to the pre-measured coffee as "pods." This job aid simply calls them "discs" because they look like a disc.
- **Make it accessible at the right place and the right time.** Rather than emailing everyone a copy of the "Seven Steps to Great Coffee," this job aid is posted directly over the coffee pot.

There are many different ways to structure a job aid beyond a step-by-step list. You can use any number of the visual organizers discussed in Chapter 5 to create effective job aids, including decision tables and flow charts.

Coffee Instructions

1. Make sure there is water in the reservoir (back of machine).
2. Choose your coffee disc and place it in the disc holder.
3. Put your coffee cup on the tray.
4. When the light turns green, press the start/stop button.
5. Wait for the light to go off & the coffee to finish brewing.
6. Remove your disc and toss it.
7. Enjoy your freshly brewed cup of coffee!

Don't forget to wash your cup!

Observing Application

Observation is critical to effective coaching. By paying attention, you can identify areas for improvement and specific examples of behaviors to share with learners. Imagine yourself as a "mirror" that reflects back the performance of the learner. When learners are able to view their performance objectively, they often notice what they might have otherwise missed. When observing, capture concrete actions that you can share to help learners get a clear picture of what is getting in the way of producing the desired result. Here's what you should focus on when observing application:

- **Walk the room.** As learners move into Practice application, it is tempting to sit down and begin to prepare for the next segment of the course. Instead, move into observation mode and check in on the progress of groups. Invest time observing each group. Make yourself available to answer questions. Be careful not to take charge of a group's activity.
- **Take notes.** Take notice of the process the group is using to apply the content. It is equally important that you coach the product of the learning assignment and the process used to generate it.
- **Record comments.** Listen to the dialogue between learners and write down specific comments you hear. These comments will be highly useful when you lead the debriefing of the exercise.
- **Ask for learner reaction.** Before sharing your feedback, ask questions to elicit the learners' experiences.

As learners apply content, you observe and make notes to share in debriefing of the activity.

Coaching and Debriefing

Coaching learning skills involves leading learners through the learning cycle. The 4MAT model provides a framework for leading, debriefing, and coaching practice activities. Let's take a look at coaching through the lens of 4MAT:

The Four-Step Coaching Model

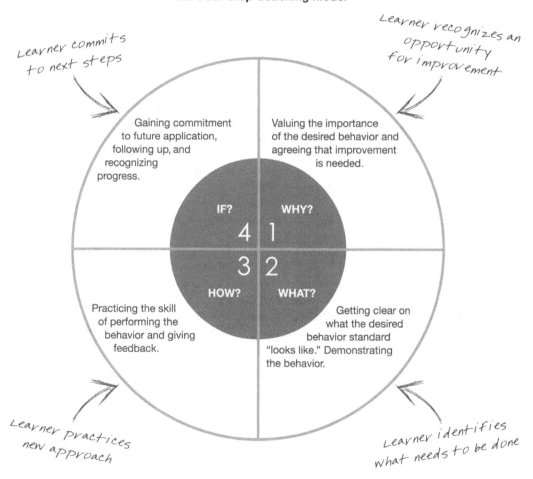

Learner commits to next steps

Learner recognizes an opportunity for improvement

Gaining commitment to future application, following up, and recognizing progress.

Valuing the importance of the desired behavior and agreeing that improvement is needed.

IF? 4

WHY? 1

3 HOW?

2 WHAT?

Practicing the skill of performing the behavior and giving feedback.

Getting clear on what the desired behavior standard "looks like." Demonstrating the behavior.

Learner practices new approach

Learner identifies what needs to be done

Using Questions to Focus the Learner's Attention

The neurons in your brain communicate with each other through electrochemical signals. These signals are triggered by incoming sensory information. What you notice and pay attention to over time shapes the neuronal connections in your brain. In the article, "A Brain-Based Approach to Coaching," Jeffrey Schwartz, M.D., shares (Rock, 2006, pp. 32-43):

"The questions you ask of your brain significantly affect the quality of the connections it makes, and profoundly alters the patterns and timings of the connections the brain generates in a fraction of a second. Now, substitute the concept of 'attention' for the phrase 'the question you ask,' and you get the statement: Where you focus your attention, you make connections."

If you want to create sustained behavioral change, you must generate focused attention on the behaviors that must be executed consistently to generate the desired training result. In the Practice step, the questions you ask are aimed at focusing the learners' attention on the quality of the practice application of the content being learned in the course.

Choosing the right question to focus the attention of the learner is critical in this step. As Schwartz points out (Rock, 2006, pp. 32-43):

"…asking one question rather than another, or focusing our attention on one item or another, influences the connections the brain makes and profoundly alters the patterns and timings of the connections the brain generates in each fraction of a second."

To enhance the learning connections, point out what is working along with what needs attention. Be careful to frame questions to direct learners' attention in the direction it needs to go. For example, asking the questions, "What worked well? What could you do more of?" emphasizes the successful aspects of the practice, whereas "Where did things go wrong?" focuses attention on what didn't work.

Let's explore how the 4MAT learning cycle can guide you in developing questions to apply in coaching practice activities.

Choose the right question to focus the learners' attention.

ENGAGE: AGREEING THAT IMPROVEMENT IS NEEDED

If you have ever tried to coach someone in an area in which the person believes him- or herself to be proficient, you know that this is an impossible task. Learners become interested in coaching when they are asking themselves, "How can I improve?" In the first part of the coaching model, the coach focuses on creating a shared perception of what improvement is needed. The coach invites the learners to share their observations and perceptions and the coach asks questions to guide the learners' attention to opportunities for improvement. Let's look at some examples of coaching questions you might use when coaching learners or peers:

learner identifies areas of improvement

PART OF THE COACHING CYCLE: ENGAGE

Learners' attention is directed to identifying areas of improvement.

Learners
- Will you share with me what happened in this exercise?
- How are you feeling about…?
- What went well?
- What would you do differently?

Peer: Peer
- How do you feel about the presentation?
- Where do you feel strong?
- What would you do differently?

1

SHARE: DEFINING WHAT CAN BE IMPROVED

Once the learner recognizes an opportunity for improvement, the coach shares a clear picture of the desired performance. In this step, the coach focuses the learner's attention on what he or she could do differently to get different results.

2   **PART OF THE COACHING CYCLE: SHARE**
Learners' attention is directed to what contributes to current results and what could be done differently to generate different results.

Learners

- Here's what I observed....

- During the exercise, I observed that your group was in deep dialogue for 10 minutes and then you suddenly shifted into action. Will you share with us what happened in your group?

- Will you walk me through how you arrived at this solution?

- What I noticed that you could do differently is....

Peer: Peer

- May I share what I observed?

- If you were to approach this differently, how would you do it?

- May I share an idea that has worked successfully for me in a similar situation?

- Have you experienced this before? What do you think is the common element?

Defining what can be improved

PRACTICE: TRYING NEW BEHAVIORS

In this step, you move the learner into action. You might begin by role playing. It is important that the learner has an opportunity to explore the skills needed to improve performance. In this step, the coach directs the learner's attention to trying new behaviors that will produce new results.

PART OF THE COACHING CYCLE: PRACTICE
Learner's attention is directed to experimenting with new behaviors.

3

Learner
- I'm going to challenge you to apply what we just discussed to this activity. How will you approach this differently?
- Let's pretend that I am a client. How would you respond to me if I asked the same question?
- We are now moving to Round 2 of this exercise. Are you ready to apply the strategy we refined in this next round?

Peer: Peer
- Let's try this ... pretend that I am the learner and you are responding to my question.
- Let's go back to the situation that happened today. How would you handle that differently?
- Let's take a few minutes to work through the workshop you are doing tomorrow and see how you can apply this.

Learner experiments with new behaviors

PERFORM: COMMITTING, IMPLEMENTING AND FOLLOWING UP

The last step of the 4MAT coaching process is focused on gaining commitment to future implementation and establishing follow-up. The coach guides the learner's attention to performing new behaviors in the real world.

Learner commits + implements

PART OF THE COACHING CYCLE: PERFORM
The learner's attention is guided to implementation, follow-up, and what success looks like.

Learners
- What do you need to anticipate to be successful in applying this?
- Take a few moments to write down two actions you will take to apply what you have learned in this exercise.

Peer: Peer
- We talked about several strategies. Which one do you feel most comfortable applying in your next session?
- So, what I heard is that you are going to try this in your next workshop on the 15th. Let's schedule a call for the 16th. I'm interested to hear how this goes.

4

Many situations require the coaching skills of a trainer. In the next part of this chapter, you will find some common scenarios that require coaching. How would you approach the coaching conversations in the examples? You can reference the Coaching Assessment Tool on page 201 to help you think about what might work. You will also find examples of questions that might work for each scenario.

COACHING SCENARIO: "OFF-PURPOSE" LEARNERS

You are leading a workshop and have assigned a team exercise in which you asked each team to address a real-world problem using the model you have just taught in the course. Each team has been asked to present a 5- to10-minute summary of the findings. Group B comes to the front of the room and begins their presentation. You realize that the team has worked through the problem, but they have not used the model shared in the course. How do you coach the team?

Here are some possible questions that might work well:

Do you feel comfortable taking this approach in the next round of this activity?

I'm going to challenge you to apply what you just outlined in the next round of the activity. When we wrap this next activity, we will come back to your group to hear about your progress.

How do you feel about the presentation?

What worked well?

Anything you would do differently?

4 | 1
3 | 2

Let's go back to the beginning of the process: how would you have approached this differently using the model we are exploring?

Will you walk us through how you arrived at the solution?

How might your outcome be different if you applied the model we shared today?

What I noticed is....

COACHING SCENARIO: "HOSTAGE LEARNERS"

You are leading a required, one-day HR training. The majority of the learners are actively engaged in the training activities you are leading, with the exception of one table group. At the beginning of the workshop, you noticed that this table of five participants seemed to be rushing through the activities. You have now assigned a group task and you noticed that they are actively engaged in a conversation on an entirely different topic. How do you coach the group?

When we debrief this as a group, I will invite you to share what shows up in your application. I think the rest of the group will be very interested to see what emerges in your practice.

If you had to choose one question around this topic that interests you, what would it be?

(or)

If we could only explore one problem, issue, or question around this content, what would it be?

4 1
3 2

If you were to apply this model to the issue you just identified, how would you go about this?

Here's what I observe...

How do you see that successful application of this content might help you address (the problem, issue, or question you shared earlier)?

COACHING SCENARIO: COACHING A FELLOW TRAINER

You observed John facilitating training workshops in the past and you know that John is a highly entertaining trainer. He uses stories and humor to engage learners and receives high praise on learner reaction surveys.

In the session you observed, you notice that John is uncomfortable with exercises that rely on learner dialogue. John rushed through the Engage step of the design phase as he delivered the training. You felt that the learners were just getting "warmed up" and that John missed an opportunity to engage the learners on a personal level. John asks you for feedback on the class. How do you coach John?

Do you feel comfortable trying this in your next workshop?

I would love to hear how it goes. I'll make a mental note to call you the next day. When is your session scheduled?

Let's start with what you felt were the strongest parts of the workshop. At what point in the training do you believe the learners were most engaged?

Are there any places in the delivery where you felt you struggled to capture the learners' attention?

4 | 1
3 | 2

Let's go back to the opening today. How could you have encouraged the group to go deeper with the dialogue?

What I observed that worked really well was….

What I noticed that you could do differently was….

Coaching Assessment Tool

After completing a coaching conversation, you can reflect on the effectiveness of your approach by answering the questions below. As with any good assessment tool, you can also use this to prepare for your next coaching interaction.

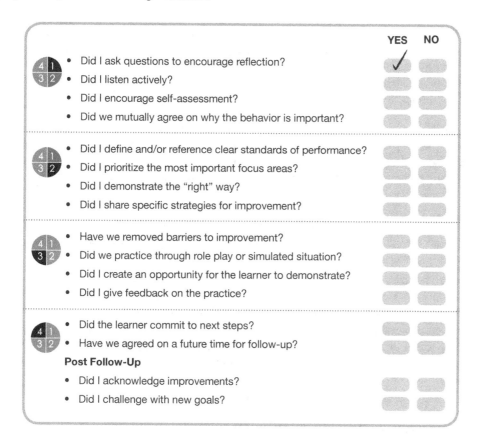

	YES	NO
4 1 / 3 2 • Did I ask questions to encourage reflection?	✓	
• Did I listen actively?		
• Did I encourage self-assessment?		
• Did we mutually agree on why the behavior is important?		
4 1 / 3 2 • Did I define and/or reference clear standards of performance?		
• Did I prioritize the most important focus areas?		
• Did I demonstrate the "right" way?		
• Did I share specific strategies for improvement?		
4 1 / 3 2 • Have we removed barriers to improvement?		
• Did we practice through role play or simulated situation?		
• Did I create an opportunity for the learner to demonstrate?		
• Did I give feedback on the practice?		
4 1 / 3 2 • Did the learner commit to next steps?		
• Have we agreed on a future time for follow-up?		
Post Follow-Up		
• Did I acknowledge improvements?		
• Did I challenge with new goals?		

Strategies That Work in Practice

There are many different ways to generate practice for learners. Here are some examples which work with any type of training content:

CASE STUDIES

When most people think of "case study," they think of lengthy, in-depth analyses of a real-world issue with an example of how an individual or an organization resolved the issue. In a workshop environment, case studies are typically smaller in scope and focus on a situation in which the content being learned might be applied. A case study typically includes an example of content application and provides an opportunity for the learners to assess the application.

For example, in a consultative selling skills course the case study might describe how a sales person conducted the needs analysis process with a client and which product solutions were recommended. Using the case study information, learners analyze the effectiveness of the needs analysis and determine whether the correct product solutions were recommended. Here are some other ways you can use case studies:

1. You can use case studies to evaluate whether learners understand information. For example, you might provide a case study and ask learners to identify how a model being learned in the course was applied in the study.

2. You can use case studies to develop the learners' ability to assess application. For example, you might provide a case study of how an organizational change process was implemented. Learners are asked to assess what worked and what they would change.

3. You can use case studies to creatively apply what they have learned. You can present learners with a case study problem and invite learners to creatively apply what they are learning in the course to solve the problems presented in the study.

When creating case studies, here are some things to keep in mind:

1. Frame the study as a problem to be solved.

2. Provide any assumptions that are made.

3. Invite learners to provide suitable solutions.

4. Give clear assessment criteria to evaluate their application of the content to the case study.

ROLE PLAYS AND SIMULATED PRACTICE SITUATIONS

Role-play activities focus on replicating real-world situations in which learners might apply the content being learned. Typically, learners use the reference materials provided in the course, including job aids, to determine how they would apply the information being learned in a given situation.

Using a template to develop the role-play approach helps learners prepare for their application. You can create a role play template by outlining the steps the learners will use to apply the information in the role play. For example, in a practice activity focused on "raising difficult issues with colleagues," the template may include guidance on:

1. How they will raise the issue

2. What examples of the issue they will provide

3. What questions they will use to elicit feedback

4. What possible solutions they will offer

When facilitating role plays, it is beneficial to include three learners in a group. There are three roles that will be filled in a role play activity: role player, partner, and observer. The role player is practicing the skills being learned. The partner plays along and fills a role such as customer, colleague, supervisor, etc. Adding a third "wheel," the observer, will generate greater compliance in the implementation of the role play.

The observer observes the interaction and offers feedback using questions you provide such as:

• Was the issue clearly defined?

• Did the "role player" use questions to invite feedback?

• How did the "role player" put his or her partner at ease?

You can invite learners to generate their own role-play situations. For example, for the "raising difficult issues" workshop, the learners might choose to practice difficult conversations they need to have with others. Or you might create common situations and invite learners to choose one. Another option is to write situations on individual index cards and place them in a bowl for learners to choose from.

KNOWLEDGE CHECK GAMES

Games are an engaging way to check for understanding. There are many books on how to incorporate games into your training design. You can also look to popular game show or board game formats, which can easily be replicated in the classroom learning environment.

ASSESSMENT OR "TESTS"

To check for understanding of knowledge before the learner moves into practical application, you can develop a written assessment. Written assessments can be delivered in many formats, including multiple-choice, essay, true/false, or fill-in-the-blank. Keep in mind that any written assessment can easily be converted into a knowledge check game. Many trainers will begin with an individual written knowledge check and then create teams to participate in a knowledge check game to review test answers.

VIDEOTAPED PRESENTATIONS

In any group of learners, you will find that that most learners have the capability to record video using their mobile phones. When conducting practice simulations such as role play, consider asking the observer to record the interaction. You can then provide a series of questions or an assessment tool for the team to use to assess their application.

GROUP PROBLEM SOLVING

In group problem-solving activities, you can give small groups a challenging situation or problem to solve using the information learned in the course. You can also invite learners to apply the content being learned to solving the real-world problems they encounter.

Summary

It is important to focus on providing learners with practice that prepares them to apply the content being learned in the real world. Focus on choosing activities that most closely simulate how the learners will apply the information in the real world.

As the learners move into the Practice portion of the learning cycle, the trainer moves to the sidelines and takes on the role of Coach. It is important that you focus on developing the learners' ability to recognize any gaps in performance at this point. Focus on asking questions to draw the learners' attention to both the process used in applying the content and the final product generated through the practice.

STEP IN THE CYCLE: PRACTICE

What the learner is doing:
- Practicing skills learned in Inform
- Hands-on application of the information learned

What the trainer is doing:
- Coaching practice activities
- Providing projects, scenarios, or worksheets
- Setting up situations in which the learners use the information being learned

Activities that work well:
- Role plays
- Worksheets
- Field work
- Simulations
- Game show–style reviews
- Problem-solving situations
- In-field work

After the "Reflect" and "Act" section of this chapter, you will find examples of activities that work well in the Practice part of the learning cycle. Review "Your Training Style in Practice" and reflect on your training style strengths related to this part of the learning cycle.

YOUR TRAINING STYLE IN PRACTICE

If you have a natural strength in the Type Three training approach, it is likely that you already rely on coaching skills in your training delivery. If your area of strength lies in one of the other three training approaches, be aware of what you will need to focus on to be successful in this step.

	HIGH STRENGTH IN TYPE ONE TRAINING APPROACH	**HIGH STRENGTH IN TYPE TWO TRAINING APPROACH**	**HIGH STRENGTH IN TYPE THREE TRAINING APPROACH**	**HIGH STRENGTH IN TYPE FOUR TRAINING APPROACH**
	Be aware of some learners' impatience to move into real-world application. When giving feedback, focus on being direct and giving helpful guidance.	Be careful not to spend too much time in lecture. Be aware of the impatience of some learners to get into practice and be careful not to linger too long in giving directions or over-explaining.	You excel in this part of the learning cycle. Be aware that some learners are hesitant to "jump right in."	Be careful to give clear direction on activities. Be aware that some learners need a clear definition of "good," "better," and "best." Create these distinctions for learners.
	Type One Trainer comment: "I sometimes tend to focus on the effort the learner puts into the exercise, rather than the end results. I have to consciously give feedback that will improve performance. Acknowledging what worked is always easier for me."	Type Two Trainer comment: "I have a tendency to spend too much time explaining what I want them to do. I am constantly reminding myself that experimentation is a big part of the learning process, even if it is messy sometimes."	Type Three Trainer comment: "I am most comfortable when I am leading hands-on practice. Sometimes, I can be a bit direct, but I think learners appreciate the feedback."	Type Four Trainer comment: "I have to be careful to clearly give directions on activities. Sometimes, I leave it too open-ended. I recognize this immediately when they begin to ask clarifying questions. Or, worse, when the group just looks at each other, hoping that someone understood the directions I just gave."

How will you check to make sure that the learners understand the necessary information to be prepared to practice?

What is the most effective activity to use to simulate the way that learners will apply this in the real world?

In the next training you design and/or deliver, which strategies will you include?

	YES	NO
• Design a knowledge check activity before asking learners to dive into real-world practice	✓	
• Include a multiple-choice test, matching test, true-false test, or short-answer test or a combination of all to check for understanding		
• Videotaped application		
• Job aids		
• Provide templates to guide learners in preparing for application		
• Create simulated practice		
• Use role play		
• Include an "observer" role in practice situations		
• Initiate real-world problem solving		

Examples of Practice Activities

In this section, you will find examples of activities that work well in Practice. The activities are presented within the context of a training course. The directions related to leading each activity are presented in a generic format that can be adapted to work with any type of content.

PRACTICE ACTIVITY EXAMPLE: TECHNICAL TERMS TRAINING

In a pharmaceutical sales training, the desired skill outcome requires that learners understand clinical terms that will be referenced throughout their training program. To reinforce learning, learners play a matching game with key terms and definitions.

PRACTICE: MEMORY MATCH

Focus: Checking for understanding of key ideas, terms or definitions.

Resources Needed
- Pre-made Memory Match cards

Description

Prior to the class:

1. Develop a set of twenty or more questions. Terms and product information questions work particularly well for this exercise. For example, "What does the symbol 'P' mean?" might be paired with an answer card that reads, "Pressure is the force per unit area applied in a direction perpendicular to the surface of an object."

2. Create two cards per question: one with the answer and one with the question.

3. Make one set of all cards for each team.

Facilitating the Exercise

1. Divide the class into groups of three or four people.

2. Give each group a set of cards.

3. Learners place the answer cards upside down on a table and arrange them into a grid.

4. Learners take turns reading the question aloud and selecting an answer card from the table. If the question and answer match, the learner keeps the cards. If the question and answer do not match, the learner replaces the answer card into the grid, face-down, and returns the question card to the bottom of the pile.

5. The game continues until all questions and answers have been matched.

Trainer Script

"Each small group has a set of 'Memory Match' cards. Turn all the cards upside down and arrange them into a grid. Every person takes a turn revealing two cards. If they are a match, remove the cards and reveal two more cards."

PRACTICE ACTIVITY EXAMPLE: COACHING WORKSHOP

In a performance coaching course, participants are introduced to a four-step model for addressing performance issues. Four flipcharts are labeled, each with a different step of the model, and posted on the walls of the classroom. In small groups, learners move to each chart and write examples of "what works" and "what doesn't work" in each step of the process.

GALLERY STROLL

Focus: Active engagement of learners in reprocessing and applying information learned.

A gallery stroll is an excellent way to get groups moving while processing information learned. On flipcharts, write one topic or question on each chart. Allow groups to dialogue on the topic and write their responses. Rotate the groups, until all groups have processed all charts.

Description

1. Determine the questions or topics to be discussed.

2. Write one topic or question at the top of each flipchart page.

3. Divide the learners evenly among the charts.

4. Ask each group to write their responses to the prompt on the chart.

5. Rotate the groups to the next chart.

6. Continue until all groups have processed all charts.

Resources Needed
- Paper chart for each topic or question
- Markers for learner groups to write responses on the charts
- Tape to secure charts to the wall

Notes:

_____

_____

_____

_____

_____

_____

_____

_____

PRACTICE ACTIVITY EXAMPLE: CALL CENTER TRAINING

In a call center training on phone skills, participants are asked to address common customer complaints in a role-play format.

ROLE PLAY

Focus: Applying information in real-world scenarios.

Resources Needed
- Role-play scenarios
- Assessment criteria

Description

1. Develop examples of real-world situations in which learners will apply the information being learned.

2. Divide learners into teams of three. Assign the roles of "role player," "partner," and "observer."

3. Share directions for the activity. If observers will be asked to record the role play, ensure that each group has a mobile phone with video capability.

4. After each round of role play, invite learners to assess their application using criteria you have provided.

5. Continue rounds of activity until all three team members have played all roles.

6. Debrief.

Trainer Script

"We will now have an opportunity to apply what we have learned to real-world situations. In teams of three, you will take turns addressing common customer issues you will encounter using the approach we explored this morning. One of you will play the role of call 'center team member,' one will play the role of 'customer,' and one of you will play the role of 'observer.' The observer's role is focused on observing and taking notes. Use the checklist provided to help guide your observations. Everyone will have an opportunity to play all three roles."

Notes:

_____

_____

_____

_____

_____

_____

PRACTICE ACTIVITY EXAMPLE: PRODUCT KNOWLEDGE TRAINING

In a product knowledge training, sales team members test their knowledge by answering common customer product questions. Each time the correct answer appears on their Bingo cards, participants mark off the spot. The first person to fill a diagonal, vertical, or horizontal row on his or her card wins a prize.

GAME SHOW STYLE REVIEW: BINGO ACTIVITY

Focus: Knowledge check to ensure that learners understand the information presented before moving into creative application

Description
1. Create a Bingo card. Insert answers to the questions you will be asking in each square.
2. Explain how the game works.
3. Introduce the prizes for winners (optional).
4. Define the start and end times of the contest.

Bingo Rules
- Each player receives a Bingo card.
- As the player finds the correct answer on his or her Bingo card, he or she must circle or "x" the answer.
- To win, the circled challenges must form a vertical, diagonal, or horizontal line on the Bingo card.

Resources Needed
- Bingo card for each participant with answers in different squares on the board. The easiest way to create the cards is to generate a list of review questions with correct answers. Place the answers on several cards in such an order that the player using the card may win. For the remainder of the cards, randomly place the answers in the Bingo card squares. You can create multiple copies of the non-winning cards.
- List of questions to call out to the group.
- Prizes (optional)

Facilitator Script:
"Has everyone played Bingo? I will ask questions created from the content we explored today. If the correct answer is found in a square on your game card, mark the square with an 'X.' To win, you must have a series of X's that are vertical, diagonal, or horizontal. The first person to declare 'Bingo' who has all the answers correct wins the game."

Notes:

_____

_____

_____

_____

PRACTICE ACTIVITY EXAMPLE: MODEL REVIEW IN AN INSTRUCTIONAL DESIGN COURSE

In our 4MAT Advanced Instructional Design course, we build on the four-step model introduced in this book and advance this to include right- and left-mode presentation strategies. This results in an eight-step model for instructional design. After explaining the model in the "Share" portion of the course, learners are asked to complete a "Pieces of Eight" exercise in which they review and assess their understanding of what is happening in each of the eight steps of the model.

MODEL MATCH-UP

Focus: Applying knowledge of a model's application.

Description

1. Identify the key steps of the model or process being taught. Create a "game board." This may be a flow chart, a wheel, or any other visual organizer that aligns with the structure of the model you have taught. For example, in a course sharing a six-step sales model, the game board may have a flow chart with the six boxes, each representing one step in the model.

Resources Needed
- Activity cards (one set per team per round)
- Gameboard (one per team)
- Answer key (one per team per round)

2. On individual cards, write an example of what someone might say or do in a particular step. One card is created for each step with an individual question on it. In the six-step sales model course example, the trainer might create six cards, each with one question which corresponds to one of the steps of the model.

3. Create an answer key. You can do this easily by labeling each card with A, B, C, D.... The answer key handout should show the correct placement of each card in the model.

4. Introduce the activity to learners. Invite them to place the activity cards in the appropriate part of the cycle. When teams have placed their cards, give them the answer key to check their work.

Facilitator Script

"To check our understanding of how the model works in the real world, we are going to practice identifying the steps of the model in action. To do this, I will be providing each table group with a game board that visually illustrates the model. [Show the game board.]

"Next, I will provide your team with a set of activity cards. The activity cards describe what might happen in each step. Your task is to place the activity card in the appropriate part of the model. For example, the first round of cards focuses on the type of questions a sales person might ask in each step of the cycle. You will read each question and decide where the question would be asked in the selling cycle."

"The path to success is to take massive, determined action."

~ Anthony Robbins

Chapter 7

Perform: Assessing and Implementing

Many training and development professionals are being asked to produce more results with fewer resources. The ability to sustain the learning process outside of the formal learning environment is a challenge that must be addressed. A recent survey of learning and human resource professionals revealed that three-quarters of the respondents thought that learners apply only 50 percent or less of what they learn. Gaining learner commitment to the implementation process is essential to improving this result. This chapter offers strategies that sustain learner commitment and improve post-training implementation results.

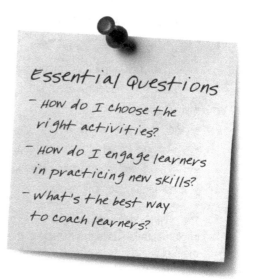

Essential Questions
- How do I choose the right activities?
- How do I engage learners in practicing new skills?
- What's the best way to coach learners?

WHAT HAPPENS IN PERFORM

In this step, the learners ask the question, "If?" They synthesize new learning into their real-world context and begin to develop an implementation plan for new learning. In addition, the learners consider potential implementation barriers and ways to adapt for success.

In the fourth part of the 4MAT learning cycle, Perform, the trainer plays the role of supportive evaluator. You focus on learning strategies that help the learners assess their hands-on practice and prepare to take what they have learned out into the real world.

The types of activities included in this part of the learning experience, self-assessment, action planning, group feedback, and celebrations of learning, are designed to encourage learners to:

- Assess their application of the skills in Practice
- Explore criteria for assessing their level of mastery
- Build competence
- Plan for implementation
- Anticipate implementation barriers
- Take ownership of the learning transfer
- Share future commitments

The shift from Practice to Perform is the shift from simulated practice to real-world implementation as learners assess their own application success and move toward mastery in the real world.

The goal in Perform is adapting, refining, re-working, re-presenting, integrating, evaluating progress, and, most of all, performing.

What You Are Doing

THE METHOD IS LEARNER IMPLEMENTATION AND ASSESSMENT

In this part of the learning cycle, learners integrate new knowledge and skills learned back into their own lives. You create an opportunity for the learners to evaluate their application of the information and build an implementation plan.

In this part of the learning cycle we will focus on three things: encouraging learner self-assessment, gaining commitment on future action, and setting up a post-training implementation plan.

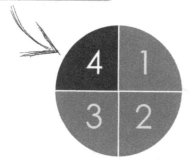

PERFORM/ADAPTATION
OUTCOME

• Learner self-assessment

• Gaining commitment on future action

• Setting up a post-training implementation plan

Encouraging Self-Assessment

Mastery is rooted in the ability to make distinctions. The learners' ability to develop mastery outside of the formal learning environment is dependent on their ability to make distinctions regarding the quality of their own implementation. In Perform, you create an opportunity for learners to assess their own application to develop awareness of the distinctions among good, better, and best performance.

WAYS TO ENCOURAGE ASSESSMENT

- **Provide examples of "good," "better," and "best" application.** Help learners see the distinctions that separate levels of performance by giving concrete examples linked to assessment criteria. For example, in the Perform step of a coaching skills workshop for managers, learners might be asked to generate a list of criteria that distinguishes a "good," "better," and "best" approach to coaching team members to higher performance. Learners then use these criteria to evaluate their role-play simulations of conversations they plan to have when they return to the work environment.

- **Self-assessment criteria.** Provide learners with clearly defined criteria that they may use to evaluate their application. Ideally, the criteria should reflect the expert knowledge you presented in the Share portion of the learning experience. For example, in a workshop on financial best practices for small business owners the trainer might provide a self-assessment tool to encourage review of the frequency of financial reporting.

Encourage learners to assess their performance

Gaining Commitment on Future Action

Overwhelm is the enemy of implementation. When a learner is overwhelmed by too much information, the tendency is to linger in reflection rather than moving into action. To leave a learning experience in a motivated state, the learner must perceive a balance between the challenge at hand and the resources available to meet that challenge. When the challenge is high and resources are low, overwhelm shows up.

The goal in Perform is to focus the learners on the right behaviors, equip them with self-assessment skills, and to move them quickly into action. In this final step of the learning experience, the learner commits to implementing key behaviors that will lead to the desired results.

WAYS TO GAIN LEARNER COMMITMENT TO ACTION

- **Define the challenge with the learner.** What do learners hope to accomplish with the information learned? How will they measure their success? What actions will they take? Weave the insights gained from the Engage portion of the workshop into the action planning. Focus the action planning on the big issues that learners hope to address related to the content being learned.

- **Create an action plan.** Action planning is an important part of the learning process. By allowing time for learners to plan next steps, you create an opportunity for them to envision successful implementation of the information. This also creates an opportunity to identify and address any potential barriers to implementation.

- **Identify and provide needed resources.** Imagine yourself in the real-world environment of the learner. Think about what the learner will need to be able to apply the information in the real world. When will they be applying this information? What resources will they have available? Encourage learners to anticipate barriers and strategize how they will overcome them.

When a learner is overwhelmed by too much information, the tendency is to linger in reflection rather than moving into action. To leave a learning experience in a motivated state, the learner must perceive a balance between the challenge at hand and the resources available to meet that challenge.

Setting Up a Post-Training Implementation Plan

A widely embraced model on learning suggests that between 70 and 80 percent of learning impact happens "on the job" (Betts, 2011). This means that on-the-job distractions, competing work priorities, and lack of sustained attention are just a few of the many barriers that must be addressed to ensure learning impact.

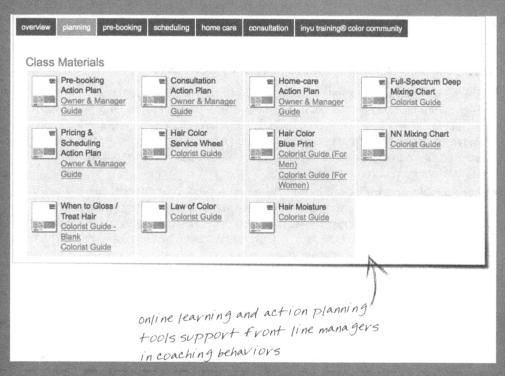

online learning and action planning tools support front line managers in coaching behaviors

The 24/7 Rule

Learning retention increases when information learned is revisited within 24 hours and again within the next seven days—thus the 24/7 rule. It's a good guideline to keep in mind as you develop your implementation plan. Think about how you can encourage learners to consciously revisit the information. Without this conscious focus the likelihood of successful workplace implementation is greatly reduced. By anticipating and planning for the factors that stand in the way of implementation such as conflicting priorities, lack of feedback, and inability to access needed information, you increase the chance of success.

WAYS TO INCREASE POST-TRAINING REVIEW OF CONTENT

- **Follow-up emails.** One of the easiest ways to reach learners within 24 hours is via email. Because it is critical to get this out quickly, design the email prior to launch of the learning experience. In the email, check in on learners' progress and connect the learners back to the commitments made during the session. Think about how you might receive feedback on their progress. You can easily embed an online survey with a simple question or two that directs the learners' attention to implementation.

- **Accountability partners.** At the end of a learning session, you can encourage learners to partner up with fellow learners to share their action plans and learning commitments. This makes for a powerful closing of the learning experience and encourages learners to stay in touch with each other after the event. Ask learners to identify one to three key action items they will implement within a specified period of time. Ask learners to choose partners to share their action plans with, establish a time to reconnect on these key learning goals, and share contact information. To take this to the next level, you can provide a structure for the partners to use when they conduct their follow-up sessions. A simple set of questions to use during the meeting lends value to the session. You can include questions such as:
  - "What are your three most important actions?"
  - "How are you progressing?"
  - "How have you overcome barriers to applying this?"
  - "What has been your biggest success as a result of what you learned?

- **Conduct follow-up interviews.** When you begin the design of the learning experience with clear outcomes that link to business goals, it is easy to uncover how learners are successfully applying what they have learned. Follow-up serves the dual purpose of reinforcing learners' commitments and assessing the overall impact of the learning experience. You can conduct follow-up interviews using free online survey tools, which makes data collection much easier. Or you can facilitate follow-up focus groups or one-on-one sessions. The types of questions you might include in this format:
  - "What have you applied from this learning experience?"
  - "What value have you seen from the application of what you have learned?"
  - "What success story would you like to share?"

- **Reunion calls.** Reunion calls are phone or web sessions designed to reinforce key learning points, discuss implementation strategies, or provide an opportunity for learners to network and to share success stories. Too often, learners create relationships in a learning experience and then never have an opportunity to connect again. The idea of a "reunion" is appealing to many learners. Prior to the reunion call, invite learners to share success stories. You can do this with an email which includes a few survey questions. Begin the reunion call session by sharing highlights of the success stories individuals shared. If you are facilitating the session via web, you can include pictures of participants captured during the learning experience along with their comments.

Slide From Reunion Web Call

Share learner success stories

Charnie

Include learner photos

Recently I applied the 4mat structure process for an observation visit that I had at one of our campuses. Initially, I found myself repeating the same "advise/behavioral coaching" that I felt like I had applied multiple times over the last year that had not shifted the behavior. Instead of providing my feedback the same way, I reflected first on using the 4MAT coaching model to get the person on the receiving end to really understand the purpose "full circle." As I applied the process myself, I felt confident that I was giving a clearer picture of the expectation, purpose and intended outcome rather than "just because this is what we expect/ or because that was the job."

4MAT 4BUSINESS

©4MAT 4Business, no reproduction allowed

4MAT 4Leadership

- **Lunch and learn sessions.** The "lunch and learn" concept was developed by a creative trainer who realized that time is a big issue in managing follow-up learning strategies. Lunch and learn sessions are typically scheduled during the lunch hour and participants are invited to bring a brown-bag lunch to the session (live or online).

- **Podcasts.** As you design your learning experience, you can easily record quick podcasts that reinforce key learning points. These podcasts can be delivered as links in an email or in the online class forum.

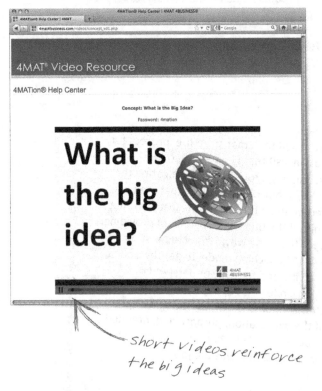

short videos reinforce the big ideas

- **Celebrating success stories.** Capturing success stories of learners can be accomplished in one-on-one interviews, reunion calls, or via survey. Think about how you might share success stories with other learners in the course or across the broader organization. Company newsletters are an example of a delivery structure that can spread the message of the value generated through the learning experience.

- **Recognition awards.** How are you celebrating the success of the learners in implementing the key behaviors? Think about how you might track and celebrate progress. The field manager and on-the-job coaches can support this process. Get creative with rewards. You can offer gift cards, books, or other perks to learners who excel in applying the information.

- **Using social media to connect learners.** When learners develop a sense of community in the formal learning environment, the natural evolution is to extend that connection out into the real world. Social media offer many ways to stimulate conversation long after the training session ends.

- **Twitter.** Twitter is a microblogging tool that allows users to publish posts called "tweets." The posts are a maximum of 140 characters and delivered in chronological order. You can use Twitter to continue conversations by offering daily questions or topics for discussion. Post an idea of the week or pose a question to get conversation started. Keep in mind that Twitter is best for an unstructured dialogue and quick answers.

- **Facebook.** Facebook is a site that enables sharing of messages, photos, videos, PowerPoint slide decks, events, and discussion topics. You can also create polls and post links to other resources such as blogs and articles.

- **Blog.** A blog is an online "journal" that allows you to post text, videos, audio, links, and documents. All content is stored chronologically. You can use a blog to host content from the course. You can also update with new content and invite learners to comment in response to questions you pose.

- **Online social forums.** An online social forum is a site for sharing content and creating interaction. There are many free resources to create an online social space that enables photo sharing, discussion, and other interaction between learners.

We will cover utilizing social media in greater detail in Chapter 8. Here are a few things to consider as you create your post-training implementation plan:

- What is the delivery system for sharing follow-through support tools? (e.g., online learning portal, social forum, manager toolkit, email, job aid)
- What does the front-line manager need to know to support execution of the behaviors?
- Do you need front-line coaches to support the key behaviors?
- Who will fulfill the role of on-the-job coach?
- How will you equip coaches to coach effectively?
- What is the optimal frequency of interaction to ensure transfer?
- What is the measure of success?
- How will you share measurement with learners?
- What online tools can you leverage?
- How will learning be celebrated?
- Who has to "buy in"?

Integrating a post-training follow-up strategy into the instructional design and delivery will greatly improve the learning results.

Organizing an On-the-Job Support Team

Because so much of the impact of the learning experience is influenced by factors outside of the formal learning environment, consider establishing an on-the-job training support team to reinforce learning. The key members of the on-the-job training team include the training sponsor, the front-line manager, the coach, and the learner.

Each member has a role and clear responsibility:

- **The sponsor** is someone who has influence in the organization and actively champions the focus on the learning initiative. The sponsor:
    - Sells the initiative to upper management
    - Gains resources
    - Maintains focus on the follow-through
    - Celebrates results internally
- **The team leader** is the primary supervisor of the learner. The team leader typically has the greatest level of influence on the successful transfer of the learning initiatives. The team leader:
    - Reinforces the key behaviors by inspecting
    - Allocates time and resources for training follow-up
    - Partners the learner with a qualified coach
    - Assesses the learner's application
    - Provides valuable feedback and measurement needed to assess training success
- **The on-the-job coach** follows up on the implementation of the key behaviors in the real-world work environments. The coach:
    - Organizes follow-up sessions
    - Shares valuable feedback with the learner
    - Is available to answer questions
    - Provides valuable feedback and measurement needed to assess training
- **The learner** is responsible for owning his or her part of the learning process.

Engaging Team Leaders in Training Support

PRE-TRAINING SUPPORT	POST-TRAINING SUPPORT
Assess the Business Case: • Determine which learners should attend. • Identify right time to attend for learners.	**Action Planning:** • Review the insights gained and action plan with the learner.
Pre-Event Meeting: • Jointly set learning and performance expectations. • Develop an action plan on post-event implementation of the information. • Schedule a post-event recap meeting.	**Provide Coaching Tools:** • As the learner implements the information, the team leader observes, coaches, and provides recognition. **Accelerate the Learning Curve:** • Identify opportunities for the learner to creatively apply the information, i.e., projects.

WAYS THAT TEAM LEADERS CAN SUPPORT TRAINING

Here are some ways you can invite team leaders to become involved in the training process.

Pre-Training

- Send an overview of the training program, including defined learning outcomes and description of the target audience.

- Outline how learners will benefit from the training and what the team leader will see in performance results.

- Encourage team leaders to identify an appropriate project for learners to apply the information being learned.

- Ask team leaders to schedule a post-event follow-up session.

Post-Training

- Send team leaders a recap of the learner evaluation. If possible, share individual feedback on learner progress.
- Provide team leaders with ideas on how they might ask learners to provide a demonstration of what they have learned.
- Provide team leaders with a timeline to guide assignment of projects that require use of newly learned skills.
- Provide an observation checklist of key behaviors the learners should observe.
- Provide a coaching guide with tips on leading quick, on-the-job feedback sessions.
- Give guidance on how much time the team leader should allocate for the learner to practice new skills.
- Create a series of emails with tips on implementing the post-training follow-up and celebrations of specific learning successes.
- Create a system to make team leaders aware of the level of follow-through and performance of their team members who have attended the course. For example, consider sending an email to all team leaders with a progress update on which learners are current with learning assignments.

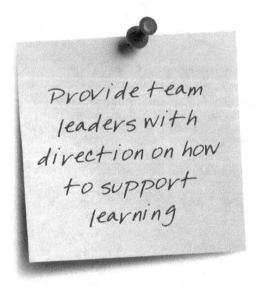

Provide team leaders with direction on how to support learning

Typically, the front-line team leader will determine who is assigned the role of on-the-job coach. To help team leaders choose the right person for this role, you can provide a checklist of the characteristics that will enable success. In the next section is a brief list of characteristics, which you can modify to suit the particular commitment you are asking for from the coach.

Choosing On-the-Job Coaches

Certain characteristics will enable an on-the-job coach to be effective. When supporting field managers in choosing on-the-job coaches, it is often helpful to give them a profile and job description of an effective on-the-job coach.

PROFILE OF AN EFFECTIVE ON-THE-JOB COACH

		YES	NO
Preparedness:	• Takes the time to prepare for a coaching session.	✓	
Competence:	• Has a high level of knowledge and skill in the area of focus.		
Compliance:	• Teaches tasks according to defined procedure.		
Availability:	• Welcomes frequent questions.		
Adaptability:	• Can adapt content based on the learner's knowledge and the situation.		
Delivery style:	• Can animate examples through personal experience implementing the content being learned.		
	• Encourages questions and trainee reflection.		
Follow-through:	• Follows through on the agreed-upon training schedule.		
Attitude:	• Is excited about the content being trained.		
	• Enjoys seeing others develop.		

WAYS TO INVOLVE ON-THE-JOB COACHES

On-the-job coaches have other priorities outside of training. Clearly defining coaching responsibilities and providing easy-to-use resources will ensure coaching success.

Here are ways you can involve on-the-job coaches in supporting the implementation of behaviors learned in a formal learning experience:

- **Summary of key learning points.** Prepare a brief summary of the key learning points from the course. Include a section in the review on the actions learners should take within a specified time window. This can be as simple as "You should expect to see learners applying _____ (skill) within the first week after the course." Or it can be much more detailed with a timeline of when each key point should be reviewed along with supplemental learning content the coach can use to reinforce the content delivered in the course.

- **Observation checklist.** An observation checklist will help a coach home in on the key behaviors learners should be implementing as a result of the training. Observation checklists can also be used as part of the measurement strategy for the course.

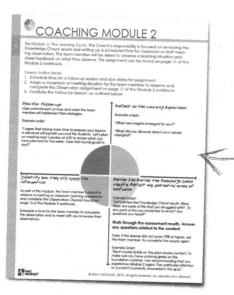

A coaching conversation template for on-the-job coaches maintains focus on key learning points.

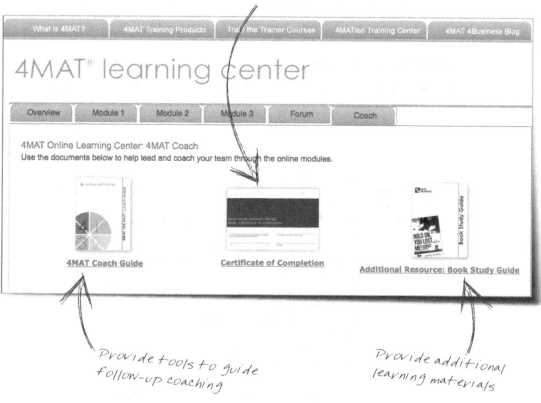

include tools for measuring and acknowledging learner progress

4MAT® learning center

| Overview | Module 1 | Module 2 | Module 3 | Forum | Coach |

4MAT Online Learning Center: 4MAT Coach
Use the documents below to help lead and coach your team through the online modules.

4MAT Coach Guide

Certificate of Completion

Additional Resource: Book Study Guide

Provide tools to guide follow-up coaching

Provide additional learning materials

- **Review of job aids.** Include job aids in any summary you provide to coaches. Encourage coaches to schedule a time to review the job aid with the learners.

- **"In-the-field" accountability meeting.** Prior to the beginning of a learning session, ask coaches to schedule a post-training accountability meeting with learners. The purpose of the meeting is to review action items the learners committed to in the training session. To maximize the effectiveness of this meeting, you can provide a simple agenda, including questions the coach might ask the learners.

- **Moderate a forum.** To enable dialogue between coaches and learners, you can create a social forum and assign coaches moderator status. With moderator status, the coach can initiate discussions on the forum and invite learners to post proof of application of the content. We will discuss online learning tools further in Chapter 8.

PREPARING ON-THE-JOB COACHES

- **Coaching checklist.** Providing coaches with tools to focus coaching conversations will ensure consistency. Here is an example of a self-assessment checklist that coaches can use to prepare for and assess their coaching conversations:

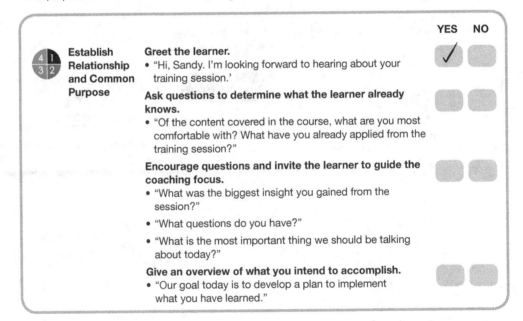

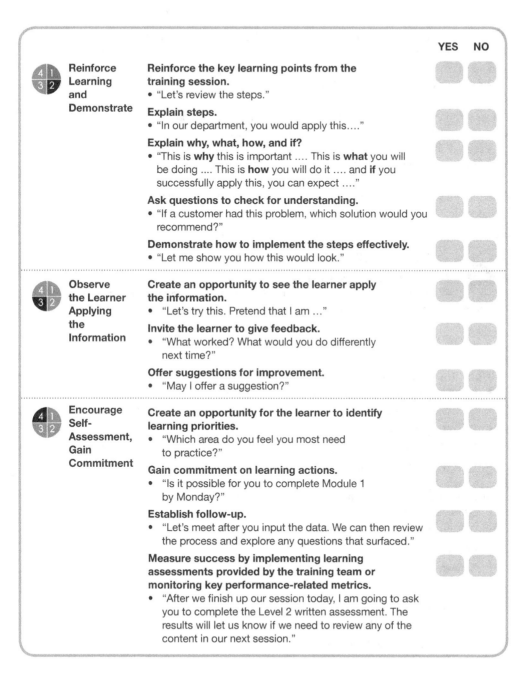

		YES	NO
Reinforce Learning and Demonstrate	**Reinforce the key learning points from the training session.** • "Let's review the steps."		
	Explain steps. • "In our department, you would apply this...."		
	Explain why, what, how, and if? • "This is **why** this is important .... This is **what** you will be doing .... This is **how** you will do it .... and **if** you successfully apply this, you can expect ...."		
	Ask questions to check for understanding. • "If a customer had this problem, which solution would you recommend?"		
	Demonstrate how to implement the steps effectively. • "Let me show you how this would look."		
Observe the Learner Applying the Information	**Create an opportunity to see the learner apply the information.** • "Let's try this. Pretend that I am ..."		
	Invite the learner to give feedback. • "What worked? What would you do differently next time?"		
	Offer suggestions for improvement. • "May I offer a suggestion?"		
Encourage Self-Assessment, Gain Commitment	**Create an opportunity for the learner to identify learning priorities.** • "Which area do you feel you most need to practice?"		
	Gain commitment on learning actions. • "Is it possible for you to complete Module 1 by Monday?"		
	Establish follow-up. • "Let's meet after you input the data. We can then review the process and explore any questions that surfaced."		
	Measure success by implementing learning assessments provided by the training team or monitoring key performance-related metrics. • "After we finish up our session today, I am going to ask you to complete the Level 2 written assessment. The results will let us know if we need to review any of the content in our next session."		

Summary

Many trainers share that Perform is the part of the learning cycle that is most often missed. This is unfortunate because learning design begins with determining what performance will be delivered as a result of the training. When the final learning step, Perform, is not fully developed and implemented, results suffer dramatically.

Before you begin your training design, think about how you will measure success after the learning event. Structure your Perform activities to ensure that these measurable outcomes will be achieved. Include front-line managers, fellow learners, and on-the-job coaches as part of your training team to leverage your ability to reinforce the learning.

After the "Reflect" and "Act" sections of this chapter, you will find examples of activities that work in Perform.

STEP IN THE CYCLE: PERFORM

What the learner is doing:
- Taking ownership of the information by assessing his or her own progress and performance
- Demonstrating original applications of the learning
- Action planning

What the trainer is doing:
- Encouraging learners to evaluate their own application
- Giving feedback
- Reviewing key points
- Gaining commitment
- Establishing feedback loops

Activities that work well:
- Self-assessment
- Scaling criteria
- Peer feedback
- Refinement of learning
- Demonstrations
- On-site applications
- Sharing commitments
- Follow-up progress reporting sessions

YOUR TRAINING STYLE IN PERFORM

If you have a natural strength in the Type Four training approach, it is likely that your style encourages self-assessment and adaptation of what is being learned. If your area of strength lies in one of the other three approaches, consciously focus on including new strategies to improve your skill in leading this part of the learning cycle.

	HIGH STRENGTH IN TYPE ONE TRAINING APPROACH	HIGH STRENGTH IN TYPE TWO TRAINING APPROACH	HIGH STRENGTH IN TYPE THREE TRAINING APPROACH	HIGH STRENGTH IN TYPE FOUR TRAINING APPROACH
	Use your natural strength in building relationships to sustain the learning process outside of the formal learning environment. Be careful to focus learners on clear, actionable steps to reinforce learning.	Be open to the learner's adaptation and interpretation of the information being learned. Encourage learners to own the information by developing their own set of assessment criteria and/or developing individual action plans.	Your natural focus on action will serve you well in the final part of the learning experience. Allow time for learners to come up with their own answers and evaluate their own work. Be patient with learners who need time to assimilate what they have learned into an actionable plan.	Be careful to create structure around the self-assessment. Pay particular attention to sharing clear criteria. When leading planning, create a structure for defining priorities. Establish how learning will be supported post-training.
	Type One Trainer comment: "I tend to emphasize the value of the learner's experience. I consciously focus on targeting the right behavior-based action steps to make sure the learning creates a visible impact."	Type Two Trainer comment: "I tend to emphasize things being right. When it comes to assessment, I am strong at giving clear 'black and white' criteria. Sometimes, it is more difficult to be comfortable with the gray areas."	Type Three Trainer comment: "I enjoy the process of sharing the 'next steps' with learners. Sometimes, it is more difficult to watch them struggle with coming up with their own answers when I can clearly see what they need to do first."	Type Four Trainer comment: "I enjoy when learners start to take ownership and get creative with the content. I need to focus on giving clear criteria for evaluating their success."

REFLECT

Reflect on a powerful learning experience that inspired you to apply the information learned. What was it about this experience that encouraged application of the content? What strategies can you apply from this experience to learning experiences you create?

Think about the participants in the learning experiences you deliver. What support do they need most to best apply the information being learned?

What follow-up delivery structures already exist within your organization(s) such as weekly team meetings or a company e-newsletter. Make a list of the possible ways you might tap into existing delivery structures to follow up with learners.

Identify strategies you will use in your next training to extend learning into the real world:

	YES	NO
• Follow-up emails	✓	
• Podcasts		
• Celebrating success stories		
• Online discussion forum		
• Facebook posts—idea of the week, question of the day, or call for comments		
• Blog articles with discussion		
• Recognition awards		
• Reunion calls via web		
• One-on-one follow-up sessions		
• Lunch and learn sessions		
• On-the-job coaching team-coach follow-up action plan		
• Accountability partners		

Activities for Perform

In this section, you will find examples of activities that will work in Perform.

PERFORM ACTIVITY EXAMPLE: ACTION PLANNING IN A FIRST-TIME MANAGER COURSE

In a learning agility course for first-time managers, participants discover their natural learning strengths and begin to identify how they can maximize these strengths and minimize potential weak areas. At the completion of the course, each participant builds a "10-10-10" plan. The plan will be used as a framework to structure the first follow-up conversation with the on-the-job mentor assigned to each participant.

10-10-10

Focus: Planning activity focused on implementation of the learning in the next ten days, ten weeks, and ten months.

Resources Needed
- Reflection section in the learners' workbook or a handout

Description

1. Develop a worksheet that invites learners to plan their implementation in increments of ten days, ten weeks, and ten months.

2. Invite learners to reflect on their plan for implementation by writing specific outcomes to be delivered in each time increment.

Trainer Script

"We have come to the end of our time together. Please refer to the last page in your workbook, entitled '10-10-10 ' In the first text box, create your goal for the next ten days. What do you want to have accomplished with your new skills in the next ten days? Next, think about ten weeks from now—2 ½ months. How will you keep the momentum going? Where do you want to be on your learning path? How will you know you are successfully implementing your plan? Write this down in the next box. If you were to identify one key behavior/commitment that you would like to be consistently be executing ten months from now, what would that behavior be? Write this behavior/commitment in the last '10' box."

Notes:

_____

_____

_____

_____

_____

PERFORM ACTIVITY EXAMPLE: ACCOUNTABILITY COACHING WORKSHOP

Line managers in the distribution arm of a product manufacturing company have just completed an "Accountability Coaching" workshop. To encourage reflection on the key learning points and to allow time for action planning, participants are asked to interview partners using a series of questions provided by the facilitator.

EXIT INTERVIEW

Focus: As a closing activity, participants interview each other.

Resources Needed
- Copies of interview questions for each learner

Description
1. Encourage learners to reflect on the content and review the interview questions found in the workbook.
2. Learners find partners and take turns interviewing each other using the questions provided.
3. Debrief by inviting volunteers to share interesting responses shared in the interview process.

Trainer Script
"In your workbook on page_____, you will find an 'Exit Interview.' Take your workbook and a pen with you and find a learning partner. Please give your workbook to your partner. Your partner will now interview you and record your answers in your own book. Find a quiet spot and interview each other. You have 20 to 25 minutes. Return to the classroom when you have finished. Please remember to be respectful to those who are still interviewing when you return."

Sample Questions
- What is one thing you learned today?
- What is the first change you will make when you return to the workplace?
- How would your performance be improved by this change?
- What is your goal from this class? What would be the biggest impact from achieving this goal?
- What would you try if you knew you could not fail? How will you define success in applying this?
- What are your greatest strengths that will help you implement your learning? What are three actions you could take this week?
- On a scale of 1 to 10, how motivated are you to take those steps? How could you increase that score?
- How will you get more information if you need it?
- Who or what will continue to inspire your learning and implementation in the days ahead?
- What was this learning really about? What was meaningful to you?

PERFORM ACTIVITY EXAMPLE: DIVISIONAL SALES MANAGEMENT CONFERENCE

At the completion of a multi-day conference, divisional sales managers are encouraged to build an action plan on how they will share the information learned with the sales team members within their respective divisions. The focus of the event was the successful launch of a product. Using the visual metaphor of a roadmap, the managers record their starting point (current sales metrics), points of interest along the way (phased launch plan), and refueling stations (training and coaching structure). The map integrates the deliverables shared by various teams, which presented resources, tools, and strategies that combine to create a successful launch.

ROADMAP TO SUCCESS

Focus: Learners will create an action plan (roadmap) for successful transfer of the learning.

Resources Needed
- Handout with space to write goals and support needed to accomplish each goal

Description

1. Create a workbook page or handout to support this activity, which provides a visual of a "roadmap." The workbook page can be developed map-style with stops along the way. Or the workbook page can simply be a flow chart with labeled steps and a place to write what will be needed to accomplish each step.

2. Invite learners to individually develop a plan for implementation, including specific goals, support needed, tools, and resources.

3. Invite learners to review and refine their roadmaps in small teams.

Trainer Script

"What is one focused goal you want to achieve? Write this goal at the end of the 'road.' Next, fill in all the necessary items on your roadmap that you will need to move toward this goal. You will find a place to list your 'traveling companions.' These can be your fellow classmates, teammates in the office, a mentor or coach who will support you in achieving your goal. You will find a place to record the tools you will need on your 'road to success.' This could be learning resources from this course, websites, books, or other tools you will apply. You will also find a 'rest stop' on your 'roadmap.' Record your strategy to recover for when you detour or find your progress stalled and need a jumpstart. This could be your favorite motivational quote or simply a reminder to get a cup of coffee! Share your completed 'Roadmap to Success' map with your tablemates."

Notes:

_____

_____

_____

PERFORM ACTIVITY EXAMPLE: CLOSING REFLECTION FOR THREE-MONTH ONBOARDING TRAINING EXPERIENCE

Participants from various departments in an international pharmaceutical company are completing their three-month orientation training process. The curriculum includes classroom-led, online learning, and on-the-job training. In the final session of the program, learners are invited to share "Words of Wisdom" with future course participants.

WORDS OF WISDOM

Focus: Closing reflection activity that encourages learners to pass on relevant advice and words of wisdom related to the course content.

Resources Needed
- Index cards (two per participant)

Description

1. Invite learners to reflect on their experience in the class. Ask learners to identify the most important things someone should take away from the course.

2. Ask the learners to write a paragraph to share their "words of wisdom" with the next group of learners who will experience this course.

3. Invite volunteers to share their words of wisdom in small groups.

4. Collect the "words of wisdom" index cards from the class participants. Reference information shared in a follow-up email.

Trainer Script

"'If I only knew then, what I know now.' How often have we heard this saying? Imagine if you were able to guide the next group of participants who will experience this program. What words of wisdom would you share? If you had to distill the most important ideas from this program into a single paragraph, what would you say? Think about responding to the questions: What was meaningful and relevant to you? What excites you as you look forward to implementing the material? What surprised you in class? Please record your thoughts on an index card. Share your thoughts with a partner."

Notes:

PRACTICE ACTIVITY EXAMPLE: LEARNER SELF-ASSESSMENT IN AN EMAIL MANAGEMENT COURSE

Participants in an "Effective Email Management" course have learned new skills on how to efficiently handle email communication. As learners prepare to bring the new skills back to their workplace, the facilitator invites participants to identify what "good" versus "great" application of each skill learned will look like. In the "Good to Great" exercise, the learners develop a clear set of guidelines that will help them concretely assess how well they are doing in applying what they have learned. As a follow-up to the course, the facilitator types the assessment criteria generated by the learners and emails this to them one week after the event.

GOOD TO GREAT

Focus: Assessment activity enabling learners to identify distinctions in levels of application of the skills learned in the course.

Resources Needed
- Flipcharts and a page in the workbook (or handout) to record the scale and self-report on skill level.

Description
Participants will define what is "good" application versus "great" application of skills learned in the course.

1. Identify the key skills for which learners will develop assessment criteria.
2. Write each skill on a flip chart.
3. Partner learners and invite them to choose a skill.
4. Learners develop a description of "good" and "great" application of the skill.
5. Learners use the criteria generated to assess their individual or group application of the skills practiced in the course.

Trainer Script
"We will explore the difference between 'good' and 'great' application of the content we have learned. I am going to ask you to generate a grading scale related to the use of our new skills and knowledge in the field. Around the room, there are flipcharts posted with the key skills covered in this course. In your group, you will be asked to define what this skill would look like if executed at an acceptable or 'GOOD' level. Then, define what the skill looks like if demonstrated at an exceptional or 'GREAT' level. Record what you would look for at each level on the grading scale on the flipchart of the associated skill."

Notes:

_____

_____

_____

PRACTICE ACTIVITY EXAMPLE: CLOSING REFLECTION IN A PARENTING WORKSHOP

At the close of a three-hour parenting workshop focused on positive discipline techniques, parents are invited to reflect on how they will apply the information shared. Each parent is invited to complete a "2+2+2" journal exercise in the workshop handout.

2+2+2 REFLECTION

Focus: Action planning activity.

Description

1. A handout is created with three prompts:
   - Two things I will do immediately….
   - Two things I will no longer do….
   - Note: Alternatively, the statements may be written on a flipchart and participants can write responses in a notebook.

2. Participants are invited to complete the statements.

3. Participants partner with fellow learners and share their insights and planned actions.

Facilitator Script

"To create an opportunity for you to reflect on all the ideas we have shared with each other, I am going to invite you to complete the reflection statements on _____ (page) of your workbook. When answering the questions, think back to the most important issues you raised in our opening conversation. Of all the ideas and strategies shared, which are the most important for you to focus on to achieve your desired outcomes? We will take 20 minutes to complete this and then you will have an opportunity to share your answers with a partner."

Notes:

PRACTICE ACTIVITY EXAMPLE: EFFECTIVE TIME MANAGEMENT COURSE

In an effective time management course, participants explore the importance of acting with intention versus reacting. At the end of the session, learners are invited to find accountability partners. Accountability partners are asked to connect within seven days to check in on the progress of implementing what has been learned. To help learners remember to implement the three key behaviors learned in the course, accountability partners share their individual action plans and tie string around their wrists to help them remember to apply new behaviors in the next week.

MEMORY STRINGS

Focus: Closing ceremony designed to help learners remember to implement new behaviors.

Resources Needed
• Piece of twine for each participant

Description
1. Learners are asked to define their action plan with clear steps.
2. Learners team up with "accountability partners" and share their action plans. Partners schedule a time to reconnect and review their progress.
3. Partners tie string around each other's wrists to help them remember to implement their commitments.

Facilitator Script
"What are some strategies you use to help you remember to do something? Is everyone familiar with the concept of tying a string around your finger to help you remember something? I would like to invite you to share your learning commitments with a partner. Share what you plan to do and when you plan to do it. To help you remember your new behaviors, your partner will tie a string around your wrist. You can keep the string on for the next week if you want a visual reminder to focus on your new behaviors."

Notes:

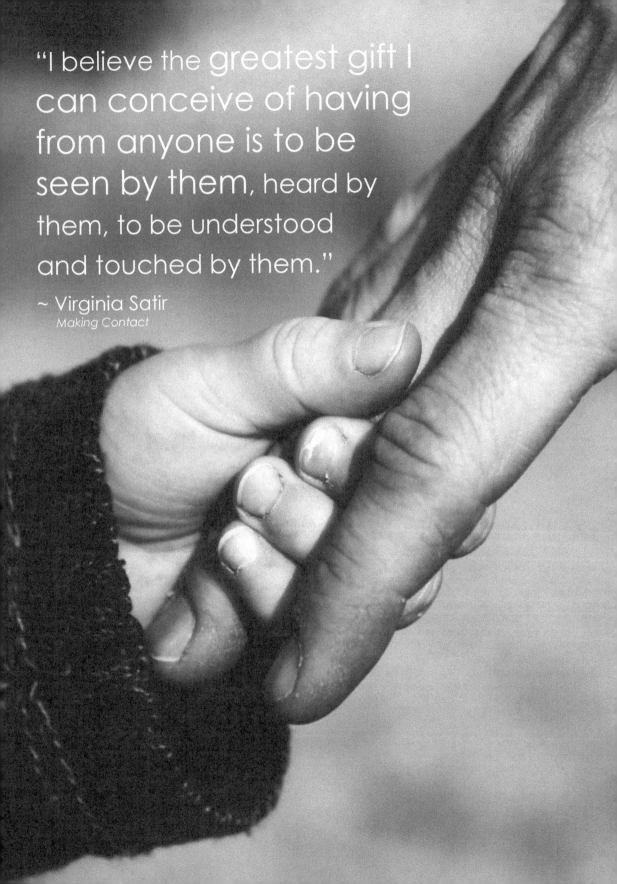

"I believe the greatest gift I can conceive of having from anyone is to be seen by them, heard by them, to be understood and touched by them."

~ Virginia Satir
Making Contact

Chapter 8

Engaging Virtual Training: How to Maximize Online Learning Impact

Imagine that you are invited to attend an upcoming learning experience. Included in the orientation email, you receive the "New Rules of Learning." The training facilitator tells you that the new rules are designed to make training more efficient by reducing the time you spend in the learning experience; your organization will also save money by eliminating travel expense and wasted employee hours.

Essential Questions

– How can I create online learning experiences that mirror the learning cycle?

Next, the facilitator outlines the following six rules:

- **Rule 1:** Chatting is strongly discouraged.

- **Rule 2:** In order to assure the anonymity of your fellow learners, please do not make eye contact with fellow learners during training or send messages before or after the session containing personal information.

- **Rule 3:** Attention must be focused at all times on the presenter; no learner-to-learner interaction, please.

- **Rule 4:** Do not ask how the information you receive relates to use in the real world. You may, however, use your imagination to determine use if you wish.

- **Rule 5:** Do not ask for handouts. They will not be provided. Instead, learners must be prepared to write a minimum of 65 words per minute to copy information presented on PowerPoint slides.

- **Rule 6:** Engagement is mandatory—no daydreaming or multi-tasking allowed—despite the lecture-style presentation format.

How much learning do you think would actually occur in this learning experience? Does this generate a vision of a learning experience that you are excited to attend? How many virtual learning sessions have you attended that follow some, if not all, of these rules?

The most basic design principles are often thrown out the window when virtual learning sessions are designed with no accommodation included for personal reflection, social interaction, multi-modal delivery, hands-on practice, or self-assessment. This chapter explores strategies for creatively addressing the needs of all learning styles in a virtual learning experience.

Designing Your Virtual Session

It is helpful to approach the design of a virtual learning session just as you would a physical classroom learning experience. Chapter 9 will explore how to define four key outcomes that will guide the design and delivery of the learning experience. Just as in a classroom experience, you begin by defining the desired learning outcomes which will serve as a filter for the content you will include in your final design; this will, in turn, guide you in choosing the right activities.

After you decide what you want to accomplish in the virtual learning experience, brainstorm possible activities appropriate for the learning experience. The challenge for most trainers in this step is envisioning how to convert classroom-led activities into an online learning format. There are many different platforms for delivering virtual learning sessions.

Many online learning platforms share features that enable the simulation of a live classroom experience:

- **Slide display.** The slide display function allows you to show visuals such as PowerPoint.
- **Chat.** The chat function allows learners to communicate with you and with others. You can use the chat function to conduct exercises and encourage dialogue. Learners can also hold conversations with each other.
- **Raise hand function.** The "Raise Hand" allows learners to indicate that they have a question, a comment or that they agree/disagree with something that you shared.
- **Whiteboard.** Think of the whiteboard function as the equivalent of a flipchart. You can use the board to capture the questions and insights of the group. Or you can invite learners to write or draw on the board.
- **Pointer.** The pointer function allows learners to position an arrow on the screen. Think of the pointer as a "mini-me." Just as you might use physical graphing (discussed in Chapter 4) in a live classroom, you can invite learners to position themselves (using the pointer) on a spectrum, in a group, or on a map, graph, or scale.
- **Markers.** Markers allow learners to draw and write on a slide or a whiteboard. You can use this function for brainstorming, recording, knowledge checks, and visual exercises.
- **Text.** Learners can type on the whiteboard using the text tool.
- **Polls.** Polls can be used to determine the learners' interests, just as a typical survey might be conducted. You can also use polls to conduct knowledge checks throughout lecture.

- **Breakouts:** Some web platforms offer the option of creating "breakout rooms" which allow smaller groups of learners to interact with each other through chat and/or audio. You can combine this feature with a whiteboard exercise which requires each breakout to generate and record ideas on the whiteboard to be presented to the rest of the group.
- **Online social forum:** An online social forum is typically not part of the web platform offering. However, you can easily link a social forum to an online course to encourage social interaction. For example, learners might be asked to post a profile, photo, and examples of websites they explore frequently related to the topic being discussed.

CREATING A SAFE ENVIRONMENT

Learners and even facilitators must overcome a learning curve when first using the technology associated with an online learning experience.

Here are some tips to help participants get comfortable with this new way of learning:

- Allow participants to answer the first few questions anonymously through chat, polls, or checking off an answer on a whiteboard.
- Call on learners after they have shared a response in the chat.
- Give learners advance notice that you will be calling on them. For example, "In a moment, I am going to invite Jim to tell us more about the experience he shared in the online forum."
- Invite learners to share by asking for volunteers to "raise their hands."
- Build on the energy of your most extroverted participants. Start by inviting them to share responses and move to include the rest of the group.

Before a session, consider sending an email with all the information required to prepare for the learning session, including any special equipment they may need to participate. It is helpful to provide a printable job aid on how to use the tools in the web platform hosting your course. Here are some of the issues you should cover in pre-communication with learners.

BEFORE THE SESSION BEGINS

Showing up for a virtual learning experience often requires more planning than simply walking into a classroom learning environment. Learners need to know how to log onto the session; they must download and set up the platform software being used for the session and ensure both audio and video functionality; they must print any necessary materials; and they must be familiar with how to use the interactive tools.

To help learners arrive at a virtual learning session engaged and ready to go, you must create a well-thought-out orientation plan. Here are some key pointers on what to include in an orientation plan:

Before the Session Begins: Focus on making sure learners have everything they need to participate fully in the session.

- **Pre-learning packet:**
  Send an electronic or physical packet that includes the participant workbook, information on how to use the web platform, and something to intrigue or stimulate thinking, such as an article to read. Include a number or email address of someone they can contact to help with any technical questions.

- **Facilitator podcast:**
  Create a short podcast welcoming the learners to the session. Focus on how the learning will benefit them. Include testimonials from learners who have previously experienced the course.

- **Sponsor message:**
  Invite the training sponsor or a senior executive to share why the learning experience is important to the learners and the whole organization.

TURN UP THE HEAT SLOWLY

Chapter 4 noted the risk of asking learners to "jump into" a learning session full-force versus the advantages of "turning up the heat slowly." Open your session by sharing slides that highlight the functionality of the course platform. The varying degrees of comfort with the technology in a virtual learning environment require that you start with activities that use the most basic application of the online participant tools. Think about how you might create an opportunity for learners to play with the functionality of the web platform at the beginning of the session. For example, as learners enter the online learning environment you might host a whiteboard with instructions for learners to write or draw answers to a question such as "How's the weather?"

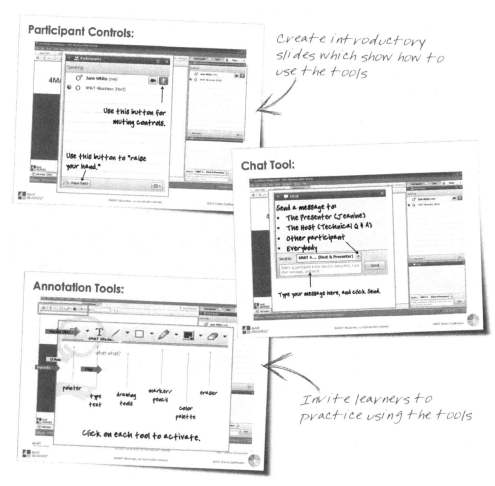

Images created using Cisco WebEx™ Meeting Center

Engage

Your goal in the opening of the learning experience is to connect the learners to each other and the content planned for the course. In the movie, *Avatar*, the Na'vi people greet each other by saying, "I see you." This form of greeting is not exclusive to the Na'vi people. You will find similarities in the Native American and Indian cultures. In India, the common greeting *Namaste* means more than a routine "hello." The greeting celebrates the presence of the divine in those being greeted (Michaelson, 2009).

One of the challenges in a virtual learning environment is the prospect of learners not "being seen." Learners feel a certain sense of anonymity in a virtual learning environment, and this invites a low level of engagement. In a classroom environment, everything a learner does is visible to other learners and the trainer. There is a generally accepted social norm that encourages learners to participate and engage at an acceptable level. In a virtual environment, learners are invisible. To create higher engagement, learners must feel that their participation is valuable to the learning experience. The challenge of learners not "being seen" goes beyond the obvious challenge of learners truly being invisible to other learners and the facilitator. To become fully engaged in the learning experience, the learners must be invited into the learning conversation in a way that encourages them to share experiences, knowledge, and beliefs that are often hidden in superficial interaction. When the learners' experiences, knowledge, and opinions are drawn out and acknowledged as valuable, learners feel "seen." This dramatically increases engagement in any learning experience, and especially in a virtual one. This section shares some ideas on how you can connect learners to each other and the relevance of the content being shared.

INTRODUCTIONS

Getting to know each other while getting comfortable with technology.

- **Chat exercise.** Invite learners to respond to questions such as "Where are you calling in from? What do you see outside of your window?"

- **Text/marker.** Learners are invited to draw images on a blank whiteboard in response to a question such as "What's the weather like where you are today?"

- **Pointer.** Learners position their pointers on a map which indicates where they are located.

- **Online social forum.** Invite learners to post a picture and brief bio.

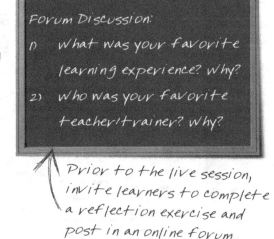

Forum Discussion:

1) What was your favorite learning experience? Why?

2) Who was your favorite teacher/trainer? Why?

Prior to the live session, invite learners to complete a reflection exercise and post in an online forum

REVIEW OF AGENDA

- **Chat or poll exercise.** "What is the biggest question you hope to have answered today?" Link the questions shared with the agenda being covered in the session.
- **Poll.** Learners vote on the learner outcomes that are most critical to dealing with their real-world issues.
- **Pointer exercise.** Invite learners to position their pointer next to the topic that most interests them.
- **Learning roadmap.** Visually share the process you will lead learners through. If this is a multi-session program, explain what is covered in each session and what is expected of learners between sessions.

INDIVIDUAL REFLECTION

- **Chat.** Ask a provocative question such as, "Why do people avoid raising difficult issues?" Invite learners to share their thoughts in the chat. Ask learners to share their insights on a pre-session reading assignment in response to a specific question such as, "How does this article relate to your own experiences?"
- **Whiteboard.** Encourage learners to reflect on their own experiences and share their insights by writing on a whiteboard. For example, you might ask learners "In your experience of productive design teams, what are the one or two most important elements that must be present? Write your answers in the box in the grid with your name on it."
- **Pointers.** Share a series of quotes or poems related to the topic. Ask learners to choose which quote represents their viewpoint on the topic or most intrigues them.
- **Online social forum.** Encourage learners to share stories in the online forum before or between sessions. Share excerpts from the stories in the PowerPoint presentation or invite learners to expand upon their stories.
- **Pointer.** Share a collection of images. Invite learners to choose an image that best represents how they view an issue or situation, using their pointers. Invite learners to share their reasoning in the chat or through audio.

Share

In the second part of the learning experience you are delivering the information that learners must understand to be able to successfully apply the information in the real world. In an online environment, this typically means lecture using PowerPoint. This section reviews how you can use common web platform tools to increase interactivity and encourage active engagement with the content being explored.

GROUP DISCUSSION CHAT

Assign each learner a partner. Invite the partners to chat with each other on an assigned topic.

- **Breakout.** Form teams and assign them to "meet" in a breakout room to perform some task.
- **Whiteboard.** After learners conduct a partner chat or breakout activity, ask each group to share their insights on a prepared whiteboard.

LECTURE

- **Poll or raise hands.** Introduce a series of controversial statements or myths and facts related to the content and invite learners to agree or disagree with each statement.
- **Whiteboard.** Pause in lecture and invite learners to each share one big idea that has captured their interest.
- **Chat.** Invite learners to generate a mock test question on the content covered thus far. You can later use the questions in review. Generate meaning around the content by periodically pausing and inviting learners to answer a question such as, "Why is this important in your role?" or "How might you apply this in your next project?" or "How does this connect to reaching the goals you outlined earlier?"

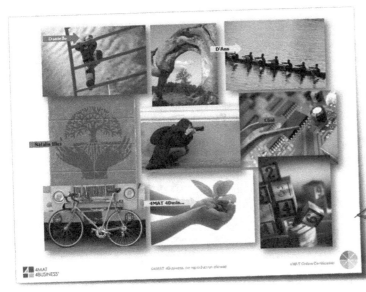

In this session, learners choose images that represent their learning styles.

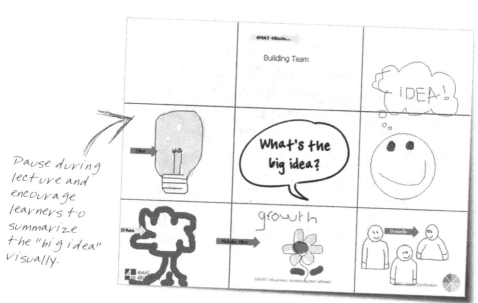

Pause during lecture and encourage learners to summarize the "big idea" visually.

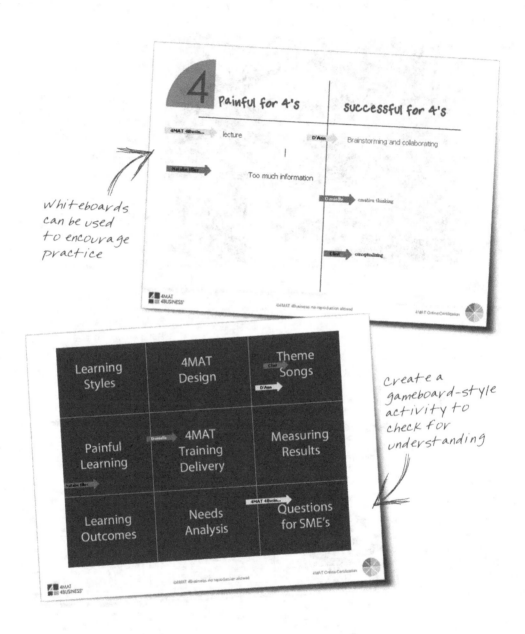

Whiteboards can be used to encourage practice

Create a gameboard-style activity to check for understanding

Practice

In the third part of the learning experience, you create opportunities for the learners to apply the knowledge in a real-world context. First, you create an opportunity to check to see whether learners understand the necessary information needed for application. Just as in a live classroom environment, you can check for understanding using worksheets, knowledge tests, and games. Once you establish that learners have a good grasp of the content, you create opportunities for them to apply the content in a real-world situation. The practice activities that work in a classroom environment will also work in a virtual one, including role plays, problem-solving scenarios, and case studies.

CHECKING FOR UNDERSTANDING

- **Chat.** Create game show–style review activities. Present questions on a slide and have learners answer using the chat feature.
- **Whiteboard.** Post a whiteboard and invite learners to generate responses to a question that requires use of the information shared in lecture. For example, learners might be asked to generate examples of "painful and successful learning experiences for Type Three learners."
- **Polls.** You can use the poll function to generate true/false or multiple-choice formatted questions.

HANDS-ON PRACTICE

- **Polls.** You can extend this beyond knowledge check into practical application by giving learners a simulated problem and asking them to choose the approach they would take. For example, the slide might show a real-world safety challenge. The associated poll could give learners four options on how they would address what they see.
- **Chat or whiteboard.** Invite learners to partner up and work on a real-world problem. Using the content shared in the course, learners should generate a possible approach or answer. Invite learners to record or draw in response to an application exercise.
- **Role plays with chat.** Create simulated practice for learners to apply the information being shared. In a customer service workshop, participants might role play how they would handle a customer issue. Fellow learners are invited to assess the application and share helpful feedback in the chat.

DEBRIEFING EXERCISES

- **Whiteboard.** Invite learners to capture insights gained from an exercise by writing on a whiteboard. Any debriefing exercise you have developed for a live classroom setting that involves a flipchart and marker can be converted for an online environment.

Perform

In the fourth part of the learning cycle, Perform, you encourage learner self-assessment, give feedback, help them develop action plans, and gain commitment for future implementation of the learning. Perform activities happen in the formal learning environment and may extend out into the real world.

ASSESSING APPLICATION

- **Pointers.** Ask learners to position their pointers on a scale to assess their commitment to application of the information being learned.
- **Polls.** Invite learners to assess their comfort level in applying the content using a scale you provide.
- **Chat.** As fellow learners observe someone role playing, invite feedback in the chat and/or provide a scaling criteria for learners to use to assess each other's applications. Invite learners to compare assessments in partner chat.

ACTION PLANNING

- **Whiteboard.** Develop a four-frame activity on the whiteboard. For example, you might use the dimensions of "High-to-Low Impact" and "Easy-to-Hard to Implement" to form the four squares. Invite learners to generate action strategies and post within the appropriate frame.
- **Chat.** Assign accountability partners and invite them to share their action items with each other. Challenge partners to establish a time to reconnect and follow up on commitments.
- **Online forum.** Include resources to support action planning such as job aids or action checklists. Require posting of assignments to serve as evidence of implementation.

CELEBRATE LEARNING

- **Polls or whiteboards.** Generate an assessment of information learned using a variety of question formats.
- **Whiteboard.** Design reflection questions for learners to complete. Invite learners to share responses on a whiteboard or chat.
- **Surveys.** Follow up with a survey to assess reaction, knowledge, and skills applied within two to four weeks of the learning event.
- **Assessment.** Consider scheduling one-on-one interviews to determine the impact of the learning on key behaviors and overall business.

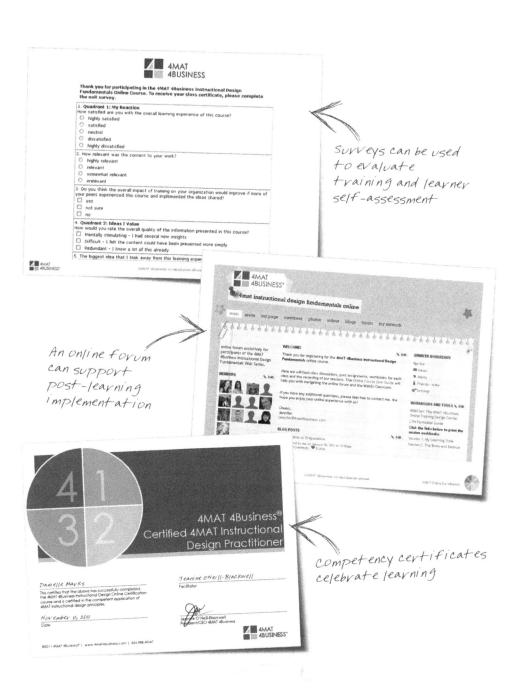

Surveys can be used to evaluate training and learner self-assessment

An online forum can support post-learning implementation

Competency certificates celebrate learning

Summary

More and more, learning is happening in an online learning environment. Creative use of learning strategies to physically and emotionally engage learners in this environment will dramatically improve the learning results. Many, if not all, of the strategies shared in this book can be adapted for the online environment. As you review the ideas shared, consider how you might adapt them for the online learner.

Where will I need to stretch in the online learning environment to reach the learning styles that differ from my natural training style approach?

REFLECT

The next time you lead a web learning experience, record the session. Review the recording and assess the balance of activities and delivery style.

Some questions you might consider:

	YES	NO
Is the orientation to the online learning tools effective?	✓	
Do learners seem comfortable?		
Are learners sharing their experiences and real-world issues?		
Are learners doing something every two or three minutes?		
Do you vary the balance of activities to appeal to different learning styles?		
Are you using a variety of tools versus relying only on one such as chat?		
Are learners practicing the content?		
Do learners have an opportunity to assess their application?		

Have you attended web classes hosted by a variety of presenters? Schedule time to participate in online workshops in order to increase your activity inventory and refine your delivery approach. Identify exercises you have used successfully in a live learning environment. How might you adapt these activity structures for online use?

	Activities I have used successfully in the live learning environment	How I might adapt this activity for online use:
Engage: Activities that connect learners to the relevance of the content while establishing a sense of community.		
Share: Activities that animate the delivery of the essential knowledge to the learners.		
Practice: Activities that check for understanding and challenge learners to apply the content in a real-world context.		
Perform: Activities that encourage learners to assess their own applications and plans for successful implementation.		

"20% of any process will yield
80% of the results."

~ Vilfredo Pareto
The Pareto Principle

Begin with the End in Mind

It should be no surprise that creating great training requires you to follow a process that author Steven Covey articulated so well in his classic book, *The Seven Habits of Highly Successful People*—begin with the end in mind. For training professionals this means that you begin with a clear idea of important learning outcomes, achieving desired business impact through knowledge transfer, and behavior shift on the job. In this chapter, we will explore the steps you will follow to develop a framework for the design of a learning experience that delivers measurable results.

Essential Questions

- *How do I know how to edit and focus my content?*

- *How do I generate measurable impact from the training I design?*

1 Clarifying Expectations and Analyzing the Performance Gap

In this step, you will guide the training request process and define the desired training impact.

2 Defining Four Critical Learning Outcomes

With a clear picture of the desired result, you can analyze current versus existing levels of performance and define the "performance gap." To bridge this gap, you will define four critical learning outcomes which, when achieved, will generate the desired results.

3 Working with Subject Matter Experts to Focus the Content

Trainers often work with subject matter experts to harvest content. In this step, you will work with subject matter experts to identify what high performers value, know, and do differently that delivers an elevated level of results. You will use this to focus the learning experience on the right content and skills practice.

Step 1: Clarifying Stakeholder Expectations and Analyzing the Performance Gap

One of the biggest challenges trainers face is focusing the learning experience on the right outcomes. Sponsor expectations, available resources, and lack of a common definition of training success are just a few of the many issues that affect learning transfer. The lack of a clear focus around defined learning outcomes leads to other issues: lack of clarity on what content to include in a design, a slower design process, activity choices that do not "flow," a low level of learner engagement, and/or diminished learning impact. Analyzing the performance gap takes additional effort, yet this first part of the design process is the most impactful in delivering results.

Trainers often get requests for training content, rather than performance outcomes. Before you begin to determine what content should be included in your training, there are two things you need to know: what outcome you are tasked with generating and what shift in learner behavior will produce it.

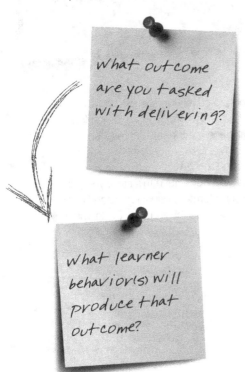

By analyzing the performance issue with key stakeholders, you can mutually define the desired outcomes of the training course you are tasked with designing. A stakeholder may be the manager or leader who requests training, a senior level executive who assesses the value of the training, or any influencer who evaluates budgeting for your area of accountability. The right questions will guide the needs analysis conversation and lead to the identification of the performance gap and the four outcomes that will help you bridge this gap. Gaining a mutual definition of success for your training program will guide development and accelerate the design process. In the next section of this book, we will explore examples of questions you can use to define the performance gap and articulate the four key learning outcomes.

QUESTIONS TO USE WHEN DEFINING THE PERFORMANCE GAP

"Performance gap" refers to the difference between the desired level of performance and the actual level of performance that currently exists. When you receive a request for training, the first thing you will do is define the performance gap. When processing the training request from a stakeholder, the following questions will help guide the conversation to define the gap.

Questions to Define the Desired Performance Level
- What is the desired result of this training program?
- How will you measure the success of the program? Is there a metric you are currently using to assess this area of performance?
- If you were to fast forward thirty days from the completion of this course, describe what new behaviors you would observe that would lead you to believe the training was successful?
- Do you have any team members who are already performing at this level? Can you share their results?

Questions to Establish the Current Performance Level
- How would you describe the current level of performance?
- What measurement are you using to assess performance now?

Questions to Analyze the Cause of the Performance Gap
- What do you see as the source of the issue?
- Can you identify performers who are achieving desired results?
- How do high performers think differently? Act differently?
- What actions have you already taken to address the performance gap?
- How do managers support and/or coach the behaviors?
- How are performers acknowledged or rewarded for the desired performance behavior?

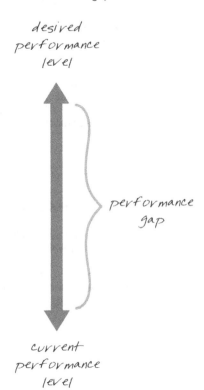

desired
performance
level

performance
gap

current
performance
level

Step 2: Defining the Four Critical Learning Outcomes

Once you have identified the performance gap, you can begin to identify the learning outcomes that must be reached to address the gap. Four dimensions of performance must be addressed for learning impact: values, knowledge, skills, and adaptation.

ADAPTATION: IF?

What the learner must be able to assess and adapt in order to perform at a high level.

Learning outcome example: Sales trainees will assess the reaction of the buyer and adapt their selling strategy to produce increased sales results.

VALUES: WHY?

What the learner must value, honor, and/or appreciate to perform at a high level.

Learning outcome example: Sales trainees will appreciate the value of negative feedback from potential buyers.

SKILLS: HOW?

What the learner must be able to do to perform at a high level.

Learning outcome example: Sales trainees will identify appropriate questions to apply based on the feedback from the buyer.

KNOWLEDGE: WHAT?

What the learner must understand and know to perform at a high level.

Learning outcome example: Sales trainees will know what questions to apply to redirect negative feedback and guide the sales conversation forward.

Successful fulfillment of these four outcomes will ensure that the right behaviors are targeted and the desired business impact is delivered. When you begin with these four outcomes clearly defined, you will have a strong framework for measuring the impact of your training design. If you are familiar with the popular Kirkpatrick assessment model, you can see how the four learning outcomes of the 4MAT model overlay on the Kirkpatrick four levels of assessment (Kirkpatrick and Kirkpatrick, 2010).

KIRKPATRICK'S MODEL

The Kirkpatrick model is one of the most widely used models for evaluating training impact. In the Kirkpatrick model, there are four levels of training evaluation:

LEVEL 1 FEEDBACK: REACTION

This level of feedback measures the degree to which learners react positively to a learning experience. Reactions and perceptions of the learners represent the type of data captured at this level. Examples of learning measurement at this level include reaction surveys, exit slips, post-training follow-up conversations, and surveys.

For example, in a phone skills training for call center employees, a Level I evaluation strategy might involve sending a post-training evaluation survey that measures the learners' satisfaction with the course.

LEVEL 2 FEEDBACK: LEARNING

This level of feedback measures the degree to which learners have acquired the knowledge, skills, and attitude required to generate the desired performance. Examples of measurement at this level include knowledge checks, written tests, and pre- and post-event knowledge samples.

In the example of a phone skills training for call center employees, a Level 2 evaluation might include a written test on call procedures.

LEVEL 3 FEEDBACK: RESULTS

This level of feedback measures the degree to which learners have applied what they have learned in the course. Examples of learning measurement at this level include post-training observation and tracking of key behaviors, front-line manager interviews, and customer experience measurement.

In the example of a phone skill training for call center team members, a Level 3 evaluation might include an on-site observation of the call center employees or recorded calls being monitored to evaluate the implementation of the procedures shared in the training course.

LEVEL 4 FEEDBACK: RESULTS

This level of measurement is focused on identifying the business impact of the learning outcomes achieved. Examples of measurement of learning at this level might include increase in sales, reduction of costs, or increase in customer retention.

In the example of the phone skill training for call center employees, a Level 4 evaluation might include a comparison of average sales dollars per customer transaction, pre- and post-training.

DEFINING THE LEARNING OUTCOMES

One of the easiest ways to define the outcomes for a course is to think about how high performers generate the desired results. Think through the lens of the four quadrants and notice the differences in performance, both behavioral and attitudinal, between high and low performers:

 Value

Is it a difference in what they value? What personal shift has to occur in the learner to ensure transfer? What has to be appreciated? Valued? Perceived as meaningful?

 Knowledge

Is it a difference in what they understand or know? What knowledge is needed to serve as a foundation for transfer? What content must be understood?

 Skill

Is it a difference in competency level? What skills are needed? What will the learner need to know how to do? What behaviors must be consistently demonstrated?

 Adaptation

Is it a difference in the ability to adapt the information to different settings? If the learner is going to successfully apply this content in the real world, what potential barriers to implementation require adaptive skills? What will successful transfer look like in the real world?

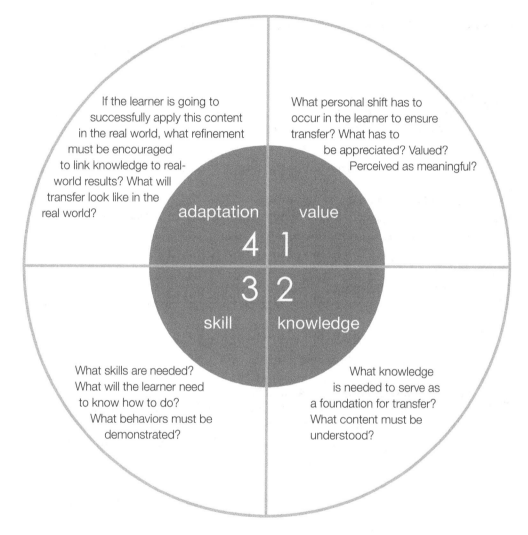

If the learner is going to successfully apply this content in the real world, what refinement must be encouraged to link knowledge to real-world results? What will transfer look like in the real world?

What personal shift has to occur in the learner to ensure transfer? What has to be appreciated? Valued? Perceived as meaningful?

adaptation

value

4 1

3 2

skill

knowledge

What skills are needed? What will the learner need to know how to do? What behaviors must be demonstrated?

What knowledge is needed to serve as a foundation for transfer? What content must be understood?

QUESTIONS TO USE WHEN DEFINING THE FOUR OUTCOMES

To help define the four outcomes, here are examples of questions you might use in your stakeholder or subject-matter-expert interviews:

 Engage: 4MAT Quadrant 1 — Value and Appreciation

- What differences exist in the appreciation for the content's value between the expert/high performer and the novice/low performer?
- What does an expert have an appreciation for that a novice does not?
- What would someone need to have a strong appreciation for in order to perform well?

 Share: 4MAT Quadrant 2 — Knowledge

- What knowledge does the expert/high performer possess that the novice does not?
- What does the expert/high performer understand?
- What concepts does the high performer grasp that the novice does not?

 Practice: 4MAT Quadrant 3 — Skill

- What tactical skills does the expert/high performer possess that the novice has yet to develop?
- What do they do differently?
- Where do most people struggle in applying this?

 Perform: 4MAT Quadrant 4 — Adaptation

- What differences exist between the expert/high performer's ability to adapt, innovate or overcome barriers to implementation?
- If this training program were 100% effective, what behaviors would you observe in the participants? What results would you see?

DEFINING OUTCOMES FOR CUSTOMER SERVICE TRAINING

Let's imagine that you were tasked with delivering customer service training for the front desk staff at a luxury hotel. Through your interviews, you determine that the performance gaps lie in the front desk attendant's ability to respond to the guests' issues in a courteous manner while following the hotel's customer service policies. In your analysis of the high performing team members, you discover a combination of knowledge, skills, and attitude that enable these team members to perform at the desired level. A front desk team member who consistently receives five-star ratings on guest feedback surveys might have differences in all four performance dimensions—value, knowledge, skills, and adaptation—or any combination of them. Let's take a look at an example of what the desired learning outcomes for this customer service course might be:

Quadrant 1
Learners will value the importance of the check-in and check-out process in the overall guest experience. (value)

Quadrant 2
Learners will understand and know when to apply the appropriate guest service system. (knowledge)

Quadrant 3
Learners will apply the appropriate service system to common check-in and check-out situations. (skill)

Quadrant 4
Learners will be able to assess guest reaction and adapt their approach, leading to higher guest satisfaction. (adaptation)

By defining the four outcomes before you begin the design process, you create a clear picture of what results will be generated from the course. Choosing the appropriate activities to deliver on each outcome is the next step.

They **appreciate** the importance of the first few moments of a guest's experience

They confidently interact with guests because they **understand** the guest care systems and know what to do to make a guest happy

Just calling to make sure you are happy with your room ...

They know how to **assess** the guest's reaction and **adjust** their approach, as needed

They quickly **address** issues by using the options available to them

ADDITIONAL QUESTIONS TO ASK A SPONSOR

Is this a training issue? There are instances when training cannot solve a performance issue. When is a performance issue not a training issue? Below, you will find some of the many factors that inhibit performance which cannot be addressed solely through training.

The performance issue may not be a training issue when:

- Employees are not clear on the performance expectation.
- There is no way for employees to measure their performance against standard.
- There is no coaching or front-line support.
- The cost of not doing anything is less than the cost of implementing a training intervention.
- Support tools, job aids, or resources are inadequate.
- There are conflicting priorities that impact employee behavior.
- Employees perform at the desired level "some of the time."
- Employees are rewarded for behaviors that conflict with the requested training outcomes.
- There are barriers in communication that negatively impact performance.

The table on the next page is a tool you can use to assess whether the issue you are analyzing is a training or performance issue.

IS THIS A TRAINING ISSUE?

		YES	NO
What is the performance gap?	• Is the desired level of performance clearly defined? Describe the desired performance.	✓	
If the gap significant enough to warrant allocation of training resources?	• Is the cost of not doing anything less than the cost of training (including missed opportunity cost)?		
Value and Appreciation	• Are expectations clear to the performer? Does the performer see the value in performing at the desired level?		
Knowledge	• Are standards of performance, policies, and procedures clearly defined?		
	• Do support tools provide enough detail? Are resources, tools, and job aids readily available?		
Skill	• Does the performer receive concrete feedback on this behavior? Describe this process.		
	• Is the performer qualified to perform the task? Can he or she do it some of the time? (If the answer is "yes," knowledge and skill are likely to be adequate.)		
	• Are the skills performed frequently enough to maintain competency? (If "no," opportunity for practice may be the issue.)		
Perform	• Does the performer receive objective feedback around the desired performance and quality of the work produced? Is measurement part of the feedback process?		
	• Does the performer receive rewards based on the desired feedback? Do the rewards align or conflict with the desired behavior?		
	• Are there competing priorities that hinder execution of the desired performance?		
	• Are there barriers in communication with supervisors or fellow stakeholders in the process?		
	• Is the performer able to perform the behavior in some situations and not others?		

To help a novice gain competency, trainers must create an opportunity for the novice to "see" what the competent already see. By asking the right questions of a subject matter expert, you can uncover the important concepts that must be conveyed in your training. Our team had the opportunity to work with a beauty product manufacturing company in designing a curriculum to be used globally to train hairdressers in haircutting. To define the outcomes for this project, we interviewed stakeholders, including customers, trainers, and master hairdressers, to define an agreed-upon ideal set of learning outcomes.

One of the most interesting discoveries came out of the process of working with a group of highly skilled master hairdressers. Using a series of questions, we began to unearth some of the surprising ways that hairdressers view their work. When asked to describe how they approach their work, one hairdresser described the process of cutting hair as being similar to carving a sculpture. He went on to compare haircutting to the process of sculpting a large slab of granite into a statue. He shared that when the sculptor approaches the granite, he has to see what needs to be removed to get to the desired result. Haircutting is similar to this process in that the hairdresser must see the "weight" that needs to be removed to give the desired result.

By asking the right questions, we were able to discover a powerful concept to guide the curriculum design process. The concept of "weight distribution" became one of the key concepts shared to help novice hairdressers begin to see what master hairdressers already see. Effective subject matter expert interviews enable you to define the conceptual focus of your course.

[Experts'] knowledge is not simply a list of facts and formulas that are relevant to their domain; instead their knowledge is organized around core concepts or 'big ideas' that guide their thinking about their domains.

~John Bransford (Medina, 2008, p. 84)

Step 3: Working with Subject Matter Experts to Focus Content and Skills Practice

Training design is focused on improving the skills and competency of a learner. Observing and questioning masters, or subject matter experts, will help you identify what to include in your training design. Subject matter experts can help you identify what concepts must be valued, what content should be included, what skills must be practiced, and what follow-up and support must be offered.

In *Brain Rules*, author John Medina references the work of John Bransford, an education researcher who answered the question, "What separates novices from experts?" Bransford identified six characteristics. One of the characteristics is relevant to the conversation around how to help novices gain mastery in a particular area of competency. "[Experts'] knowledge is not simply a list of facts and formulas that are relevant to their domain; instead their knowledge is organized around core concepts or 'big ideas' that guide their thinking about their domains" (Medina, 2008, p. 84). When working with subject matter experts, the trainer must focus on determining these concepts, the "big ideas."

One way to discover why high performers perform better could be to simply ask high performers what low performers need to do differently. This sounds like a simple solution, but one of the outcomes of growing expertise is the tendency to forget what it is like to be a novice. When working with subject matter experts, the trainer must help them remember what they know that others don't. You can do this by asking the right questions in your subject matter interviews.

Unconsciously Incompetent → Consciously Incompetent → Subject Matter Expert → Subject Matter Expert

QUESTIONS TO ASK A SUBJECT MATTER EXPERT

Asking the right questions of subject matter experts will help you target the right learning outcomes and elicit the content that should be included in your training design.

Here are examples of questions you might use in a subject matter expert interview:

- Was there ever a moment when you had an "aha!" around this and suddenly it all made sense? If so, will you share this with me?
- If there were "one thing" that most people don't get about this area of content, what would that one thing be?
- What does someone need to understand to do this well?
- Of all the information you shared, what is most important?
- If someone were to get "all caught up in the details" around this content, what "big picture" might they miss?
- When you picture how all this information fits together, what image comes to mind?
- If you were assigned to give someone feedback on applying this, what would you look for?
- If you were watching a high performer and a low performer applying this side-by-side, what differences would you see?
- What kind of situations would require someone to be creative in applying this information?
- Where might the "wheels come off of the track"?
- What advice would you give people to help them prepare for the barriers they might run into when applying this content?

1. Whats the problem
2. How do high performer solve it

This helps you see what to teach learners.

3. What are jedi tricks do y have to help y be great

What's the growing tip doing?

4. What do most people not get

5. What are the rabbit holes.

How did they get there?
How do they think
How can that help your learners.

CHAPTER 9 283

Example: Defining Outcomes for a Sales Training Course

If you were tasked with designing a high-impact sales training, where would you start? You begin by defining the four outcomes for your course.

 Quadrant 1
What value shift must occur in the learners? How must they think about this differently?

 Quadrant 2
What knowledge must the learners have?

 Quadrant 3
What skills must the learners possess?

 Quadrant 4
What adaptations will the learners need to make to ensure transfer in the real world?

In the next section of this chapter, we will examine how you might apply this process to the development of a sales training course. To identify the outcomes for your course, you will analyze the gap between current and desired performance.

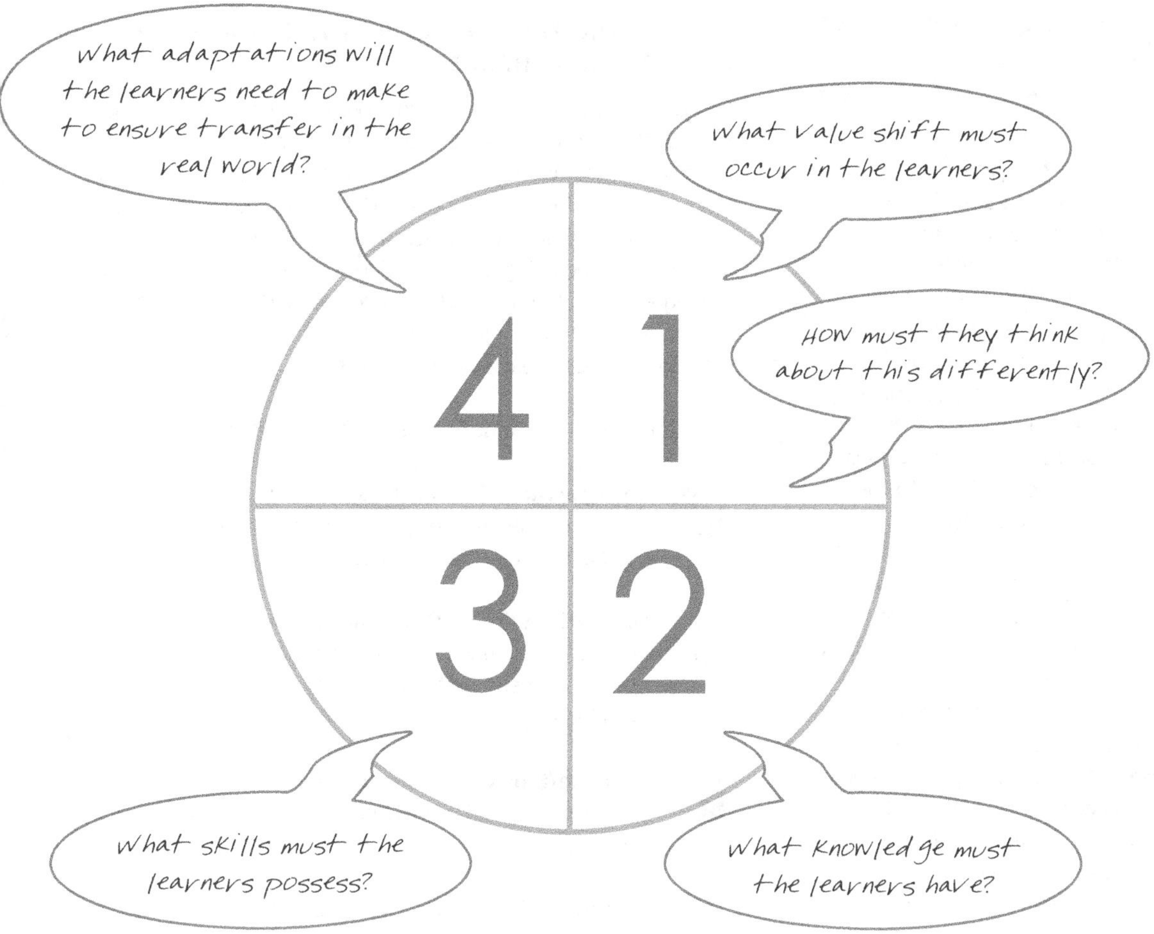

Begin with the End in Mind

In the article titled, "What Makes Great Salespeople Tick" psychoanalyst Rapaille shares that great salespeople are "happy losers" (*Inc.* Staff, April 2010). Rapaille shares that great sales people see rejection as a challenge. Rapaille goes on to explain that our first experiences in selling shape our views. When we sold (or didn't sell) that first box of Girl Scout cookies, a foundational view of sales was formed.

When designing training, simply sharing what the learner needs to know and practice is often not enough. To motivate the learner to apply the knowledge and skills, we must define the value outcome. What do high performers appreciate or value differently than those who struggle? In the case of dealing with rejection, great sales people value negative feedback. A high performing sales person sees the negative response as a valuable clue that redirects his sales approach. To create this mindset in low performing sales team members requires a reframing of their existing beliefs that are a direct result of their previous experiences.

STEP 1: ANALYZING THE PERFORMANCE GAP FOR A SALES TRAINING REQUEST

Imagine that the VP of sales in your organization, Mark, comes in to your office and shares, "Our global sales meeting is coming up in a few months. We want to do a breakout session for new sales team members focused on how to deal with rejection in sales calls. Can you put something together for a 90-minute session?" You respond by scheduling time with Mark and several regional sales managers to analyze the performance gap and determine the outcomes you need to generate in the session using some of the questions explored earlier in this chapter.

An example of the four outcomes for this course might be:

 Engage/Value Outcome: Learners will learn to *value* rejection or negative responses from customers as useful feedback in the sales process.

 Share/Knowledge Outcome: Learners will *understand* how to *apply* "redirect" questions to adjust their sales approach based on the positive and negative responses from the prospect.

 Practice/Skill Outcome: Learners will successfully *apply* the appropriate redirect questions to common sales scenarios.

 Perform/Adaptation Outcome: Learners will *assess* and *adjust* their approach, based on customer response.

STEP 2: DEFINING THE OUTCOMES IN A SALES TRAINING COURSE

You have now defined four learning outcomes that will help guide development of your training course:

PERFORM/ADAPTATION OUTCOME

Learners will assess and adjust their approach, based on customer response.

ENGAGE/VALUE OUTCOME

Learners will learn to *value* rejection or negative responses from customers as useful feedback in the sales process.

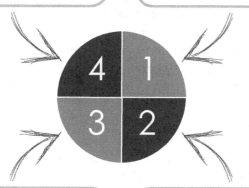

PRACTICE/SKILL OUTCOME

Learners will successfully apply the appropriate redirect questions to common sales scenarios.

SHARE/KNOWLEDGE OUTCOME

Learners will understand how to apply "redirect" questions to adjust their sales approach based on the positive and negative responses from the prospect.

STEP 3: WORKING WITH SUBJECT MATTER EXPERTS IN A SALES TRAINING

At this point, you have met with Mark, the VP of sales, and spent some time interviewing the regional sales managers. You have clearly defined the desired outcomes of the training program and you are now ready to determine the content for your course. To help you filter through all of the possible content choices, you have decided to meet with some of the salespeople who are "high performers." Because you are tasked with creating a training course that targets the behavior of "dealing with rejection" in sales calls, you ask the regional sales managers to each identify one sales person who is highly effective at making "cold calls." Cold calls require a sales person to call upon a potential customer that he or she does not know and who has not requested information on the company's products or services. Being effective at cold calling requires a high level of skill in dealing with rejection.

- You interview high-performing sales team members Bob, Sue, and Mark based on some of the "Questions to Ask a Subject Matter Expert" shared earlier in this chapter. Here are examples of some of the responses:

- You: Was there a moment when you had an "aha" when you realized how to deal with rejection?

- Sue: I had a mentor when I first started in sales. She said to me: "The person doing the most talking is the person who is most committed in the process. I learned quickly that sales is about asking questions and getting the customers to talk about their problems. It's definitely not about me doing all the talking."

- You: If there were "one thing" that most sales people don't get about dealing with rejection, what would it be?

- Mark: It's not always about you. Yes, people buy from people they like. But there has to be a connection between their problems and our solutions. When I don't make a sale, I know that the connection wasn't there. Rather than beat myself up, I ask myself if I could have dug deeper into figuring out where their pain lies.

- You: When you picture how dealing with rejection plays in being a high-performing sales person, what image comes to mind?

- Bob: I see it like a roadmap. We have a lot of products to offer a customer. When I ask a question, they might say "yes" and they might say "no." Either way, it tells me which direction I need to go.

- You: What advice would you give to a new sales person on how to deal with rejection?

- Bob: Every time a customer tells me "no" in response to an offer, I get clearer on what they might say "yes" to. You have to think of each answer as a clue that tells you which way to go next. You have to learn to read each response as a sign that points you in the right direction.

In your interviews with the high-performing sales people, you determine that one thing that all of these performers have in common related to dealing with rejection is that they view rejection as an integral part of the sales process. You determine that this ability to find value in both positive and negative responses from customers will be the focus of your course design.

Engage: Delivering the Value Outcome

In Chapter 4, we explored what the learner and trainer are doing in the first step of the learning cycle, Engage. In this step, the trainer plays the role of "facilitator" and uses reflection and dialogue to connect the learners to what they already know about the content and establish personal relevance. Here the trainer introduces the big idea, or concept, that subject matter experts appreciate that leads to learner engagement in the topic being explored.

For example, in this sales training course example learners might be asked to reflect on early experiences in "selling" something and being faced with rejection.

Learners describe that experience in small table groups and answer the following questions:

- What were the commonalities in your experiences?
- How did this experience shape your view of "selling"?

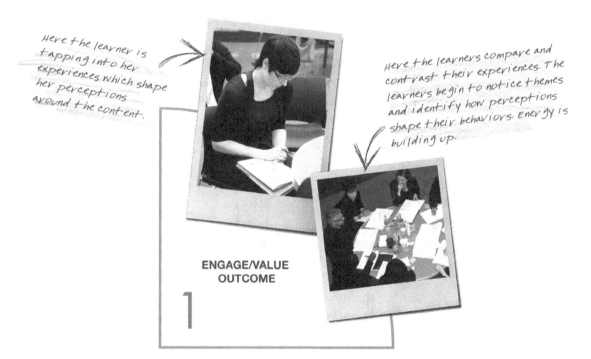

Here the learner is tapping into her experiences which shape her perceptions around the content.

Here the learners compare and contrast their experiences. The learners begin to notice themes and identify how perceptions shape their behaviors. Energy is building up.

ENGAGE/VALUE OUTCOME

1

Share: Delivering the Knowledge Outcome

In Chapter 5, we explored what the learner and trainer are doing in the second step of the learning cycle, Share. In this step, the trainer plays the role of "presenter" and shares the knowledge and resources needed to prepare the learners to apply the skills. The opportunity for the learners to see the bigger picture and how all the content fits together is created.

In this sales training example, learners might be asked to use materials provided by the facilitator to create a visual which illustrates how positive and negative feedback from a potential "buyer" impact their sales approach. Imagine a learner sharing a visual with "positive = negative" written across the paper chart while sharing a comment such as, "Positive and negative cues from a buyer give me equal value. Each points me in the right direction."

In this part of the learning cycle, the trainer shares the "meaty" content of the training program in an engaging, multi-modal lecture format. In this sales training course example, the facilitator shares a lecture on "Redirecting Negative Responses from the Customer."

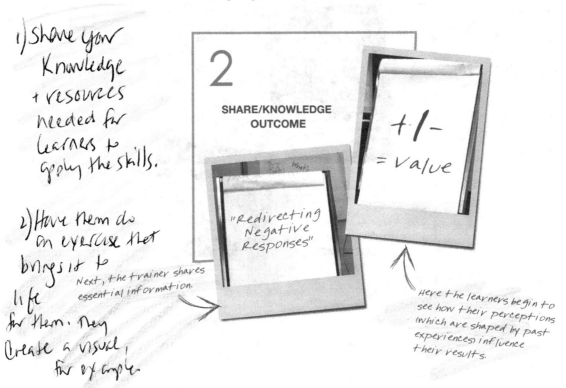

1) Share your Knowledge + resources needed for learners to apply the skills.

2) Have them do an exercise that brings it to life for them. They create a visual, for example.

2

SHARE/KNOWLEDGE OUTCOME

"Redirecting Negative Responses"

+/− = value

Next, the trainer shares essential information.

Here the learners begin to see how their perceptions (which are shaped by past experiences) influence their results.

Practice: Delivering the Skill Outcome

In Chapter 6, we explored in detail what the trainer and learner are doing in the third part of the learning cycle, Practice. In this step, the trainer plays the role of "coach" and creates an opportunity for the learners to practice the necessary skills needed to deliver the desired behavior.

In this sales training example, learners are asked to check their understanding of how common sales objections link to the need for more information by playing a competitive game which requires matching of customer responses to the appropriate next step in the sales process. Next, learners form teams of three and role play common sales scenarios. Learners take turns playing the role of sales person, customer, and observer while practicing "redirecting" skills.

Learners apply content to real-life problems.

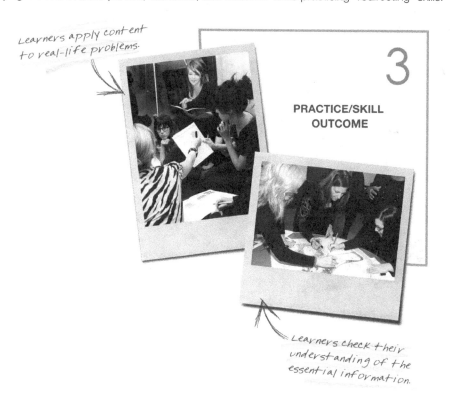

3

PRACTICE/SKILL OUTCOME

Learners check their understanding of the essential information.

Perform: Delivering the Adaptation Outcome

In Chapter 7, we explored in detail what the trainer and the learner are doing in the fourth and final part of the learning cycle, Perform. In this step, the trainer plays the role of "evaluator" and creates an opportunity for the learners to assess and adapt their performance. In this final step, the trainer gains commitment for post-training action and establishes follow-up commitments.

In this sales training example, learners are asked to assess their application of the redirect questioning technique using the self-assessment tool provided by the trainer. Learners receive feedback from fellow learners and refine their approach. Learners commit to using their refined approach with each customer in the coming week and plan to share their results with their manager in a previously scheduled follow-up session. Prior to the training, all managers received a "Follow-Up Action Plan," which includes how to lead the follow-up session and coaching tips to improve results.

Lead follow-up sessions

Learners commit to an agreed-upon action plan.

PERFORM/ADAPTATION OUTCOME

4

Learners self-assess their application.

4MAT DESIGN

The complete 4MAT-based instructional design for this course might look like this:

PERFORM/ADAPTATION
OUTCOME

ENGAGE/VALUE
OUTCOME

4 | 1

3 | 2

PRACTICE/SKILL
OUTCOME

SHARE/KNOWLEDGE
OUTCOME

Summary

Many trainers share with us a desire to move from training "order taking" to true "performance consulting." Encouraging training stakeholders to invest time in defining the true performance issue is the first step. This chapter is a basic introduction to this process. For more in-depth resources on how to lead the needs analysis process, visit the companion site to this book.

What questions have you used during the training request intake process that have helped you shape your outcomes?

What questions will you add to your needs analysis process?

Which outcome is most often missing in training designs you have seen, created, or experienced? Why do you think it is missed?

Reflect on an area of mastery that you possess.

Review a recent training design you have created. Were all four outcomes addressed in the design? If not, which were missing?

PERFORMANCE OUTCOME　　　　　　　　**VALUE OUTCOME**

SKILL OUTCOME　　　　　　　　**KNOWLEDGE OUTCOME**

"You get what you measure. Measure the wrong thing and you get the wrong behaviors."

~John H. Lingle

Chapter 10
Assessment: Integrating Measurement into Training Design and Delivery

A well-structured assessment plan helps identify the value of the learning experiences you create. The insights gained through measurement of learning impact will help you refine the design of the experience and clearly articulate the value generated to stakeholders.

An effective assessment strategy:

- Reinforces the learning
- Creates an opportunity for learners to identify what they have learned
- Celebrates new knowledge and skills gained
- Measures the value generated in the learning experience

This chapter will examine how to structure an effective assessment plan and provide concrete examples of appropriate assessment strategies and data collection tools.

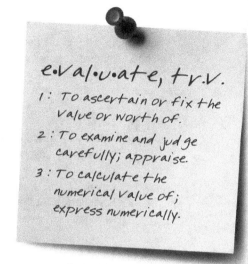

e·val·u·ate, tr.v.

1 : To ascertain or fix the value or worth of.

2 : To examine and judge carefully; appraise.

3 : To calculate the numerical value of; express numerically.

Evaluating at Four Levels

In Chapter 9, we introduced the concept of defining the four learning outcomes before designing a learning experience. The value, knowledge, skill, and adaptation outcomes defined at the front end of the instructional design process guide activity choice within the design process. The stated outcomes also serve as the basis of your assessment strategy. When developing your assessment strategy, think about how you will measure learning at all four levels. Here is the focus of assessment at each level:

Level 1
Value: At the value level, you are assessing the shift in values, perceptions, and beliefs of the learners. Level of commitment and engagement is the measurement focus.

Level 2
Knowledge: At the knowledge level, you are assessing the knowledge gained by the learners. Pre- versus post-knowledge gain is measurement focus.

Level 3
Skill: At the skill level, you are assessing the degree of competence the learner has attained in the critical skills related to the desired performance outcome. Competency attainment, consistency of execution, and quality of execution is the measurement focus.

Level 4
Adaptation: At the adaptation level, you are assessing the results generated as a result of the learning experience. Business impact is the measurement focus.

In this chapter, we will explore how to include all four levels of evaluation in your learning experience design.

"On-the-Way" Versus "At-the-Gate" Assessment

When you deliver content, you continually assess the impact of the learning experience and you adjust along the way. Before you give learners an advanced task, you likely provide an activity that allows you to determine whether the learner has mastered the basics. Creating opportunities to assess learning progress during the learning process is the focus of on-the-way assessment. At the end of a training session, you may choose to administer a comprehensive knowledge test to determine what learners gained from the learning experience. This is a form of "at-the-gate" assessment. Assessing attainment of learning outcomes as a result of completion of a learning experience is the focus of an "at-the-gate" assessment. An effective assessment plan should include both on-the-way and at-the-gate assessment strategies. Take a look at the major differences in these two assessment strategies in the table below:

	"ON-THE-WAY"	"AT-THE-GATE"
When	• Happens during instruction	• Happens after instruction
Frequency	• Happens throughout the learning process	• Happens at natural "end" points, e.g., end-of-module assessments, course completion examinations
Quantifying Results	• Emphasis is not on scoring; rather, focus is on learner self-assessment	• Quantifiable measurement is included
Focus	• Designed to guide instructor in adapting and refining design and delivery methods	• Designed to evaluate level of learning attained and overall impact of the learning experience
Examples	• Problems to be solved • Case studies • Knowledge reviews • Skills practice	• Real-world projects • Certification exams • Final knowledge tests • Observation of learner application on the job • Measurement of application results

In this chapter we offer examples of on-the-way and at-the-gate assessment in each of the four parts of the 4MAT learning cycle. Examples of strategies and tools you can use to develop an effective assessment plan are also offered.

Note that Bloom's taxonomy is referenced to give examples of learning outcome verbs related to each part of the 4MAT Cycle. Bloom's model is a widely used classification system of learning objectives. The outcome verb choice influences the choice of activities used to deliver the desired outcome and the type of assessment strategy needed to determine whether the outcome is achieved. For example, notice how the verb choices of "recall" and "apply" influence the activity choice and assessment strategy in the chart below.

Outcome Statement	Possible Activity Choice	Possible Assessment Strategy
Learners will recall...	Game Show Style Recall Activity	Multiple-Choice Test
Learners will apply...	Simulation	In-field Manager Observation Checklist

Level 1: Value—Evaluating for Learner Reaction

MEASUREMENT FOCUS: LEARNER REACTION, VALUE SHIFT, ATTITUDE, COMMITMENT, ENGAGEMENT

The first level of evaluation focuses on the learners' reaction to the learning experience. Typically, the focus of assessment at this level is on how the learners felt about the experience. You can greatly improve the depth of your assessment by expanding this focus to include the personal shift that happens in the learners. Commitment, engagement, and perceived value are all critical factors that greatly influence the level of implementation.

At this level, your assessment plan should focus on assessing the value the learner places on the ideas shared and the level of commitment to implementation. The table below provides examples of the types of assessment questions and statement completions used in on-the-way and at-the-gate assessment at Level 1.

Level 1 Evaluation Focus	• Assessing Value • The learner must have or develop an appreciation for the value of the content being shared.
Examples of Bloom's Outcome Verbs	• Commit • Accept • Demonstrate value • Adhere • Participate • Apply • Support • Embrace • Engage • Lead • Appreciate • Adapt • Receive • Combine
On-the-Way	• How do you feel about...? • How would you enroll a colleague in the concepts? • What is the benefit or value of applying? • How committed are you to...? • How likely is it that you will use this information in the next _____ (number of days)?
At-the-Gate	• I am feeling.... • On a scale of 1 to 10, I am committed to.... • On a scale of 1 to 5, I enjoyed this learning experience....

ON-THE-WAY EXAMPLES

Trainers have many ways to determine their effectiveness while delivering a learning experience.

Below are some ways to assess learning value generated during the formal learning experience:

- **Quality of Dialogue:** Pay attention to the quality of the interaction between participants. Is the conversation deep or superficial? Are you having to work hard to get the conversation going, or are the learners' interests guiding the conversation?
- **Focus of questions asked:** The types of questions that learners are asking give valuable feedback on the level of engagement. For instance, when learners begin to ask questions about next steps and how they can best apply the information, they are imagining themselves using the information, which is a positive sign.
- **Sense of ownership:** When the learners begin to guide the direction of the learning conversation, a sense of ownership of the learning has emerged.

AT-THE-GATE

In our 4MAT courses we administer a daily feedback form called an "exit slip." The exit slip invites learners to record reaction in all four dimensions of the learning experience: value, knowledge, skill, and adaptation. On the next page is an example of the 4MAT Exit Slip asking learners to complete four statements. It is one example of the type of learner reaction surveys used as part of a Level 1 evaluation strategy.

Example of a Level 1 Feedback Form: Exit Slip

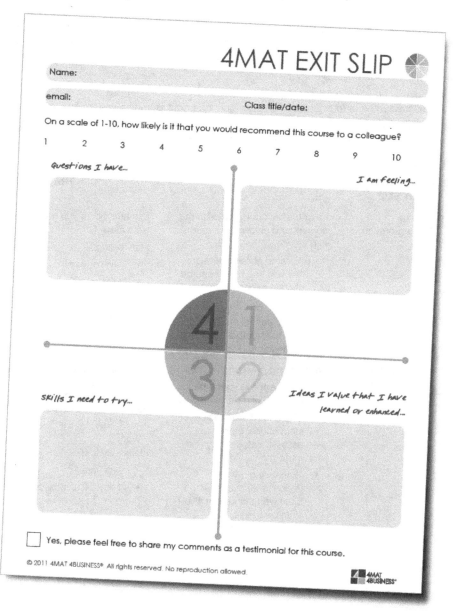

4MAT EXIT SLIP

Name:

email:

Class title/date:

On a scale of 1-10, how likely is it that you would recommend this course to a colleague?

1   2   3   4   5   6   7   8   9   10

Questions I have...

I am feeling...

4 1
3 2

Skills I need to try...

Ideas I value that I have learned or enhanced...

☐ Yes, please feel free to share my comments as a testimonial for this course.

4MAT
4BUSINESS®

Since most of our courses are multi-day programs, the facilitator collects learners' comments at the end of the day and creates slides with the feedback. For example, the beginning slide would have a header of "I am feeling…" with all the comments of learners posted beneath this header (anonymously). At the beginning of the next day's session, the facilitator begins by highlighting the themes uncovered in the exit slips. This is a valuable way to take the "pulse" of the group and determine whether learners are on track.

You can assess whether learners are "on track" or "off track" by paying attention to the comments shared in reaction surveys. Learner feedback often gives the trainer clues on what adjustments are needed in the course delivery or design.

QUADRANT OF THE EXIT SLIP	ON TRACK	OFF TRACK
Value "I am feeling…"	Learners are finding value in the content and enjoying the learning experience. • "Excited about what I am learning and how it can be used in my company." • "Great." • "More confident about how to structure my design approach."	Pay attention if you get comments such as: I am feeling.. • "Overwhelmed" • "Frustrated" • "Bored" • "Like I won't be able to do this.'
Knowledge "Ideas I value…"	Learners are grasping the content. • "I value the research base behind this model." • "That 4MAT extends beyond instructional design to assessment, delivery and performance." • "Enhancing my understanding of how the brain works and how 4MAT aligns with this."	Pay attention if you get comments that indicate that learners are not grasping the big ideas, are confused, or there is lack of interest in the content being explored: Ideas I value… • "Not sure." • "I am still unclear about how to…"

QUADRANT OF THE EXIT SLIP	ON TRACK	OFF TRACK
Skill "Skills I need to try…"	Learners are thinking about where they need to develop competency to implement the learning. • "Bringing in more right-brain stuff—I need to balance my over-use of left-brain strategies." • "Tomorrow, I am going to have to work harder on organizing my lecture better for the 2's."	Pay attention to comments that indicate the learners are uncertain of how they will use the content or where to start. • "I will need to think more about this." • "There is so much, I am not sure where to start."
Adaptation "Questions I have…"	Learners are generating new possibilities around the learning and thinking about how they will need to adapt for successful adaptation. • "What other resources can you provide to help me go further with this? Additional reading?" • "How can I apply this to a large group learning experience of 300+?"	Pay attention to whether the questions being asked are "moving forward" questions or "moving backward" questions. "Moving forward" questions focus on future application of the content, such as those referenced in the column to the left. "Moving backward" questions indicate that learners are unclear or confused and want to revisit content previously covered. • "I still don't understand the model. Why do you start with Step 1?"

Level 2: Knowledge—
Evaluating Knowledge Gained

MEASUREMENT FOCUS: LEVEL OF UNDERSTANDING

The second level of evaluation focuses on identifying the level of knowledge gained by the learner. Typically, the measurement is focused on pre- versus post-training knowledge gain. Effective measurement, at this level, is focused on identifying whether the learner has developed the capabilities to execute the behaviors linked to delivering the desired business impact. The table below provides examples of the types of assessment questions.

Level 2 Evaluation Focus	• Assessing Knowledge • The learners must understand all necessary information to prepare them to apply what is being learned.
Examples of Bloom's Outcome Verbs	• Compare • Describe • Conclude • Discuss • Evaluate • Explain • Combine • Summarize • Categorize • Define • Differentiate • Outline • Illustrate • Match • Interpret • Recall • Organize • Associate
On-the-Way	• What do you recall about…? • Match the term with the definition. • What is your definition of…? • How would you approach this problem using the model shared? • Role play using the skills learned today. • How would you teach this information back to a partner?
At-the-Gate	• Assess your level of knowledge on _____ (example) before this session and after this session. • Knowledge check questions in multiple-choice, true/false, and open-ended formats.

ON-THE-WAY EXAMPLES

As discussed in Chapter 6, the trainer's focus in Share is on delivering the essential knowledge the learners need to understand in order to apply the information in the real world.

Below are some techniques to assess the level of understanding learners are gaining during information delivery:

- **Game show reviews:** Game show–style activities create an opportunity for the trainer to reinforce key ideas and make sure that learners understand important terms and concepts.
- **Teach backs:** Periodically inviting learners to reprocess information by teaching it to a partner or group is an effective way to check for understanding.
- **Creating mock test questions:** Pausing periodically throughout a training program and inviting learners to create one question for a mock test on the subject being learned is another way to encourage learners to identify big ideas. You can also collect the questions and use them for a game show review later in the course.

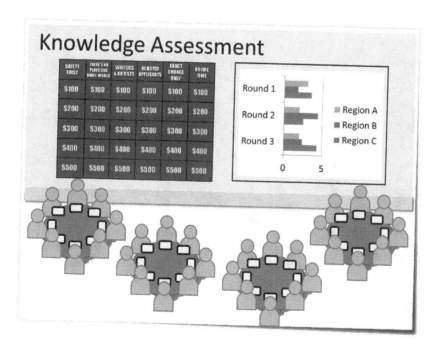

AT-THE-GATE EXAMPLES

Pre- and post-knowledge checks are a common form of measurement at Level 2 in order to assess the learners' gain of knowledge. Beyond providing proof of learning, pre- and post-knowledge checks give a trainer valuable information on the design of the learning program.

Rather than simply looking at the overall scores of learners, think about diving deeper into the results and assessing knowledge gain on each question in the assessment. When you review the pre- versus post-knowledge scoring by individual question, valuable insight is gained that will inform you about how the course design or content may need to be refined.

For example, take a look at the graph below. In this graph, the percent of learners who answered each question correctly in the pre- and post-knowledge check is compared.

Notice the following:

A. On Question 4, 100 percent of learners answered this correctly in the pre-test.

B. On Questions 6, 9, and 10, no noticeable improvement was made.

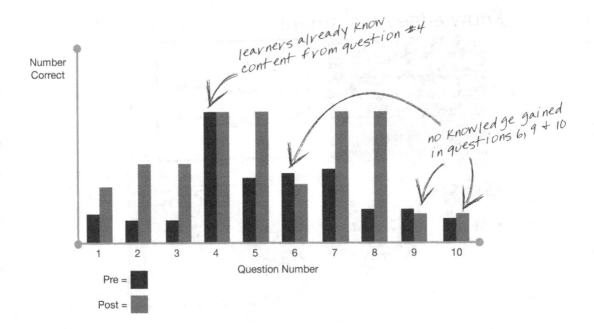

This feedback would prompt the trainer and instructional designer to review both content and delivery. On Question 4, it might be possible to remove this content from the course or invest less time in delivery. On Questions 6, 9, and 10, the way the content was covered might need to be re-examined and adjusted.

EXAMPLE OF A PRE- AND POST-KNOWLEDGE CHECK

You can administer a knowledge check before the formal learning experience to assess current level of knowledge. After completion of the learning experience, the same assessment tool can be administered again to determine knowledge gain.

EFFECTIVENESS OF COURSE TRAINER	Strongly disagree 1	2	3	4	Strongly agree 5	Didn't cover
10. Provided a well-organized presentation	☐	☐	☐	☐	☐	☐
11. Communicated material in clear and simple language	☐	☐	☐	☐	☐	☐
12. Provided appropriate examples relevant to Child Welfare	☐	☐	☐	☐	☐	☐
13. Trainer motivated me to incorporate new ideas into practice	☐	☐	☐	☐	☐	☐
14. I would recommend this training to a co-worker	☐	☐	☐	☐	☐	☐

EFFECTIVENESS OF PRESENTATION	Not effective				Very effective	
15. Material was presented in multiple formats:	1	2	3	4	5	Didn't use
a) Lecture	☐	☐	☐	☐	☐	☐
b) Facilitated discussion	☐	☐	☐	☐	☐	☐
c) Small group breakouts	☐	☐	☐	☐	☐	☐

EXAMPLE OF A PRE- AND POST-KNOWLEDGE GAINED SELF-ASSESSMENT

You can combine the pre- and post-knowledge check by administering a self-assessment survey at the completion of the learning experience. The survey should invite learners to assess their knowledge "before training" and "after training."

BEFORE TRAINING	SELF-ASSESSMENT OF KNOWLEDGE AND SKILLS RELATED TO:	AFTER TRAINING
1 2 3 4	Assessing the learning style of learners.	1 2 3 4
1 2 3 4	Understanding my learning style strengths.	1 2 3 4
1 2 3 4	Defining four critical learning outcomes: value, knowledge, skill, and adaptation.	1 2 3 4
1 2 3 4	Understanding what is happening in the four parts of the learning cycle: Engage, Share, Practice, and Perform.	1 2 3 4
1 2 3 4	Choosing activities that appeal to all learning styles.	1 2 3 4
1 2 3 4	Including "on-the-way" and "at-the-gate" assessment.	1 2 3 4
1 2 3 4	Designing a 4MAT instructional design.	1 2 3 4
1 2 3 4	Defining an assessment strategy for my instructional design.	1 2 3 4
1 2 3 4	Evaluating training at different levels of evaluation.	1 2 3 4

Level 3: Skill—Evaluating Skills Gained

MEASUREMENT FOCUS: COMPETENCIES GAINED, CONSISTENCY OF EXECUTION, QUALITY OF EXECUTION

The third level of evaluation focuses on the learners' skill in applying the information. Typically, the focus of assessment is on measuring the degree of mastery of the learners in key competency areas. A solid measurement plan assesses whether learners consistently execute the behaviors required to generate the desired business impact. Assessment strategies may include self-assessment, peer assessment, customer surveys, and assessment by a leader or coach. The table below provides examples of the types of assessment questions and statement completions used in on-the-way and at-the-gate assessment at Level 3.

Level 3 Evaluation Focus	• Assessing skill • The learner must acquire the necessary techniques and skills to demonstrate the desired behaviors in the real-world environment.
Examples of Bloom's Outcome Verbs	• Consistently apply • Demonstrate • Demonstrate • Re-enact • Generate • Role play • Master • Script • Perform • Simulate • Adjust
On-the-Way	• What worked well in this case study? • What went wrong in this case study? • How might you combine this model with your current approach? • What solutions can be generated for this problem? • Demonstrate how you would apply…. • Role play your approach to….
At-the-Gate	• In-field observation tracking tools • Project portfolios • Customer surveys

ON-THE-WAY EXAMPLES

In the third part of the learning cycle, Practice, learners apply the information being learned. When you create an opportunity for the learners to assess their success at application, you empower learners to make distinctions that support them as they continue to develop content mastery. Incorporate self-assessment and action planning by using a tool such as the Action Planning Tool.

Action Planning Tool

TRAINER COMPETENCIES	I HAVE LOW STRENGTH IN THIS AREA	I HAVE HIGH STRENGTH IN THIS AREA	WAYS I WILL BUILD STRENGTH IN THIS AREA
I am comfortable using questions to generate meaningful learner dialogue.		✓	
I can use strategies to focus learner conversation on the learning topics.	✓		*I will practice using visual tools to capture the comments of learners such as mindmapping the expectations of a group.*
I am comfortable using facilitation techniques to identify the themes emerging in the learners' dialogue.	✓		*I need to work on identifying a task for the learners that encourages them to figure out the commonalities in their experiences.* *I will incorporate paper chart tasks that encourage learners to identify the common themes showing up in their experiences.*

AT-THE-GATE EXAMPLES

A measurement of the competencies gained should be part of a Level 3 at-the-gate assessment. Developing a list of competencies needed to generate the desired learning impact can be an effective self-assessment tool for learners. Think about how you can engage the on-the-job support team to implement the assessment on the job.

Example of a Competency Assessment Tool

Skill Area: Understanding the learning styles of others.	1	2	3	4	5
Using the four questions to develop a presentation.	1	2	3	4	5
Including activities for each learning style.	1	2	3	4	5
Beginning by defining the four outcomes my design should achieve.	1	2	3	4	5

USING SOCIAL MEDIA IN LEVEL 3 EVALUATION

There are many creative ways to use social media to assess information application by your learners. Here are a couple of examples:

- **Blog post.** In a training course for property and casualty claims adjustors, participants were trained in how to assess water and fire structural damage. As part of the post-training evaluation, adjustors were asked to videotape the damage they assessed in real-world on-site visits. Adjustors posted the videos of structural damage observed to a private course forum, along with comments on how they assessed the damage and their reasoning. Instructors monitored the forum and provided feedback.

- **Discussion board in SharePoint®.** As part of the assessment strategy for a course on "Effective Communication," a discussion board was created within SharePoint. (SharePoint is a Microsoft product that allows an organization to host intranet-based web pages.) Course participants posted their communication goals in the discussion board. Within the first two weeks of the course, participants were asked to review their goals with their manager and receive feedback and needed approval for resources. Every two weeks for 90 days, participants were asked to post progress updates in response to discussion posts. E-learning modules were delivered via the company's learning management system to support execution of goals. SharePoint was programmed to automatically generate updates to participants to generate postings. Bi-weekly, managers received a report on participation percentages by manager and by department on posting requirements and completion of e-learning modules.

Level 4: Adaptation—Evaluating Performance and Business Impact

MEASUREMENT FOCUS: BUSINESS IMPACT AND RESULTS

The ultimate measure of the success of a learning initiative is rooted in the defined performance outcome. At the fourth level of evaluation, the focus is on measuring the business outcomes generated as a result of the learning experience. The table provides examples of the types of assessment questions and statement completions used in on-the-way and at-the-gate assessment at Level 4.

Level 4 Evaluation Focus	• Assessing adaptation and performance • The learner must be able to adjust, refine, and adapt in different situations to successfully apply and continuously improve the application of the information.
Examples of Bloom's Outcome Verbs	• Adapt • Grade • Assess • Measure • Evaluate • Rank • Consistently apply • Integrate • Produce • Generate results • Solve • Master • Interpret • Synthesize
On-the-Way	• Develop assessment criteria to evaluate your application. • Describe what "good," "better," and "best" application looks like. • Develop an action plan for implementing this information. • What do you think is the best thing about your plan? • What does your plan need most? • What are the three most important actions that must be executed to achieve success? • How might you integrate the new behaviors learned with your current approach?
At-the-Gate	• Tracking business metrics linked to results

A self-assessment tool can be administered before a learning session and guide

4MAT learning styles

Note: This part of the workshop is designed to get your team engaged at a personal level. The dialogue and "personal-ness" of the content particularly appeals to Type 1 Learners.

assessing your current reality

		good	better	best
Financial Performance	I review the financial reports of my company...	within 21 days of month end.	within 14 days of month end.	within 7 days of month end.
	Utilizing a cash flow planner:	I create a 12-month plan and update monthly.	I create a 12-month plan, update monthly with actuals and adjust for differences.	I create a 12-month plan, update monthly, adjust actuals and communicate our goals with the team.
Sales Drivers	I project sales growth by analyzing service and retail opportunity...	by projecting a % increase.	by comparing actual against benchmarks.	by analyzing individual performance vs. benchmark, as well as team performance.
	I review my salon software sales reports...	monthly.	weekly.	daily.
Operations	Job descriptions and clarity on roles:	All roles are defined.	All roles are defined with clear measures.	All roles are defined with measurable daily results for accountability.
Training and Performance	Training program links directly to desired financial results:	Our monthly meetings focus on the key sales opportunities.	Our training is focused on the key business opportunity. Team meetings and individual coaching focus on the key behaviors that will deliver results.	Our training is focused on the key business opportunity. Team meetings, individual coaching and technical training focus on key behaviors that will deliver results.
Measurement and Results	I communicate actual results to goal...	in monthly staff meetings.	in daily huddles.	in daily huddles with a clear link to behaviors needed.
	I conduct one-on-one performance coaching sessions with service providers...	quarterly.	monthly.	weekly.

optimizing the 5 key sales drivers

AT-THE-GATE EXAMPLES

- **Manager observation checklist.** A manager or coach observation checklist can help focus the on-the-job training team on following up on the learner's action plan. An example of a job aid for coaches of participants included in our asynchronous 4MAT instructional design course is on page 230. This is a one-page job aid designed to support coaches in implementing action items and leading coaching conversations. Notice that the coach is directed to perform specific follow-up actions.

- **Tracking and celebrating results.** To deliver Level 4 evaluation, you must link learner behaviors to positive business results. Consider how you might track both behaviors and associated business metrics. Celebrate results by posting individual and group progress. Involve managers by acknowledging which learners are implementing behaviors and generating results.

- **Projects.** Define projects on which learners can put newly learned skills to use. Choose projects that will generate measurable business impact.

HOW TO DETERMINE WHAT LEVEL OF EVALUATION YOU MUST DELIVER

In a recent survey, organizations were asked to assess which levels of evaluation they use to any extent.

The reporting organizations shared the following:

- Using Level 1 evaluation: 92 percent
- Using Level 2 evaluation: 81 percent
- Using Level 3 evaluation: 55 percent
- Using Level 4 evaluation: 34 percent

The higher the level of evaluation, the more planning and effort required to measure. Sometimes, the expectations of training sponsors will require that you deliver evaluation at all four levels. For example, if the expectation from training sponsors of a train-the-trainer course for subject matter experts is that participants will be able to generate higher learning retention of the content they are teaching, then Level 4 evaluation will be required. However, if the expectation is simply that participants will value and understand learning style differences, a Level 2 evaluation will suffice. In the table, you can see how the focus of the learning experience determines how deep the assessment strategy must go.

EXPECTATION	OUTCOME LEVEL	FOCUS OF THE LEARNING EXPERIENCE	PRIMARY FOCUS OF ASSESSMENT STRATEGY
Learners will value and understand the differences in learning styles.	• Level 1: Value • Level 2: Knowledge	• Create an experience that develops appreciation for the unique value each learning style brings.	• Level 1: Participant reaction surveys • Level 2: Pre- and post-knowledge check
Learners will be able to apply strategies to engage all learning styles in a presentation.	• Level 1: Value • Level 2: Knowledge • Level 3: Skill	• Equip learners to address the needs of all four learning styles in a learning experience.	• Level 1: Engagement results of learners • Level 2: Pre- and post-knowledge check • Level 3: Engagement scores of learning workshop participants • Level 3: Skill assessment on ability to apply the model to learning experience design
Learners will improve engagement and learning results by reaching all learning styles in a presentation.	• Level 1: Value • Level 2: Knowledge • Level 3: Skill • Level 4: Adaptation and Performance	• Equip learners to engage all learning styles while targeting key learning behaviors.	• Level 1: Participant reaction surveys • Level 2: Pre- and post-knowledge check • Level 3: Skill assessment on ability to apply the model

Summary

A strong assessment strategy enables the trainer to correct along the way. It also includes metrics that can be assessed to determine the value generated through the learning intervention. When choosing activities for your instructional design, think about how each activity will deliver "proof of learning."

Before you begin the design process, it is important that you clearly define the desired results of the learning experience. Clarifying stakeholder expectations and defining measurable learning outcomes are the first steps in enabling effective activity choice.

With a clear vision of the desired results you intend to create, you can intentionally craft a learning experience that transforms the learner and generates lasting learning results. In the final section of this book, you will find case studies sharing how other organizations have successfully used the 4MAT model to create learning results. In the "Next Steps" section, you will find how you can continue to grow your skill in 4MAT. We look forward to hearing of your successes.

Are my assessments:

Linked to the defined learning outcomes for the course?

Connected to meaningful learning targets?

Integrated within the "flow" of the instructional design, rather than separate from it?

Easy to administer?

Easy to score?

Providing valuable feedback that guides instructional design and delivery?

Linked to the scaling criteria or rubrics I provide to learners in lecture?

REFLECT

ACT

What new assessment strategies will I include in my next training design and delivery?

ENGAGE	SHARE	PRATICE	PERFORM
On-the-Way:	**On-the-Way**	**On-the-Way**	**On-the-Way**
☐ Personal sharing	☐ Game show style reviews	☐ Role play	☐ Quality of action planning
☑ Assessing quality of small group dialogue	☐ Knowledge check activities	☐ Projects	☐ Assessment of commitment
☐ Depth of group reporting	☐ Learners generating mock test questions	☐ Case studies	☐ Quality of self-assessment of practice
☐ Prioritization of key issues		☐ Real-world scenarios	☐ Learners' questions generated
At-the-Gate:	**At-the-Gate:**	**At-the-Gate**	**At-the-Gate**
☐ Learner reaction surveys	☐ Pre- and post-knowledge tests	☐ Assessment of learner behavior on the job	☐ Application of action items
☐ Exit slips	☐ Final certification	☐ In-field manager observation forms	☐ Impact on business initiatives
	☐ Demonstrations of knowledge	☐ Metrics on consistency of execution of behaviors, e.g., in-field surveys	

[4MAT] … allows learners to not just absorb information, but interact with it and apply it immediately, with the ultimate goal of helping them reach their professional and personal potential.

~Shelley Barnes,
Executive Director for Aveda Field Education
and Program Development,
Aveda

USING 4MAT TO CREATE A POINT OF DIFFERENCE THROUGH
ENGAGING EDUCATION EXPERIENCES

Aveda creates high-performance, botanically based products for beauty professionals and consumers worldwide while continuously striving to conduct business in an environmentally sustainable manner.

Why 4MAT? Aveda was seeking a proven method to train technical subject matter experts with no formal instructional training on how to design and deliver engaging learning experiences to their employees and customers around the globe.

CASE STUDY

Headquartered in Blaine, Minnesota, Aveda manufactures innovative, plant-based hair care, skin care, makeup, and lifestyle products, available in Aveda Experience Centers and more than 7,000 professional hair salons and spas in more than 30 countries.

As an industry leader, Aveda is a culture of innovation that is always seeking new, exciting ways to engage and meet the needs of their customers. New products, treatments, and trends require constant training for the thousands of professionals in the Aveda network. Aveda adopted the 4MAT methodology to address critical training issues that many organizations face:

- The need to equip subject matter experts with a simple and effective framework for delivering engaging learning experiences
- The need to eliminate inconsistency and duplication of effort by leveraging training resources across multiple training design and delivery channels
- The desire to create a sustainable point of difference through education by creating a common language for learning shared by Aveda employees and customers

Why 4MAT?
Aveda was seeking a proven method to train technical subject matter experts with no formal instructional training on how to design and deliver engaging learning experiences to their employees and customers around the globe.

EQUIPPING SUBJECT MATTER EXPERTS TO ENGAGE EVERY LEARNING STYLE

Aveda first introduced 4MAT as a tool for educators within the Aveda Institutes—cosmetology and esthiology schools that prepare beauty professionals for licensure. Educators at the Aveda Institutes are subject matter experts with a high level of technical skill. Aveda partnered with the 4MAT 4Business team to develop a customized train-the-trainer curriculum that would equip the educators with effective teaching skills.

Research on 4MAT learning styles across industries consistently indicates a correlation between roles and learning style preferences. When Aveda assessed the Institute learners with the 4MAT Learning Type Measure, the results indicated that the vast majority preferred the Type 3 and Type 4 learning approaches.

Based on this insight, the Aveda team focused on designing a curriculum that appealed to the preferences of their audience while also addressing potential weaker areas. To do this, the curriculum design team moved learners through the complete learning cycle.

Shelley Barnes, Executive Director for Aveda Field Education and Program Development, believes that 4MAT is essential to the success of Aveda's education strategy. "4MAT gives Aveda a consistent framework for curriculum design that engages every learning style—so each learner becomes an active participant and connects with the information in a meaningful way. The result is a dynamic learning environment that allows learners to not just absorb information, but interact with it and apply it immediately, with the ultimate goal of helping them reach their professional and personal potential," says Barnes.

CREATING CONSISTENCY ACROSS TRAINING CHANNELS

In-field education to Aveda customers is delivered through corporate or distributor-led education by subject matter experts. In order to create and maintain consistency in delivery, educators are required to demonstrate a working knowledge of 4MAT. As part of the rigorous educator certification process, potential educators are trained in 4MAT.

Product knowledge, product launch information, technical content, and soft-skills content are all delivered to Aveda educators within the 4MAT training design, complete with visual icons that reference the advanced, eight-step 4MAT model. As a result, the instructional design team, educators, and customers use the shared language of 4MAT to convey information systematically and consistently across the entire Aveda network.

USING 4MAT TO CREATE EDUCATION EXCLUSIVELY FOR SALON/SPA OWNERS AND MANAGERS

To support salon/spa owners and managers in growing sustainable businesses, Aveda offers advanced business education through Aveda™ Business College (ABC). Each ABC course focuses on meeting business benchmarks and running a profitable salon/spa business. In ABC, learners discover their learning styles by completing the 4MAT Learning Type Measure. Once they understand their own learning styles, they are able to consider the learning styles of their team and bring the language of 4MAT back to their salon/spa and re-create the dynamic learning experiences created by Aveda.

Lupe Voss, owner of Julian August Salon, completed the 4MAT certification to prepare for her accreditation as one of a select team of global technical educators for Aveda. Voss shares, "I really believe that 4MAT has made me the trainer I am today. It is the tool that every trainer can use to bring out potential in both themselves and their learners. 4MAT helps me speak in different 'learning languages' and serves as a guide for me."

WHAT WE CAN LEARN FROM AVEDA

1. **Understand the learning styles of your audience.** When you understand the learning style preferences of your team and customers, you identify both strengths and potential weaknesses. With an awareness of the weak areas, you can better plan curriculum that supports your audience in implementing for success. This may mean that you pay particular attention to the audience's weaker quadrants in your design approach. For example, if your audience has a low percentage of learners with a Type 3 approach, you might include more action planning tools and job aids.

2. **Create consistency across all training channels.** For large or global companies with many educators, consistency is essential to ensure every learner receives the same information and learning experiences. 4MAT provides a simple, effective framework that makes it easy to train and receive information in a clear, consistent way.

3. **Share the language of 4MAT with your staff and customers.** Consider how your team, company, and customers might benefit from having a common language to share information.

With 4MAT, we could have substantive conversations about the [instructional design and delivery] work we shared.

~David Horth,
Senior Fellow and Senior Designer,
The Center for Creative Leadership

Case Study:
The Center for Creative Leadership

USING 4MAT TO POSITION "DESIGN AS A STRATEGIC ADVANTAGE"

The Center for Creative Leadership (CCL) is a top-ranked, global provider of leadership education. The CCL faculty of over 550 offers leadership programs in the Americas, Europe, and Asia.

Why 4MAT? CCL was looking for a solid instructional design model that their entire faculty of experienced learning professionals could embrace as a common methodology to enable collaboration.

CASE STUDY

The Center for Creative Leadership (CCL) is a top-ranked, global provider of leadership education. The CCL faculty of over 550 offers leadership programs in the Americas, Europe, and Asia. In 2007, CCL adopted the 4MAT model as their global platform for instructional design and delivery. With a vision of establishing their needs analysis and instructional design approach as a competitive advantage, CCL implemented a four-step approach to bring 4MAT into their culture:

Step 1: Create a common language for design and delivery
Step 2: Assess existing programs through the lens of 4MAT
Step 3: Design a peer review process
Step 4: Create a design database enabled through the common language of 4MAT

CCL was looking for a "container" to hold and organize the 40+ years of experience of their vast faculty of over 1,100 global faculty and team members. Many of the faculty members of CCL have a background in the academic teaching environment and/or instructional design. CCL was lacking an agreed-upon common design methodology that would enable efficient collaboration. To accelerate the design, testing, and delivery feedback process, CCL was looking for a way to standardize their approach to both public and custom course design.

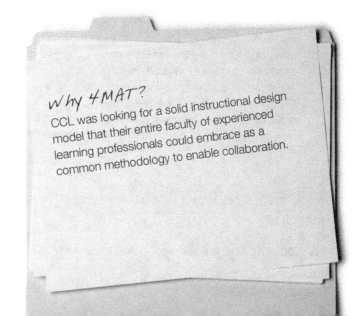

Why 4MAT?
CCL was looking for a solid instructional design model that their entire faculty of experienced learning professionals could embrace as a common methodology to enable collaboration.

STEP 1: CREATE A COMMON LANGUAGE FOR DESIGN AND DELIVERY

To facilitate the training of the global faculty, 4MAT 4Business® certified a core group of CCL trainers to deliver the 4MAT 2.5-day Advanced Instructional Design course. In the course, faculty members discovered their learning and training style strengths and gained a high level of competency in applying the eight-step 4MAT instructional design model. This team was equipped with the tools and content needed to train the global faculty over the next 18 months. David Horth, Senior Fellow and Senior Designer and one of the 4MAT CCL Certified trainers, shares the following story:

"As we trained our design and delivery faculty in 4MAT, one of the more senior faculty members shared with the whole class that this was the best internal training he had experienced in CCL and that what made it the best was that it provided us with a common language for talking about the designs we create. With 4MAT, we could have substantive conversations about the work we shared."

STEP 2: ASSESS EXISTING PROGRAMS THROUGH THE LENS OF 4MAT

With a common language for collaboration, the CCL team began to assess the existing strengths of their curriculum. In a series of practice "lab" sessions, the design team used the 4MAT coaching tools provided to assess the strengths of each program. As a research-based organization, CCL is known for delivering strong, proven methodology. Looking through the lens of 4MAT, the CCL Program Development team identified a high strength in knowledge sharing (Share). The models and information shared in their courses are well-researched, proven, and well-documented. Davida Sharpe, Director of Programs and Services, Global Product Development, led the process of enhancing the CCL core course offerings. Davida shares the following:

"After an intense assessment of our offerings from a design perspective, we realized that we may have overplayed our strength in providing people with knowledge (Quadrant 2—Share) and that we needed to increase the amount of time we give participants to practice and apply the knowledge (Quadrant 3—Practice). 4MAT gave us a common language and frame for being equally adept at designing both the "know-how" and "how to" of leadership development. In fact, an epiphany that many of us have had with all of our experience, education, and training is that activity doesn't necessarily equal application. Unless your objective is to teach learners how to discuss or create dialogue, a 'talking, discussing activity' is not necessarily one that provides learners with adequate practice to develop the capability you're trying to develop."

STEP 3: Design a Peer Review Process

In addition to the public course offerings of CCL, the faculty consults with organizations to develop custom leadership development curriculum. The CCL team is one of the top 10 global providers of custom leadership education programs. One of the most common issues trainers share in 4MAT courses is the challenge of how to help clients (both internal and external) identify the right content to be included in a course design. More often than not, clients show up with clear opinions of what the training program should look like. The CCL team began to use the four key learning outcomes (described in Chapter 9) to guide the interaction with clients in the design process. This is where the opportunity to demonstrate value shows up and the concept of "design as strategic advantage" becomes apparent.

To ensure consistency and facilitate skill development, the CCL design and delivery directors created a peer review process in which proposed custom designs by faculty are reviewed by peers through the lens of 4MAT.

STEP 4: CREATE A DESIGN DATABASE

The common language of 4MAT enabled CCL to develop a shared database of designs. Each course is captured using the 4MAT framework, which enables designers to quickly review the design and understand what they are seeing.

SUMMARY

Learner satisfaction scores and overall client satisfaction improved immediately as a result of the enhancements to existing programs, particularly redesign of the Engage portion of courses.

The CCL Global Faculty continues to build upon the 4MAT foundational skills learned. Newly hired faculty members participate in the 4MAT 4Business® Online Instructional Design Fundamentals Course to get "onboard" with the 4MAT model and become fluent in the "language" of design shared by the CCL team. The CCL 4MAT-certified trainers receive advanced training in courses such as "Leading the Training Needs Analysis Process" and "4MAT 4Delivery." The CCL 4MAT trainers provide advanced skill development for the CCL Global Faculty by delivering these courses globally.

WHAT WE CAN LEARN FROM CCL

1. **Begin with a critical mass of committed team members.** A handful of committed team members can quickly animate the power of 4MAT.

2. **When enrolling team members in the value of 4MAT, focus on the idea that 4MAT provides a context for learning that enables a *common language* for learning design and delivery.** When internal team members have differing and valid opinions on methodology, experience shows that most can easily find common ground in the simplicity and research-based credibility of the 4MAT model.

3. **Make a commitment that this is more than the "flavor of the month."** New models, ideas, and strategies for improving learning impact come and go. To sustain 4MAT within your organization, select a core group of trainers to gain advanced teaching and coaching skills through 4MAT certification. Your in-house team can bring deeper and deeper layers of this model to your team, continually enhancing the skill level of the team.

It warms me that from a simple concept you can keep on learning in new areas. There are always new dimensions to it.

~Lars Holmgaard Mersh,
Senior Education Consultant,
Grundfos Pumps

USING 4MAT TO BUILD SALES COMPETENCY

Grundfos is one of the world's leading pump manufacturers with companies in more than 50 countries throughout the world.

Why 4MAT? Grundfos was searching for a learning platform to support development of the The Poul Due Jensen Academy curriculum (PDJA).

CASE STUDY

In 2001, Grundfos invested in their commitment to build sales competencies with the design of a global sales and leadership curriculum. This focus initiated a search for a learning philosophy that could serve as a platform for the design and delivery of the curriculum. The Grundfos faculty was searching for a learning platform that met the following criteria:

* Grounded in sound pedagogy, yet was not complex
* Could be easily adapted by trainers, also outside PDJA
* Could support learning beyond the formal learning environment

WHY 4MAT?

In 2000, Grundfos chose 4MAT as their model and began building competency in applying 4MAT. The Academy completed 4MAT certification and began the work of designing the global curriculum. The process of moving from basic to advanced application of 4MAT began with the team's awareness that Grundfos was very good at "what-how" teaching with room for improvement in "why-if." The momentum around building skill in 4MAT accelerated as the training team began to see immediate results in both learner reaction and learning results. Lars Holmgaard Mersh, Senior Learning Consultant at Grundfos, shares, "As you start practicing it, you can very quickly sense the difference when you are more 'full circle' rather than 'what-how,' as we used to be. You can see that it gives results. Your own motivation grows very fast."

Why 4MAT?
Grundfos was searching for a learning platform to support development of the The Poul Due Jensen Academy curriculum (PDJA).

SHARING A COMMON LANGUAGE OF LEARNING

With companies in more than 50 countries, building a common language for learning was critical. 4MAT became a shared language amongst trainers globally in Grundfos. "If you were to listen in, you might think .... 'Wow, what language are they speaking?' It is a tribal language, I suppose," shares Mersh.

Global Grundfos trainers are introduced to the 4MAT language as they participate in the PDJA "The Grundfos Trainer". The "tribal" language of learning and performance began to spread as Academy participants discovered their learning style preferences using the Learning Type Measure. Line Wilgaard Wittrup, Learning Consultant at Grundfos, shares, "It is a language we use to understand our individual and team preferences."

MOVING FROM BASIC TO ADVANCED SKILL IN 4MAT

For over 10 years, PDJA trainers have experienced basic- to advanced-level skill development in 4MAT. "What I like is that you keep on discovering things. In terms of getting enlightenment as you go through the years. You keep learning with 4MAT. It warms me that from a simple concept you can keep on [learning] in new areas. There are always new dimensions to it," shares Mersh.

Skill development in applying 4MAT begins with self-awareness of individual learning strengths. As 4MAT skill grows, the ability to impact performance at broader levels in the organization grows.

- **Foundation for leadership and coaching skill development**—4MAT is a simple framework for leading, managing, coaching, and performance improvement.
- **Model for execution**—the 4MAT four-step model is a framework for getting things done. Project teams can utilize this framework to build a plan and identify potential barriers for successful execution.
- **Improving the impact of training**—4MAT dramatically increases the measurable impact of training by focusing on the essential content and eliminating the non-essential.
- **Framework for engaging others**—the four-step model directly applies to planning meetings, sales presentations, coaching and marketing.
- **Building complementary teams**—team members and leaders can apply 4MAT to communication, conflict resolution, and assembling teams with complementary skill sets.
- **Increase self-awareness**—individuals discover how their natural styles interact with the styles of others

FOCUSING ON THE "WHY" FRAME

In Grundfos speak, the first part of the 4MAT Cycle, Engage, is referred to as the "Why Frame." There is great emphasis on making learning relevant in the hearts and minds of learners in the Grundfos learning culture. The Grundfos team has recognized that without this critical component, learning is less likely to extend into the real world and create business impact. "4MAT is a more wholesome approach and also a constant reassurance that this is going to bring something new. Training does not become an event. Quite often, when you talk instructor-led training, whether online or face-to-face, it is out of context. But, we must address the daily context of participants. The learning is initiated in their hearts and executed in their business context. That's an advantage from having a common language," shares Mersh.

CREATING ENGAGING ONLINE LEARNING EXPERIENCES

The PDJA was tasked with extending the global curriculum into an easily accessible online learning format alongside the classroom learning to build a truly global blended learning architecture. PDJA was committed to maintaining the personal connection to the learning content that begins in the first step of 4MAT. PDJA challenged themselves to develop 4MAT-based designs that moved learners through the entire learning cycle. Line Wilgaard Wittrup shares, "Rather than focusing on the technology, we focused on how the technology could support the learner moving through the complete learning cycle. We asked ourselves 'What is good learning? What elements must be present? 'Only then did we ask, 'How can the online learning features enable this?' This focus enabled PDJA to develop creative strategies for extending offerings into engaging online programs maintaining high learning impact.

As Mersh shares, "You need the full 4MAT circle to perform. People like that. They like performing and they get rewarded for performing."

WHAT WE CAN LEARN FROM GRUNDFOS

1. **Share 4MAT as a performance language.** PDJA embedded 4MAT into their culture. The language spread as global Grundfos trainers experienced 4MAT and the Learning Type Measure in their Academy courses.

2. **Build a professional development plan for instructors and trainers using 4MAT.** From basic awareness of learning styles to organizational performance consulting, 4MAT provides a framework learning professionals can build on to continuously contribute at a higher level.

3. **Focus on the "Why?"** Begin by assessing which parts of the 4MAT learning model you currently emphasize and which parts need greater focus.

4. **Focus on the learning process when designing online learning.** Focus on leading learners through the complete learning cycle when designing online learning. Consider how you can extend effective classroom learning strategies using the features available in the online learning environment.

It is not over-reaching to say
that adopting the 4MAT model
can transform an organization's
training department.

~Brian Johnson,
Director of Corporate Training and Development,
Holland America Lines

Case Study:
Holland America Line®

USING 4MAT TO ENGAGE A DIVERSE AUDIENCE

Holland America Line is a recognized leader in the cruise industry. Holland America Line's fleet offers more than 500 cruises annually to 350 ports in more than 100 countries.

WHY 4MAT?

Holland America Line was seeking a solution for delivering engaging learning experiences to an international, multi-cultural, and multi-lingual audience.

CASE STUDY

Holland America Line (HAL) was looking for a platform for instruction that would enable their team to deliver engaging learning experiences to an international, multi-cultural, and multi-lingual audience. In 2007, Brian Johnson, Director of Corporate Training and Development, discovered the 4MAT model and recognized that the simplicity and interactive nature of 4MAT would appeal to the audience his team served.

DESIGNING AN OUTCOME-BASED CURRICULUM

The process of bringing 4MAT into the Holland culture began with advanced training on the application of the eight-step 4MAT model. Soon after the initial training, the team began development on a company-wide leadership and professional development curriculum for a catalog of 36 shoreside courses. The team used the 4MAT framework to build an integrated, outcome-based learning experience. "By using 4MAT to construct a course to the specific needs of all learners, the effectiveness of each module is increased significantly. In the model, the learner has the opportunity to practice, refine and extend their learning, and this provides a measurable way to determine if participants have grasped new concepts and to identify if learners are prepared to apply the new information in the workplace," shares Brian Johnson.

One of the advantages of understanding and using the language of 4MAT is the flexibility and speed gained in design. As the team developed curriculum, they identified which steps in the design could be treated as unique "learning objects" that could be easily customized for different audiences. The flexibility of the 4MAT model allowed for the same concepts to be delivered in a variety of ways as audiences changed, while

Why 4MAT?
Holland America Line was seeking a solution for delivering engaging learning experiences to an international, multi-cultural, and multi-lingual audience.

EQUIPPING DELIVERY TEAM MEMBERS TO REACH ALL LEARNING STYLES

"We recognize one of the keys to training success is ensuring the facilitators are familiar with the design of the curriculum ... and fully understanding the 4MAT framework is key. The training team at Holland America are avid users of 4MAT and have been through the train-the-trainer courses offered by 4MAT 4Business. We licensed a shortened version to ensure the HAL facilitators are prepared to instruct any class. This training has been incorporated into the standard Holland America Train-the-Trainer program, which is attended by all incoming team members, as well as shipboard and shoreside trainers throughout the company," shares Johnson.

Understanding how the trainer's natural approach can be adapted to reach all learning styles has accelerated the skill development of the training team. "The Learning Type Measure is a key component of teaching facilitators about the 4MAT methodology. We have found when people understand the other three learning styles, not just their primary, they become more effective facilitators," shares Jaime Seba, Manager of Training and Development.

"While the course offering is newly launched, feedback on the new 4MAT-based program has been extraordinarily positive. Each course has an associated action plan which is supported by the learner's supervisor. Integrating front-line leaders into the training process has extended the 'Perform' part of the learning process into the real world. Demand for internal training and performance consulting has increased significantly as a result of the positive impact of the new curriculum," states Johnson.

The success of the new curriculum has been overwhelming, as more than 35 percent of corporate employees voluntarily attended training in the four months following the program's launch. Of those who attended, more than half returned for a second course or more.

According to Johnson, "It is not over-reaching to say that adopting the 4MAT model can transform an organization's training department."

WHAT WE CAN LEARN FROM HOLLAND AMERICA LINE

1. **Equip your delivery team with training in 4MAT.** When delivering "around the wheel," the trainer plays four very different roles: facilitator, presenter, coach, and evaluator. Build a long-term development plan that supports team members in building skill in all four roles.

2. **Use the model to build flexibility into your curriculum design.** When working on large-scale curriculum projects, make sure that all involved parties understand the language of 4MAT. This will help accelerate the design process. Think of the activities within each step of the 4MAT model as a "learning object" that serves a particular learning function. You can easily customize curriculum for different audiences by offering alternate activities.

3. **Involve front-line managers in "pushing" learning out into the real world.** When designing the "Perform" step, involve front-line managers in supporting implementation and measuring learner success.

How do you plan to maximize your strengths to create engaging learning experiences?

STEP 1—IDENTIFY YOUR STRENGTHS

Take the FREE online Training Style Inventory assessment at **www.trainers-guide-to-learning-styles.com** designed to identify your preferred training approach. You'll receive a summary of your natural strengths as a trainer.

You can also take the Learning Type Measure to identify your strengths in taking in and making meaning of new information. You will discover your thinking strengths along with how they show up in your role as a trainer, leader, parent, and more.

STEP 2—START WITH THE FUNDAMENTALS

Read through this book and complete the "Reflect" and "Act" sections at the end of each chapter. If you work with a team of learning professionals, create a book study group and review each chapter together. You will find a book study guide on the companion site for this book—**www.trainers-guide-to-learning-styles.com**.

STEP 3—INVEST IN YOURSELF

Take time to explore the companion site to this book, where you will find downloadable resources and FREE web events focused on applying the strategies shared. Some of what you will find:

- Training Style Inventory
- Free web events and advanced course schedule
- Videos
- Downloadable tools

STEP 4—CONTINUE TO GROW YOUR SKILL

Join learning expert Jeanine O'Neill-Blackwell and the 4MAT team in an advanced live or web-based course to practice, apply, and master the strategies shared in *Engage*. We can come to you, or you can join one of our open courses. Grow and expand your skill by becoming certified to lead one or all of the 4MAT course offerings within your organization.

- Advanced Instructional Design
- 4MAT 4Leadership
- 4MAT 4Coaching
- Leading the Needs Analysis Process
- 4MAT 4Teams
- **Visit www.4mat4business.com**

Bibliography

American Cancer Society. (November 21, 2011). Cigarette Smoking. Retrieved from the American Cancer Society Web site: http://www.cancer.org/Cancer/CancerCauses/TobaccoCancer/CigaretteSmoking/cigarette-smoking-who-and-how-affects-health.

Bozarth, J. (2010). *Social Media for Trainers; Techniques for Enhancing and Extending Learning*. San Francisco: Pfeiffer.

Betts, B. (2011). The Ubiquity of Informal Learning: Beyond the 70/20/10 Model. Retrieved from *Learning Solutions* magazine web site: http://www.learningsolutionsmag.com/articles/715/the-ubiquity-of-informal-learning-beyond-the-702010-model.

Buzan, T. (1991). *Use Both Sides of Your Brain*. New York: Penguin, pp. 89-95.

Carter, R., Aldridge, S., Martyn, P., & Parker, S. (2009). *The Human Brain Book*. New York: Dorling Kindersley.

Chapman, Alan. (n.d.). Conscious Competence Learning Model. Retrieved from Businessballs.com web site: www.businessballs.com/consciouscompetencelearningmodel.htm.

Covey, Stephen R. (1989). *The 7 Habits of Highly Effective People*. New York: Fireside, p. 99.

Dempsey, D. (2010). *Present Your Way to the Top*. New York: McGraw-Hill.

Drucker, Peter F. (January 2005). *Managing Oneself*. Retrieved from HBR.org web site: http://hbr.org/2005/01/managing-oneself/ar/1.

Duarte, N. (2008). *Resonate: The Art and Science of Creating Great Presentations*. Sebastopol, CA: O'Reilly.

Duke, Alan. (Feb. 2009). '867-5309' Bids up to $365,000. Retrieved from CNN.com web site: http://articles.cnn.com/2009-02-03/entertainment/ebay.jennys.number_1_bidding-war-ebay-area-code?_s=PM:SHOWBIZ.

Edwards, B. (1989). *Drawing on the Right Side of the Brain*. New York: Penguin Putnam, p. 4.

Einstein, Albert. (n.d.). Thinkexist.com. Retrieved November 1, 2011, from Thinkexist.com web site: http://thinkexist.com/quotation/if_you_can-t_explain_it_simply_you_don-t/186838.html.

Gallo, Carmine. (2010). *The Presentation Secrets of Steve Jobs: How to Be Insanely Great in Front of Any Audience*. New York: McGraw-Hill, pp. 7, 92, 105.

Goldstein, Daniel. (November 2011). The Battle Between Your Present and Future Self. Retrieved from TED.com web site: http://www.ted.com/talks/daniel_goldstein_the_battle_between_your_present_and_future_self.html.

Goleman, Daniel. (1996). *Emotional Intelligence*. London: Random House, p. 18.

Hyland, A., Kennedy, D., Ryan, & N. (n.d.) *Writing and Using Learning Outcomes: A Practical Guide*. Retrieved from the University of Gothenburg web site: http://www.externarelationer.adm.gu.se/digitalAssets/1272/1272565_Writing_and_Using_Learning_Outcomes.pdf.

Inc. Staff. (April 2010). The Secret of Sales Success. Retrieved from *Inc. Magazine* web site: http://www.inc.com/magazine/20100401/the-secret-of-sales-success.html.

Keen, S. (2010). *In the Absence of God: Dwelling in the Presence of the Sacred*. New York: Harmony, p. 56.

Kegan, R., & Lahey, L. (2001). *Seven Languages for Transformation: How the Way We Talk Can Change the Way We Work*. San Francisco: Jossey-Bass, p. 30.

Kirkpatrick, J., & Kirkpatrick, W. (2010). *Training On Trial: How Workplace Learning Must Reinvent Itself to Remain Relevant*. New York: AMACOM, p. 8.

Krishnamurti, Jiddu. (1895-1896). A quote by J. (Jiddu) Krishnamurti on transformation, world and you. Retrieved from Gaiam.com web site: http://blog.gaiam.com/quotes/topics/transformation?page=4.

Lakoff, G., & Johnson, M. (1980). *Metaphors We Live By*. Chicago: University of Chicago Press, p. 3.

Leonard, George. (1992). *Mastery: The Keys to Success and Long Term Fulfillment*. New York: Plume, p. 55.

Lingle, John H. (n.d.). Performance Measures Quotations. Retrieved from Corpslakes.usace.army.mil web site: http://corpslakes.usace.army.mil/employees/perform/quotes.cfm.

McCarthy, Bernice. (2000). *About Teaching: 4MAT® in the Classroom*. Chicago: About Learning, Inc.

Medina, John. (2008). *Brain Rules*. Seattle, WA: Pear Press. p. 74.

Metaphor. (n.d.). In *Merriam-Webster's online dictionary*. Retrieved from M-W.com web site: http://www.merriam-webster.com/dictionary/metaphor

Michaelson, J. (December 2009). The Meaning of Avatar: Everything Is God. *The Huffington Post*. Http://www. huffingtonpost.com/jay-michaelson/the-meaning-of-avatar-eve_b_400912.html.

Nadler, R. (July 2009). What Was I Thinking? Handling the Hijack. *Psychology Today*. Available: http://www. psychologytoday.com/files/attachments/51483/handling-the-hijack.pdf.

Nisbett, R.E. (2003). *The Geography of Thought: How Asians and Westerners Think Differently ... and Why*. New York: Free Press, p. xiii.

Patel, L. (2010). Overcoming Barriers and Valuing Evaluation. Retrieved from ASTD.org web site: http://www.astd.org/ LC/2010/0510_patel.htm.

Phillips, Christopher. (2001). What Is the Socratic Method? Retrieved from Philospher.org web site: http://www. philosopher.org/en/Socratic_Method.html.

Reynolds, Anthony. (n.d.). Quotes.net. Retrieved November 1, 2011, from Quotes.net web site: http://www.quotes.net/ quote/16952

Reynolds, Garr. (2008). *Presentation Zen*. Berkeley, CA: New Riders Press.